Post-Automobility Futures

Post-Automobility Futures

Technology, Power, and Imaginaries

Robert Braun and Richard Randell

ROWMAN & LITTLEFIELD
Lanham • Boulder • New York • London

Published by Rowman & Littlefield
An imprint of The Rowman & Littlefield Publishing Group, Inc.
4501 Forbes Boulevard, Suite 200, Lanham, Maryland 20706
www.rowman.com

86-90 Paul Street, London EC2A 4NE

Copyright © 2022 by Robert Braun and Richard Randell

Cover picture: George Grosz: Das Tempo der Straße (The tempo of the street), 1918.
© George Grosz/Artists Rights Society
Private Collection, Courtesy Richard Nagy Ltd., London

All rights reserved. No part of this book may be reproduced in any form or by any electronic or mechanical means, including information storage and retrieval systems, without written permission from the publisher, except by a reviewer who may quote passages in a review.

British Library Cataloguing in Publication Information Available

Library of Congress Cataloging-in-Publication Data
Names: Braun, Róbert, 1966- author. | Randell, Richard (Sociologist), author.
Title: Post-automobility futures : technology, power, and imaginaries / Robert Braun and Richard Randell.
Description: Lanham : Rowman & Littlefield, [2022] | Includes bibliographical references and index.
Identifiers: LCCN 2021059547 (print) | LCCN 2021059548 (ebook) | ISBN 9781538158852 (cloth) | ISBN 9781538158876 (paper) | ISBN 9781538158869 (ebook)
Subjects: LCSH: Transportation, Automotive—Philosophy. | Automobiles—Social aspects. | Transportation, Automotive—Forecasting. | Posthumanism.
Classification: LCC HE5611 .B685 2022 (print) | LCC HE5611 (ebook) | DDC 303.48/32—dc23/eng/20220124
LC record available at https://lccn.loc.gov/2021059547
LC ebook record available at https://lccn.loc.gov/2021059548

Erzsébet and Monika

Diana, Flavie and Rudy

Ein *Bild* hielt uns gefangen. Und heraus konnten wir nicht, denn es lag in unsrer Sprache, und sie schien es uns nur unerbittlich zu wiederholen.

—Ludwig Wittgenstein, *Philosophische Untersuchungen*

Contents

Preface	xiii
Acknowledgments	xvii
Introduction: From Automobility to Post-Automobility	xix

PART 1: THE ONTOPOLITICS OF AUTOMOBILITY	**1**
1 An Ill-Named Thing: From Mode of Transportation to Automobility Studies	3
Contemporary Automobility Studies	4
The System of Automobility	5
The Automobility Regime	6
The Automobility Apparatus	8
What is Automobility?	9
Automobility *avant la lettre*	9
Early Twentieth-Century Resistance	10
Mid-Twentieth-Century Critique of "The Automobile"	10
The Ill-named Thing	13
2 The Automobility Imaginary	15
Imaginaries of the Future	17
Automobility Sociotechnical Imaginaries	19
The Automobility Imaginary	20
The Ontology of the Automobility Imaginary	22

	The Phenomenology of Automobility	26
	A Historiography and Brief History of the Automobility Imaginary	29

PART 2: RECONFIGURING THE ILL-NAMED THING   **31**

3	Dromos: The Violence of Speed	33
	The Diolkos of Corinth	36
	Dromocracies of Modernity	41
	The Railway Experience	41
	Capitalist Space-Time	45
	Futurism as Dromocracy	51
	The Ontopolitics of Dromocracy	57
4	Theatron: The Spectacle	61
	The Situationists	63
	The Dromocratic Spectacle	67
5	Hypnos: The Automobility Dreamscape	71
	The Dreamscapes of Automobility	72
	The Autoscape	73
	The Dromoscape of Automobility	75
	Automobile Dreams	77
6	Nomos: The Appropriation of Space	85
	Nomos as Ordering and Appropriation of Space	89
	Automobility Spatialities: The Appropriation of Land and Space	91
	The Road as Bracketed Space	92
	The Road as Space of Permanent Exception	93
	The Moral Economy of Automobility	95
	Road Safety Research: The Statistical Construction of Causality	96
	Dromocratic Violence: The Constitutive Center of Automobility	98
	The Rhizomatic Spatial Reordering of the World	99
	The Global Nomos of Automobility	101
	Spatial Violence	103

PART 3: FUTURE AUTOMOBILITIES AND POST-AUTOMOBILITY — 105

7 Ker: The Political Religion of Nomocracy — 107
    The State of Exception — 109
    Automobility as Political Religion — 113
    Automobility as Police State — 115
    Constructing the Facts of Road Safety Research — 118
    The Nomocratic Revolution — 121
    Sociologies of Mobility — 123
    The Ontopolitics of Automobility — 128

8 Metron: Electric and Autonomous Automobility Dreams — 131
    The Sociotechnical Automobility Imaginaries of the Twenty-First Century — 132
        Electric Dreams: The Electric Vehicle Sociotechnical Imaginary — 133
        The Autonomous Vehicle Sociotechnical Imaginary — 135
        The Dataspaces of Connected Autonomous Vehicles — 136
    Twenty-First Century Automobility Futures — 141

9 Idiotes: Destituting Automobility and Post-Automobility — 143
    A Destitute Mobility Utopia — 146
    Destitute Commoning and the Idiōtēs — 150

Epilogue — 161

References — 165

Index — 193

About the Authors — 199

Preface

Many excellent journal articles, monographs and edited collections on the topic of automobility have been published over the last several decades. The multi-disciplinary field of automobility studies has provided a spectrum of answers to the question: What is automobility? The guiding thesis of this book is that only by critically rethinking automobility can we adequately address three related questions: What would post-automobility be? Why would we want to get there? How might we get to a post-automobility future?

Readers familiar with the automobility studies literature will come to this book already with an understanding of the term "automobility." For the reader who is not familiar with this literature, we hope to have provided sufficient context and background detail to not only engage with our argument but also to come away with a reasonable overview of the automobility studies field. This book aims to disturb and decenter what we understand automobility to be, what we take to be the reality of automobility, both in our everyday lives and as automobility has been conceptualized within much of the academic literature.

One way to think about a post-automobility future is as a necessary but unwelcome future. As a loss that regrettably must be endured, not only but perhaps above all, due to the need to limit planetary greenhouse gas emissions, for which we are receiving our final warnings regarding the gravity of the climate emergency that is no longer located in the future but is already upon us (IPCC 2014; McKibben 2020; Lynas 2020) . Another way to think about a post-automobility world is as a better world than the one we currently inhabit and not as a constraining and unfortunate necessity. A world where the urban and rural spaces that have been appropriated by and for automobiles have been reclaimed for other purposes; a world absent of the routine violence of automobility; a world the natural habitats and resources of which are not being systematically depleted and destroyed; a world where there is room for other species besides ourselves (Klinkenborg 2007); a world in which the world itself is not being terminally destroyed.

Such a post-automobility world would not be a world where the automobile has simply been replaced by equally oppressive mobility technologies. That too would be no different from what now goes under the name "automobility." Post-automobility is not, we should make clear at the outset, a world of connected, autonomous, electric automobiles.

In an essay first published in 1960, Lewis Mumford predicted that "if our present system of development goes on, without a profound change in our present planning concepts and values, the final result will be a universal wasteland, unfit for human habitation." (reprinted in Mumford 1963, 223–33). Our circumstances are direr, and the wasteland we are staring into is a more profoundly uninhabitable place than Mumford could possibly have imagined in 1960. We live in a world physically, politically, experientially, aesthetically and existentially dominated by automobility. It is a world most of us grow up in and have no choice but to routinely navigate, making it a world we take to be normal, proper, unexceptional and unremarkable. It is sustained in multiple ways, including, but not limited to, the political and economic power of the automotive and associated industries, popular culture, marketing and advertising.

That world is a picture of the type described by Ludwig Wittgenstein (2009, § 115) in the epigraph to this book: "A *picture* held us captive. And we couldn't get outside it, for it lay in our language, and language seemed only to repeat it to us inexorably." It is a picture that *lies*—in both senses of the term—in language. It is repeated to us inexorably, and it holds us captive. While we might not be able to get outside this picture, it is possible to imagine what it might look like from the outside, to provide alternative interpretations of the picture, to ask what it means to live in this picture. Above all, to entertain the possibility that we live in such a picture. It might be imagined as not unlike the picture that is reproduced on the cover of this book, *Die Geschwindigkeit der Straße* (*The Tempo of the Street*) by George Grosz.

Only by reflecting on what automobility *is* can we begin to imagine what a post-automobility future might be. If something close to such a world is to come into existence, we need to articulate and disseminate alternative visions and futures of that world, to develop plans, suggestions, trajectories for getting from this world to that world, other ways of thinking about what we currently take to be unquestionably obvious, normal and desirable.

Steffen Böhm, Campbell Jones, Chris Land and Matthew Paterson, in their edited volume, *Against Automobility*, remarked that:

Every day, throughout the world, millions engage collectively in presenting possibilities that run against the current regime of automobility, and we will be very happy indeed if the publication of this book contributes to that movement of resistance.

More than fifteen years have passed since the publication of *Against Automobility*, yet automobility continues its expansion across the globe. What is required, in our view, are alternative metaphors, descriptions and narratives to those that have dominated the automobility studies field. The form of resistance we are suggesting is one that would rupture the fabric of automobility to create opportunities, or as Walter Benjamin (2005) put it in a different context, to start from scratch and make a new start.

Citing a twelfth-century proverb attributed to Saint Bernard, Abbot of Clairvaux, in *Envisioning Real Utopias*, Erik Wright (2010, 6) observed that the road to hell has often been paved with the best of intentions. It is an observation Marx (1976, 298) also once made, albeit ironically, in reference to the intentions of capitalists to make more money from the money they have advanced. Yet to forego imagining and working towards an alternative to the present is to acquiesce to the present.

The belief that what we write will change the world is an occupational hazard of academic life. We live in the hope that the pen is indeed a mighty sword. Accordingly, in this hope, we take post-automobility to be with Wright (2010) not an unrealizable utopia but a vision of a "real utopia," with Ruth Levitas (2011, 209), a utopia that is the "expression of the desire for a better way of being." A planet that is not only, as Hannah Arendt (1994, 233) put it in another but not entirely different context, "fit for human habitation," but fit also for habitation by our fellow non-human terrestrials (Latour 2018), animals just like us (Derrida 2008).

Acknowledgments

No book is an individual effort. Not only because co-authorship is writing and thinking together. We have joint and separate acknowledgements to make.

We met at a mobilities conference in Lancaster where, over drinks at the conference bar, we began what has become an ongoing conversation. We thank the Center for Mobilities at Lancaster University for providing the context for that initial exchange, which has subsequently grown into a friendship and intellectual collaboration.

The idea for this book came from Isobel Cowper-Coles, then Philosophy Commissioning Editor at Rowman & Littlefield, after listening to a paper Robert presented at the 2019 Conference of The Society for Philosophy and Technology at Texas A&M University. Scarlet Furness, Frankie Mace, and Linda Kessler at Rowman & Littlefield have supported us from start to finish.

Robert would like to thank Erich Griessler, a friend and colleague at the Institute for Advanced Studies in Vienna, for his openness to new ideas and for providing the space, peace of mind and inspiration required to go forward and explore intellectually unchartered territories. His personal warmth and intellectual openness have provided a safe space unparalleled in my career. I would also like to thank the members of the team I work with: Elisabeth Frankus, Johannes Starkbaum, Anna Gerhardus and Matthias Allinger, as well as all my other colleagues for their inspiration and assistance. Being the wind beneath my wings, they keep me flying.

While working on this book, I have been involved with two major projects funded by the European Union's 8th Research and Innovation Framework Programme, Horizon 2020. Within this framework, NewHoRRizon addressed mainstreaming responsible research and innovation (RRI) in European research policy (Novitzky et al. 2020); RiConfigure experimented with quadruple helix innovation constellations—how knowledge and innovation can be co-produced by and collaboration made to work for different societal actors: from business, academia, public service and, most importantly, civil society (Carayannis and Campbell 2009). While neither of these projects were directly related to automobility, both inspired my thinking about post-automobility. In both projects we applied participatory action research, a democratic method oriented towards experimentation and change that blurs the boundaries between researcher and research subject. Members of the social laboratories, addressing challenges in transportation research as well as doing quadruple helix collaboration in mobility, inspired my thinking about automobility and its connection with the order of late modernity.

My conversations over lunch and coffee with the distinguished policy scholar Henk Wagenaar, a fellow at the Institute for Advanced Studies, helped me better understand the challenges of commoning. Matt Green, who has been walking every street of New York, responded to my inquiries kindly and swiftly. Dagmar Rychnovska, our Marie Curie Fellow at the Institute for Advanced Studies, taught me about securitization and questions related to surveillance and potential impacts of future technologies. Our wonderful librarians, Elisabet Torggler and Doris Szoncsitz, ordered every book I needed. Thomas König, head of strategy at our institute, an ardent cyclist and car adversary, sent me excellent articles to read and reflect upon. For all these I am thoroughly thankful.

Most of all I thank my daughters, Nora and Sara who shine a light on every day of my life and my amazing wife, Krisztina Rozgonyi, with whom the roller-coaster of life is always more joyous than I would ever have imagined it to be.

Richard would like to thank his wife, Clarissa, and their two children, Thomas and Elisabeth, for their patience and support while writing this book. At Webster University Geneva, Vlad Glăveanu has been a source of support and encouragement. I would also like to thank my colleagues at Webster University Geneva and at the Institute for Advanced Studies in Vienna, in particular Matthias Allinger, for stimulating conversations on automobility and related matters. Webster University Geneva provided financial support to attend several conferences, papers for which found their way into parts of this book.

Scattered throughout the following pages are sections of text that have been published in the journals *Humanities and Social Sciences Communications* (Braun and Randell 2020) and *Mobilities* (Braun and Randell 2022), as well as a paper under review that has been submitted to *Applied Mobilities* ("Towards Post-Automobility: Destituting Automobility").

Introduction

From Automobility to Post-Automobility

The first point we would make regarding the question of what automobility might be is that "automobility" is a word. It is this word, not an independently existing automobility, that we encounter in the texts of that academic field which throughout this book we will refer to as "automobility studies." It is a word that orders the semiotic contents of the texts in which it appears. At the same time, it signifies an automobility that is assumed to exist outside those texts.

From within a realist epistemology, the appropriate place to begin would be not with "automobility" the word but with the ostensibly independently existing automobility that is assumed to exist "out there," regardless of whether or not we have a name for it, whether that word is automobility or some other name. The ubiquitous presence of automobiles suggests that automobility is indeed the correct descriptive term and that realism is the appropriate epistemological orientation. In one of the founding canonical texts of automobility studies, "The 'System' of Automobility," John Urry (2004, 26) described automobility as:

> an extraordinarily powerful complex constituted through technical and social interlinkages with other industries, car parts and accessories; petrol refining and distribution; road-building and maintenance; hotels, roadside service areas and motels; car sales and repair workshops; suburban house building; retailing and leisure complexes; advertising and marketing; urban design and planning; and various oil-rich nations.

One needs to only venture outside onto the street to experience and see automobility, where we can ascertain not only that it really exists but that it also manifestly exists as described by Urry. It would seem obvious, self-evident and beyond dispute that the signified entity, automobility, exists outside the texts that invoke and employ its corresponding descriptive signifying term, also "automobility."

In the Postscript to the second edition of *The Structure of Scientific Revolutions,* Thomas Kuhn (1970, 187–89) wrote that what he called a "shared example" enabled scientists "to see [a] problem as like a problem he has already encountered" and "to see a variety of situations as like each other." This "way of seeing," as Kuhn called it, is either what the student has been instructed in or, in the case of scientists who have come to reject an old paradigm, the alternative way of seeing provided by the new paradigm they have come to embrace. Scientists whose allegiance is to different paradigms live, in effect, Kuhn (135) insisted, in different worlds. "After Copernicus," Kuhn (117) observed, "astronomers lived in a different world." Similarly, Lavoisier, "after discovering oxygen . . . worked in a different world"; where Lavoisier saw oxygen, "Priestley had seen dephlogisticated air" (118). Similarly, there was once a time when there were "no pendulums . . . only swinging stones, for the scientist to see. Pendulums were brought into existence," Kuhn (120) argued, "by something very like a paradigm-induced gestalt switch."

To Kuhn's list we would add that there was once a time when there was no automobility, only automobiles, to see. It is a world that exists neither solely in the texts of automobility studies nor solely in the world external to those texts but at their intersection. It is, possibly, a world inhabited only by those convinced of the existence of the world that the texts of automobility studies have rendered visible. So persuaded, it is possible to venture outside and see not only the component elements of automobility described in the passage above but also to see them as interrelated components of a system. It is to enter the world inscribed and opened up by Urry's text, which is a world not of separate and loosely related things—cars, roads and gas stations, for example—but a world composed of diverse and interrelated automobility entities that together form a *system* of the type described by Urry. What one sees when one ventures outside will, however, only be "automobility" for those familiar with the term, and at that what is seen in the Kuhnian sense of the verb "to see" depends on what we understand automobility to be. The mobility scholar sees something very different from what the automotive engineer sees.

The weak, largely uncontroversial version of the constructionist account of knowledge is that what we see depends on the conceptual apparatus that is brought to the subject at hand. There are, after all, few who doubt that the theories and methods that we bring to any scientific inquiry will influence if not determine what has been, or will be, discovered, how "reality" will be represented, categorized and made available for analysis. Under a currently popular optical metaphor, it is generally acknowledged that any object of inquiry will look different depending on which "lens" is applied to examine the phenomena in question.

The strong version of the constructionist account of knowledge is that the ostensibly independently existing objects of scientific inquiry have been brought into existence by the disciplinary apparatuses of science—its texts, equipment, models, theories, methods and lenses. It is to treat discourses, as Michel Foucault (1972, 49) argued, not "as groups of signs (signifying elements referring to contents or representations) but as practices that systematically form the objects of which they speak." Or, as John Law and Annemarie Mol (2002, 19) put it, "knowing, the words of knowing, and texts do not describe a preexisting world. They are rather part of a practice of handling, intervening in, the world and thereby of enacting one of its versions—up to bringing it into being." On this strong version, there are no objects or entire worlds that are not systematically formed or brought into being. What is of interest is how they have been formed and brought into being.

Part 1, "The Ontopolitics of Automobility," focuses on the construction of automobility in this strong sense, both within the world of automobility studies and within everyday life. The third-person singular of the verb "to be" that is the copula between "what" and "automobility" in the question "What *is* automobility?" has several possible significations. Drawing, presumably, on Heidegger's distinction between the ontic and the ontological, David Chandler (2019, 384), in an essay on the ontopolitics of mobility in the Anthropocene, argues that more "work needs to be done on the ontological rather than the ontic level."

In an explanatory footnote in their translation of *Sein und Zeit,* John Macquarrie and Edward Robinson describe "ontological inquiry" as "concerned primarily with *Being*," whereas "ontical inquiry is concerned primarily with *entities* and the facts about them" (Heidegger 1962, 31, fn. 3). Read as an ontic question, the question "What *is* automobility?" invites the assembling of a list of the properties, characteristics and components of automobility—the entities of which automobility is composed—including automobility's intersections and articulations with what is held to be external to automobility. Read as a question of the ontology of automobility, it is a question that requires specifying what one understands the "reality" of automobility to be. Automobility reality is not, we argue, the sum total of empirical descriptions of automobility, an ontic list of properties, characteristics and components that ostensibly exist, what Heidegger called the "present-at-hand." Rather, it is the reality of everyday existence, what Heidegger called "Being-in-the-world." It is an ontology—a reality—that is constructed, sustained and reproduced through power/violence.

The ontopolitical, as we employ this concept throughout this book, covers both the ontic and the ontological. The construction of the entities of automobility in their details, and the construction of the ontology of the *sui generis* social order that is automobility. Traditional ontology is a discursive field within which all parties to the dispute assume the dispute takes place within the discursive realm called "metaphysics." The perennial disputes in the social sciences regarding their similarities to or differences from the natural sciences are a case in point. Attending to the ontopolitical, in contrast, requires focusing on the empirical: the politics through which entities—the ontic—are discursively constructed and the politics through which one or another ontology is established as obviously the case and not something else—as hegemonic ontological common sense. In respect to automobility, that ontology is an ontology of realism.

Chapter 1 examines the construction of the concept of "automobility" from the late nineteenth century to the texts of automobility studies in the present. It is articulated with and inseparable from its object of study—also automobility—which is no less a constructed world. The very possibility of analyzing the latter assumes the former; without a conception of "automobility," it is impossible to discuss, describe, represent or analytically circumscribe automobility "out there," to delimit it from what is not automobility, what is external to automobility. If that which we call "automobility" is the construction of those discourses that name it so, how we describe "it"—namely automobility—and what we take its referent to be, become one and the same. What is in dispute is how automobility should be constructed and *eo ipso* described.

"Automobility," as this word is understood within the textual world of automobility studies, has not been constructed *ex nihilo*. In chapter 2 we turn to what we call "the automobility imaginary." Sustained and reproduced by power/knowledge, the automobility imaginary, we argue, is none other than the reality of everyday automobility—that which we take to be real. The automobility imaginary is an indexical ontopolitical imaginary; it is both a reality-constructing apparatus *and* the reality constructed by that apparatus. It is an imaginary that speaks for itself, has spokespersons who speak on its behalf, a primary interlocutor for which is the speech actant that is the automobile. It is an ontopolitical imaginary in that the reality that has been constructed is a reality that we take to be unquestionably real within a metaphysics of ontological realism. It is within this imaginary that automobility studies itself is located, and it is this imaginary that has constructed and defined the object of study that is "automobility."

In *Of Grammatology,* Jacques Derrida (2015, 20) remarked that: "the sign is that ill-named thing"—both "is" and "thing" written, as Derrida put it, "under erasure." The sign that is "automobility" is an equally ill-named thing. It is a sign the etymological center of which is the ostensibly material, physical artifact that is the singular collective noun "the automobile." That artifact, as Urry (2004, 26) observed, is "the major item of individual consumption after housing which provides status to its owner/user through its sign-values (such as speed, security, safety, sexual desire, career success, freedom, family, masculinity)." The very employment of the term "automobility" as the sign for what we study is symptomatic of the hegemony of "the automobile," which hegemony extends to the very name that is routinely used by those—ourselves included—who set out to criticize it. It is a hegemony that marks the sign that is "automobility" as an ill-named thing.

To utter (or write) "automobility" is always to do so within a context. Conversely, "automobility" reflexively defines any context within which it appears (Wilson and Zimmerman 1979). "Automobility" is not simply one word among others; it defines automobility through reference to the automobile. Yet it is a sign it is difficult to do without: as point of departure, as point of orientation, as that which has made possible the development of a critical analysis and account of automobility. The indispensability of the term does not, however, render it exempt from analysis and critique *qua* sign.

In part 2, "Reconfiguring the Ill-Named Thing," the sign "automobility" is progressively placed under erasure. The challenge is not to develop alternative descriptions of something, whatever we call "it," that is assumed to occupy a distinct space and location, the space and location currently occupied by an automobility. Not only is there no epistemic or politically neutral location from which automobility could be represented as it "really is," from which a representation could be constructed that would correspond to that presumed reality, but there is also no independently existing "automobility as it really is." The challenge is that of constructing alternative ways of seeing, alternative worlds and alternative metaphors by shifting our attention elsewhere. Redescriptions of the experiential space occupied by automobility in everyday life and the theoretical space it occupies within academic automobility discourses; redescriptions that replace and subvert the signifier that is the name that names this ill-named thing. Anaesthetized by the familiarity of the words of the dominant modern European languages, we have searched for alternative metaphors to expand the restricted meanings of familiar words that have flattened our vocabularies.

If we think of what Kuhn called a "way of seeing" under the metaphor of inscription, one aim of this book is to inscribe—literally and metaphorically, the two are the same—an alternative "way of seeing," such that automobility ceases to look like it looked before. This requires de-reifying *the thing* that is "the automobile" such that it loses its thingness, its haecceity. Kuhn's metaphor of a way of seeing is not, however, entirely adequate. It is into another world that we hope to transport the reader. That world is not the world of realism, namely a preexisting world, only *perceived*—a term already inseparable from a realist metaphysics—differently, but an alternative world in the sense articulated by Kuhn.

The world described in the following pages is far bleaker than typically imagined by automobility's critics. The rhetorical and performative challenge is not only that of redescription but to transport ourselves from the utopian imaginary of automobility, the actually existing everyday world we inhabit, into the world that is the profound dystopia of automobility. Inhabiting that world is a precondition for imagining a post-automobility world. From within the automobility dystopia, to search for ways to underscore the two possible future worlds we face: the "universal wasteland, unfit for human habitation," glimpsed by Mumford (1963, 223–33), of intensified automobility; or an alternative post-automobility world, a planet, as Arendt put it, that is fit for human habitation. We live in a world, the automobility imaginary, where the former is being sold to us as the latter. Chapter 3 through chapter 6 focus on the characteristics of the automobility imaginary, which was only described in general terms in chapter 2.

Chapter 3 traces the genealogy of what Paul Virilio (2006) calls "dromocracy," a social order with movement, speed and violence at its center. The Greek word *dromos* signifies roads, passageways, racetracks and other enclosed spaces within which movement occurs. The chapter begins with dromocratic military technologies in the ancient world through which space and time were transformed. It then turns to space/time transformations wrought by the railway and the global expansion of capitalism in the nineteenth century, both of which transformed space/time by exploding the boundaries of previously enclosed spaces. In the early twentieth century, an automobility *dromos* based on ever greater speed and violence spread throughout urban and rural spaces.

Chapter 4 focuses on Guy Debord's concept of "The Spectacle," the ontopolitics of dromocracy, and the subversive political tactics of the Situationists. The automobility imaginary is not only a space of public performances but a space of spectacularity. The spectacle that is the automobility imaginary is a theatrical space with, like all theatrical spaces, spectators, performances and a stage. The stage is the *dromos* described in the previous chapter, which has expanded everywhere.

In Chapter 5 we take up Shelia Jasanoff and Sang-Hyun Kim's allusion to "dreamscapes" in the title of their edited volume, *Dreamscapes of Modernity: Sociotechnical Imaginaries and the Fabrication of Power.* The public-performed visions of which the automobility imaginary is composed are not simply visions but dreams, which circulate in the public space that is the automobility dreamscape. Like the dreams that visit us when asleep, they also are meaningful and require interpretation. What they mean, like all dreams, points beyond the ostensible intentions of the dream and the dreamer, to the unconscious and the repressed of automobility.

In chapter 6 we turn to Carl Schmitt's concept of a *nomos*. Like the *nomos* of the earth described by Schmitt, constructed by the European colonial powers, the automobility *nomos* is founded on land appropriation and violence. Violence has been and remains the constituting logic of automobility. *Qua nomos*, automobility is inextricably enmeshed in relations of power and violence. Automobility is a space wherein we are reduced to what Giorgio Agamben has referred to as *homo sacer*. It is a space of danger and control, a normalized version of a police state in which those who enter that space are stripped of their freedom; a network in which human-machine cyborgs and humans enact public routines that weave different types of "stuff"—artifacts, skills, signs—together.

Part 3, "Future Automobilities and Post-Automobility," turns from the present to the future. A future automobility is a temporal horizon whose limits are located in the sociotechnical imaginaries that are being promoted and disseminated by the automobile industry and other automobility interests. It is a future, they would have us believe, that is radically different from the present. Yet if the imagined utopic future is no different than the present, the very term is a misnomer. Grammatically, it would not be an automobility located in the future tense but the continuation of the singular enduring automobility, which has always existed in the present continuous.

In chapter 7 we return to the question: What is automobility? Automobility is not primarily about automobiles but about speed, movement, imaginary reality and space. It is a material-semiotic spatio-political totalitarian order with a family resemblance to fascism. Its violence needs to be made visible and unveiled for what it is: absolute violence as opposed to violence conceptualized as a means to an end.

The final two chapters, chapter 8 and chapter 9, contrast two utopias. In chapter 8, we critically examine the likely automobility future that is visible within the new automobility sociotechnical imaginaries that dominate automobility discourses and state policy. Embedded within those sociotechnical imaginaries are promises of an accident-free and sustainable automobility future. There are good reasons to doubt the claims, and they fail even on their own terms. Their most important effect, however, is in the present, by ensuring the continued reproduction and expansion of automobility.

In chapter 9, we offer an outline of what post-automobility, an alternative utopia, might, at a minimum, look like and how we might move towards such a future. How we might avoid, by rendering them inoperative, the automobility futures that are being sold to us. What is needed is a conception of a non-automobility future. Our ability to imagine what that might be, as we suggested earlier, is determined by what we understand automobility to be. It is not a future where cars as we know them now have been replaced by cars with a different propellant and a computer as driver, nor is it flying vehicles or drones. Post-automobility must be conceptualized as a form of life that is differently politicized. This is the significance of our claim that automobility is ill-named. Named as "automobility," which is in fact how "it" has been named, would trick us into thinking that *that,* a world without cars, would be post-automobility.

*****

Addressing ontopolitical questions (Mol 1999) is a key ambition of this book. Interrogating the ontopolitics of automobility is the precondition for even imagining post-automobility futures. The ambition is akin to David Chandler's quest to offer ontopolitical modes, a vital task that would enable alternative perspectives to emerge (Chandler 2018). Politics is not a separate human sphere of freedom and autonomy, but includes "the world itself that shapes and directs the content of politics" (Ibid., 15). This world, for the subject at hand, is the world of automobility. Automobility not as a separate social or sociotechnical arrangement among others that make up our world, but an apt if ill name of the world we dwell in. It is not the only world (Mol 1999, 77–79), but it is a reality in which the automobility imaginary determines possibilities, generates constraints and openings within which the world is to be interpreted, and in which assessments of identity, legitimacy and responsibility are conceived and ordered (Connolly 2004, 2).

Although the focus of this book is automobility, albeit progressively reconfigured under other names, it is about much more. Automobility is a paradigmatic order, but it is only one manifestation of a larger *dromos, nomos,* imaginary and dreamscape—a world that bewitches and enchants us with its magic (Pignarre, Stengers, and Goffey 2011; Randell 2020, 44–45)—of the technoscientific world of late-modernity that is the time and space we inhabit.

Part 1

THE ONTOPOLITICS OF AUTOMOBILITY

Before Turner there was no fog in London.

—Oscar Wilde

Chapter One

An Ill-Named Thing

From Mode of Transportation to Automobility Studies

Steffen Böhm, Campbell Jones, Chris Land and Matthew Paterson (2006, 3), in the Introduction to *Against Automobility*, describe automobility as:

> one of the principal socio-technical institutions through which modernity is organized. It is a set of political institutions and practices that seek to organize, accelerate and shape the spatial movements and impacts of automobiles, whilst simultaneously regulating their many consequences. It is also an ideological (see Gorz 1980) or discursive formation, embodying ideals of freedom, privacy, movement, progress and autonomy, motifs through which automobility is represented in popular and academic discourses alike, and through which its principal technical artifacts—roads, cars, etc.—are legitimized. Finally, it entails a phenomenology, a set of ways of experiencing the world which serve both to legitimize its dominance and radically unsettle taken-for-granted boundaries separating human from machine, nature from artifice and so on.

The term "automobility," they observe, "has become recognized shorthand for referring to these different meanings" (Böhm, Jones, et al. 2006, 4). While the term "automobility studies" is only occasionally encountered in the literature (see, for example, Graham 2007, 71, fn. 4; Randell 2020b, 211–13), it recommends itself as an appropriate name for a multidisciplinary network of scholars, research institutes and literature established around the turn of the twenty-first century, whose shared point of reference and principal object of inquiry is *automobility* in at least one of the ways listed above.

The *Oxford English Dictionary* (*OED*) defines automobility as "the use of automobiles or motor vehicles as a mode of transport," tracing early uses of the term to the late nineteenth century (3rd ed., entry for Automobility). The French "automobilisme" first appears as an entry in the 1935 edition of the dictionary of the Académie Française: "Terme Générale qui désigne tout ce qui concerne les véhicules à traction automobile." "Véhicules à traction automobile" were not, however, limited to what we today understand to be automobiles, namely cars, but included "les voitures de promenade, de tourisme, les fiacres, les omnibus pour le transport en commun, les voitures de livraison, les camions" (Rochet 1900, 69).

The definition of automobility as "the use of automobiles or motor vehicles as a mode of transport" is a conception of "automobility" considerably removed, but not entirely, from the significations it has come to assume within the automobility studies literature. The major point of difference is not that these early definitions cover diverse types of "motor vehicles" beyond cars, but that they define automobility either in terms of "transport" or in terms of their mode of propulsion—no longer the horse but an engine. How these and other instances of the use of the term "automobility" differ or are similar to how "automobility" has been conceptualized within the automobility studies literature requires beginning with what temporally comes at the end; namely, automobility as it has been conceptualized within automobility studies. It is, however, in these early references to automobility that the genealogy of contemporary conceptions of automobility can be identified, a point we return to toward the end of this chapter.

CONTEMPORARY AUTOMOBILITY STUDIES

The defining feature of contemporary automobility studies is its distinct object of empirical and theoretical inquiry. Its canonical texts have made the case for the existence of an entity that is understood to be comprised of more, both materially and conceptually, than simply automobiles. That entity is automobility, whose contours, boundaries and components have been described and analyzed across a spectrum of methodological and epistemological positions (Randell 2020b) in a now considerable and diverse corpus of empirical automobility research (Merriman and Pearce 2017). Encompassing political economy (Paterson 2007), cultural studies, the humanities, film studies, literary criticism, gender studies, race (Alam 2020) and racial domination (Sorin 2020), geography, law and policing (Seo 2019), these studies have provided empirical detail and content to our understanding of automobility.

Automobility studies has articulated not only a largely critical, alternative account of automobility to that disseminated in advertisements, the mass media, by automobile manufacturers, and within popular culture and public discourse, but it has also defined these representations of automobility as themselves intrinsic components of automobility and thus also as objects of inquiry and critique. While Böhm, Jones, Land and Paterson's shorthand description of, as they put it, "this emerging understanding of the phenomenon we and others call automobility," provides a useful overview of the field, what is not apparent in that list are the points of difference and disagreement within the field.

The System of Automobility

In "The City and the Car," an early and seminal text of automobility studies, Mimi Sheller and John Urry (2000, 738–39) represented automobility as "a complex amalgam of interlocking machines, social practices and ways of dwelling." "Civil societies of the West," they argued, "are societies of 'automobility.'" "Civil society," they write, "is significantly remade through contestations over the power, range and impact of the system of automobility" (Sheller and Urry 2000, 751). It is in this essay that Sheller and Urry first refer to a "system of automobility," which is one of a number of different systems they identify. Other systems they mention are the "criminal justice system," "mass transport systems," "the road system," "electric tramway systems," "systems of monitoring," the "freeway system," "congestion pricing systems," "traffic information systems," "information, communication and simulation systems" and "personal entertainment systems."

The term "system" covers both generic and technical designations. In everyday speech we frequently refer to "systems," such as "the system of government," "the banking system" and the kinds of systems listed by Sheller and Urry. It is this standard, generic, dictionary definition of "system" that Sheller and Urry employ in referring to "the system of automobility" in "The Car and the City." It is in Urry's (2004) later "The 'System' of Automobility" that the *systemic* characteristics of automobility are addressed, where discussion of "the system of automobility" moves from a generic to a technical definition of "system."

The two sources that Urry draws upon in "The 'System' of Automobility" are complexity theory and social systems theory from sociology. Citing Fritjof Capra (2002; 1996) and Ilya Prigogine (1997) from complexity theory and Niklas Luhmann's (1995) *Social Systems* from sociology, automobility is described by Urry (2004, 27; see also 2007, 118) as a "self-organizing autopoietic, non-linear system" with the "capacity for self-production," which, he argues, has "irreversibly locked [social life] in to [its] mode of mobility," transformation of which depends upon the automobility system being "tip[ped] into a new path" (Urry 2004, 33).

The system of automobility described here is not a system in a generic sense; it is a system in the technical sense that the term has been invested with in complexity theory and in systems theory within sociology (Randell

2020b, 213–15). It is this conceptual hybrid, described by Sheller (2014, 799) as "complex social systems theory," that informs Urry's representation of automobility as a system (see also Urry 2005a, b). While this description of automobility has not been without its critics, conceptualizing automobility as a complex system served to further direct attention away from the automobile to seeing it as one component of an interconnected set of constituent elements—automobiles, infrastructure, laws and regulations, hospital emergency centers, gas stations, oil supplies, naval forces, military dictatorships, war and human rights crimes, urban planning and so forth (Urry 2004, 26)—of which the *sui generis* entity "automobility" is composed.

Urry and Sheller's two essays did not appear *ex nihilo* but in the context of increasing scholarly attention being paid to this emerging object of inquiry (Thrift 2004; Rajan 1996; Katz 1999; Featherstone 2004). It was an automobility that was being progressively described in its details but lacked a definition of what it was that was being described. In these two early texts by Sheller and Urry, we see the outlines of a conceptualization of "automobility" that has come to define automobility studies.

The Automobility Regime

Taking issue with Urry's systems theory account of automobility, Böhm, Jones, Land and Paterson (2006, 5–6), in the Introduction to *Against Automobility*, argued that:

> The notion of system tends to underplay collective human agency in the production of automobility and to avoid the political questions about the shaping of the automobile "system." At the extreme it can create a sense of "lock-in" where the only possibilities for shaping automobility or of moving away from its dominance arise from within the system itself.

A not inaccurate portrayal of Urry's argument and assumptions, these observations echo earlier critiques of systems theory and structural-functionalism within sociology in the 1950s and 1960s (Mills 1959). With its intellectual roots in complexity theory and the social systems theory of Talcott Parsons's (1951), Urry's representation of automobility as an autopoietic, cybernetic, complex system, Joanna Latimer and Rolland Munro remark (2006, 36), "raises key theoretical issues," primarily the functionalist assumptions embedded in Parsonian systems theory (Randell 2020b, 219).*

---

* While Parsons was not in a position to connect systems theory with a yet-to-be-developed complexity theory, the analytical model developed by Parsons and his associates was marked by an extraordinary—his critics would say excessive—complexity (see, for example, Parsons 1951; Parsons, Bales and Shils 1953; Parsons and Shils 1962).

We would add that describing automobility as a complex system in the specific sense that it is so described by Urry in "The 'System' of Automobility" is to locate automobility within the two ontologies of complexity theory and of systems theory. In respect to complexity theory, it is, Brian Wynne (2005, 71) notes, an "ontology involving moral recognition of the falsehood of ambitions and pretences of prediction and control." Or, as Law and Mol (2002, 5) put it, "On the one hand there is an order that simplifies, and on the other there is an elusive and chaotic complexity expelled, produced, or suppressed by it." In respect to systems theory, it is an ontology of cybernetic, autopoietic adaptive systems, which "generate the preconditions for [their] own self-expansion" (Urry 2007, 118).

In contrast, Böhm, Jones, Land and Paterson argued that we should "speak not of a system but a regime of automobility." Describing automobility as a regime, they remark (Böhm, Jones, et al. 2006, 6), "allows us not only to emphasize the systemic aspects of automobility but also to bring out *the relations of power* that make this system possible" [our emphasis]. As they here make clear, to speak of a "regime of automobility" is not an alternative description but a supplemental account. It is this Foucauldian concept of a "regime" that informs many of the essays in their edited volume, which explore the power relations, forms of discipline, technologies of governance, automobility subjectivities and the construction of the self-evident, taken-for-granted, ideological truths of automobility.

Central amongst these ideological truths is the assumption that automobility provides autonomous mobility and freedom. Here, Böhm, Jones, Land and Paterson (2006, 11) argue, lies a "conceptual impossibility," which impossibility, they observe, "is contained in the very combination" of the two conceptual terms of which the word "automobility" is comprised: "autonomy" and "mobility." It is an autonomy belied by what is externally required, the components of the system of automobility identified by Urry, without which automobility could not function: roads, traffic rules, oil, hospitals, military forces and so forth. More fundamentally, "instead of an autonomous subject that moves freely in space . . . what we have," they argue, "is a continuously increasing disciplining of drivers." It is a regime that not only disciplines drivers but has also constructed new subjectivities and formed us as automobile subjects. Its governance practices, as Paterson (2007, 138) has put it, "shape and produce *new types of people* consistent with automobility's logics" [emphasis in original].

Not only have we been constructed as new types of people, but we have also become one component of a cyborg car-driver entity, raising existential implications regarding our *relationship* to technology. We have become components of a machinic technology (Randell 2017). "The car," as

Paterson (2007, 123) has disturbingly put it, "is partly constitutive of who it is to be us."

The Automobility Apparatus

To this Foucauldian description of automobility as regime, Katharina Manderscheid (2012; 2014) has made the further case for describing automobility as a *dispositif* (or "apparatus," as the term is usually translated into English).* "The dispositif terminology," Manderscheid (2014, 608) observes, "directs focus onto the power relations and interweaving of the elements which together produce the hegemony of the car." Those elements include, she adds—quoting Foucault (1980, 194) on one of the few occasions, an interview, when he articulated what he meant by the term *dispositif*—"a thoroughly heterogeneous ensemble consisting of discourses, institutions, architectural forms, regulatory decisions, laws, administrative measures, scientific statements, philosophical, moral and philanthropic propositions." Conceptualizing automobility as an apparatus of dispersed and decentralized power, Manderscheid (2014, 608) observed, "brings its multifaceted character to the fore which consists of automobile landscapes, discourses, formation and governance of specific subjectivities and mobility practices."

Manderscheid's contribution to Foucauldian automobility scholarship has been to provide a framework for representing automobility that extends the regime concept through insisting on the interrelatedness of the components of automobility: knowledges, classifications, discourses and hierarchies, policies, planning, marketing strategies, a socio-spatial order, regulations, institutions, laws and lifestyles. A hierarchy of different forms of transportation, wherein automobility has become defined as "normality" while public transportation, bicycle traffic and pedestrians have become associated with deviance, she argues, has been discursively produced (Manderscheid 2014, 613). As did Böhm, Jones, Land and Paterson in conceptualizing the Foucauldian regime concept as a supplemental addition to Urry's description of automobility as a system, Manderscheid similarly views the *dispositif* concept as providing the possibility to expand our understanding of the system of automobility. It represents a recuperation of Urry's description of automobility as a system, albeit with an emphasis on networks of decentralized power—"the

---

* In English translations of Foucault's work as well as in the secondary English language Foucauldian literature, either the original French *dispositif* is kept untranslated or it is translated as "apparatus." Except in the case of quotations and where otherwise unavoidable, we have opted for the English "apparatus." The English "dispositive" is no more meaningful to most English native speakers than *dispositif*. To be a subject within an "apparatus" as opposed to a "*dispositif*" carries considerably more forceful and disturbing significations (see, for example, Foucault 2007).

system of relations," as Foucault put it (1980, 194) in that same interview, between "the elements of the apparatus."

What is Automobility?

"Philosophy," Richard Rorty (1982a, 226) once remarked, "is not the name of a natural kind but just the name of one of the pigeonholes into which humanistic culture is divided for administrative and bibliographical purposes." "Automobility studies" is similarly a name for an administrative and bibliographical pigeonhole, identifiable through possession of what Wittgenstein referred to as a family resemblance. Like all disciplinary fields, automobility studies has been constituted through the application of a collection of linguistic methods and apparatuses that are passed down through the books that represent its bibliographic heritage (Vattimo 1984, 62). Although it has appropriated, incorporated and borrowed from outside its own fuzzy and blurred conceptual boundaries, automobility studies is comprised not of any and all literature about automobiles or automobility. It possesses also a pre-history, texts that retrospectively appear to have as their object of analysis automobility under at least one of the different meanings to which the term "automobility" has become a referential "recognized shorthand," such that they can retrospectively be included in the bibliography of automobility studies.

AUTOMOBILITY *AVANT LA LETTRE*

The term "automobility" allows for the discursive construction not only of an automobility in the present but also an automobility in the past, making it possible to categorize earlier accounts of what we today understand automobility to be as accounts of an ostensibly preexisting automobility. Either left unnamed or named under other names, such as "the automobile," the automobility concept makes it possible to write a history not of automobiles or transportation but a history of the system of automobility, the automobility regime, the automobility *dispositif* or, as we will argue in the next chapter, the automobility imaginary. It allows for a presentist reading of past texts (Tully 1988) as adumbrations or early contributions to the theoretical landscape of contemporary automobility studies. Matthew Paterson (2007, 33–34) has identified two earlier periods of contestation of what we today call automobility. The first can be traced to the appearance of automobiles on public roads at the beginning of the twentieth century and the second from the early 1960s until the end of the 1970s.

Early Twentieth-Century Resistance

The first period of contestation, documented by Clay McShane (1994, 57–80) and Peter Norton (2008, 21–46), was one of citizen opposition to automobiles on public roads at the end of the nineteenth century and the beginning of the twentieth century. Appearing for the first time on roads and thus against a temporal background when automobiles were absent, cars were experienced in ways we, now accustomed to their presence, can no longer experience. Experienced as loud, noxious and dangerous, automobiles steadily encroached on previously communal living areas with deadly force against those, frequently children, who either stubbornly refused to vacate the streets or did not understand this new danger that was incrementally appropriating the commons that was the road space, which, they mistakenly assumed, still belonged to them (McShane 1994, 176). Opposition to this offensive intruder and new danger found its way into newspaper reports, letters to editors, posters and local protests, including the erection in some US cities of temporary memorials to traffic victims (Norton 2008, 41–46). Criticism ranged from brief asides to more sustained criticisms of automobility and were typically critiques of "the automobile."

Mid-Twentieth-Century Critique of "The Automobile"

Despite the rapid expansion of automobile-based transportation in the latter part of the first half of the twentieth century, it was only at mid-century that what we would today recognize as scholarly and critical analyses of automobility appeared. This period corresponds to what James Flink, in a 1972 essay, "Three Stages of American Automobile Consciousness," called "Automobile Consciousness III." The most notable of these is a series of essays by Lewis Mumford written between 1953 and 1962 that were subsequently republished in *The Highway and the City* (1963). Across many of these essays, automobility-related themes are discernible: automobiles, roads and highways, cities, urban planning and sprawl, architecture and automobile cultures.

In the opening essay, Mumford (1957; 1963, 9–10) observes that both in Europe and the United States, cities have become clogged with cars, making it impossible to appreciate city spaces and architecture, describing the private motorcar and road construction as "costly . . . inefficient [and] wasteful in space and time" (Mumford 1963, 108–9). In "The Skyway's the Limit," Mumford (1963, 217) observes that "Our cities are being replanned for passing cars, not for permanent residents, and the more cars that can be induced to clutter the arteries of a city and make residence less desirable, the more 'progressive' the planning is deemed." The result of "the utopia that highway engineers have been busily bulldozing into existence," Mumford

(1963, 218–20) observed, is impoverished urban and rural environments. The proposed highway system and plans for urban parkways were described by Mumford as "a formula for defacing the natural landscape and ruining what is left of our great cities." It was made possible by a shift in investment from public to private transportation and through "stealing land from public parks, dumping traffic in urban centers that are already overcrowded."

John Keats's (1958) *The Insolent Chariots,* which was on the *New York Times* bestseller list for five weeks (McCarthy 2007, 304 fn. 13), is a critique of automobiles, automobile manufacturers, road construction, death and injury and the expense of automobiles. "We are," Keats (1958, 158) wrote, "building a nation for automobiles rather than one for people." While Mumford and Keats were unambivalently critical of, as Mumford called it, "motor transportation," their contemporary Jane Jacobs, in *The Death and Life of Great American Cities,* largely defends "automobiles" against its critics. "We blame," she writes, "automobiles for too much" (Jacobs 1961, 338).

Vance Packard's (1961) *The Waste Makers* describes the planned obsolescence and poor quality of American consumer products, of which automobiles were a particularly egregious example. While only two chapters are devoted to cars, their obsolescence was not only material but also symbolic, as Keats (1958, 38) had already observed, noting that General Motors had built what they called "dynamic obsolescence" into their products. While the physical obsolescence of American automobiles was a result of deterioration due to their poor quality and design, annual style changes created a "planned obsolescence of desirability" that rendered each model desirable for only a limited period.

Perhaps best known for his exposé of the Ford Pinto in the late 1960s, Ralph Nader's (1965) *Unsafe at Any Speed: The Designed-In Dangers of the American Automobile,* focused on American automobile manufacturers and, as did Packard, the vehicles they manufactured. As the title makes clear, it was not all automobiles that were "unsafe at any speed" (cf. Braun and Randell 2020) but *American* automobiles. They were unsafe because of design flaws that resulted in the death and injury of drivers, passengers, and other road users, which, moreover, manufacturers were aware of. Some of the design flaws were the result of cost savings, others because aesthetic styling took precedence over safety, others because drivers were not informed how to properly maintain the vehicle, others because safety equipment, such as disk brakes or safety glass, were available only as optional accessories.

Unsafe at Any Speed documents resistance by automobile manufacturers to reducing automobile pollution; blaming drivers and road design for accidents, not vehicles; denying public access to accident data and investigations while benefiting from university-funded research; and links between the automobile industry and government agencies, including road safety agencies. What should be stressed is that *Unsafe at Any Speed* is not a critique of automobility *per se*. It is a critique of specific human agents: automobile manufacturers that build unsafe automobiles, and government insofar as it allows and enables the building of unsafe automobiles. Behind his critique is the assumption that there is such a thing as a "crashworthy automobile" (Nader 1965, 344).

Published in 1974, Ivan Illich's *Energy and Equity* is a critique of energy-intensive transportation systems and their inherent inequities. The United States, Illich (1974, 11) observed,

> puts 45 per cent of its total energy into vehicles: to make them, run them and clear a right of way for them when they roll, when they fly and when they park.... For the sole purpose of transporting people, 250 million Americans allocate more fuel than is used by 1,300 million Chinese and Indians for all purposes.

The "typical American male," Illich (1974, 18–19) added regarding the irrationality of automobile transportation,

> devotes more than 1,600 hours a year to his car. He sits in it while it goes and while it stands idling. He parks it and searches for it. He earns the money to put down on it and to meet the monthly instalments. He works to pay for petrol, tolls, insurance, taxes and tickets. He spends four of his sixteen waking hours on the road or gathering his resources for it. And this figure does not take into account the time consumed by other activities dictated by transport: time spent in hospitals, traffic courts and garages; time spent watching automobile commercials or attending consumer education meetings to improve the quality of the next buy. The model American puts in 1,600 hours to get 7,500 miles: less than five miles per hour. In countries deprived of a transportation industry, people manage to do the same, walking wherever they want to go, and they allocate only three to eight per cent of their society's time budget to traffic instead of 28 per cent.

Although this mid-century literature took a reflexive and critical stance towards what we today call "automobility," automobility was conceptualized along the lines of the *OED* definition: "the use of automobiles or motor vehicles as a mode of transport." Packard's and Nader's criticisms are of a particular class of automobiles, primarily American automobiles, not criticisms *in toto* of what we today call "automobility." The umbrella terms that Mumford employs are "private motorcar," "motor transportation" and "motor traffic" (Mumford 1963, 108, 150, 232), but nowhere does he refer to "automobility." The closest Mumford gets to contemporary conceptions of automobility is a critical aside to "the current American way of life," which, Mumford (1963, 234; see also 1961, 509–11) remarks, "is founded not just on motor transportation but on the religion of the motorcar." Read from the present, the texts by Mumford, Jacobs, Packard, Nader and Illich may be considered descriptions, however inadequate by today's standards, of automobility *avant la lettre*.

Instructive here is Flink's 1972 essay, "Three Stages of American Automobile Consciousness," a history of "American automobile consciousness" read through a concept of automobility that goes beyond automobiles, cars, roads and transportation. In a footnote, Flink (1972, 451 fn. 2) writes: "For the term 'automobility' I am indebted to John C. Burnham [(1961)], 'The Gasoline Tax and the Automobile Revolution.'" "Automobility," Flink adds, "conveniently sums up the combined impact of the motor vehicle, the automobile industry and the highway plus the emotional connotations of this impact for Americans."

In the essay cited by Flink, Burnham (1961, 435, 458) observes in the context of a discussion of gasoline taxes that "Americans were willing to pay for the almost infinite expansion of their automobility" and towards the end that "Even in adverse circumstances Americans would not surrender their automobility," the adverse circumstances being the Great Depression. The term refers only to automobile transportation, not Flink's use of the term.

THE ILL-NAMED THING

Discernible in this mid-century literature is an intellectual history that began with critiques of the "the automobile," from which emerged a concept of automobility beyond transportation. Flink's use of the term "automobility" stands between early twentieth-century uses and its signification in the automobility studies literature. One of the striking properties of the term "automobility" is its persistence over time and the diversity of its contexts of use. One might be tempted to conclude that despite the presence of a common word, "automobility," in nineteenth-century engineering texts, mid-twentieth-century literature, and twenty-first-century Foucauldian texts, that those texts refer not only to very different conceptions of automobility but construct separate realities. Early documents that refer to transportation and motorized vehicles under the English sign of "automobility" and the French "automobilisme" have bequeathed us a word, a signifier, whose corresponding signified is a material technology. Either recovered from obscurity or independently conceived in the 1960s by Burnham, it is the automobile that occupies the etymological and genealogical center of "automobility." It is symptomatic of a hegemony that extends into the very name of the field that has taken as its task the analysis and critique of "automobility." The source of that hegemony is not to be found within automobility studies but within the automobility imaginary that is the subject of the next chapter.

This chapter serves as a starting point for rethinking the ill-named thing, for reflecting on the deconstruction of its ontology. First, in respect to what has been constructed under the sign of "automobility." Second, in respect to providing alternative constructions, not of what is currently signified by "automobility" but under a different sign; but through finding new names and metaphors that allow for the construction of an alternative object of inquiry; to construct a path that leads us outside of the hegemony that automobility exercises.

Böhm, Jones, Land and Paterson (2006b, 11) describe automobility as a "conceptual impossibility." Automobility's conceptual impossibility, they argue, "is contained in the very combination of autonomy and mobility." Its ideological representations are contradicted by its external requirements—the components of the system of automobility as described by Urry and the existence of a disciplinary regime—without which automobility cannot function. This already points to automobility being an ill-named thing, yet despite its ostensible displacement, the automobile remains at the conceptual center of their project, namely to "theorize automobility" (Böhm, Jones, et al. 2006, 4).

The descriptions of automobility as a system, a regime and an apparatus are meta-descriptions of automobility; descriptions of a *sui generis* entity, namely automobility. They specify automobility's components, properties and boundaries, as well as automobility's relationship to what is held to be external to automobility—other systems, regimes and apparatuses, by demarcating an automobility "out there" from what is *not* an automobility "out there."

The epistemological choice is between assuming there is an independently existing phenomenon, automobility, which has been subsequently discovered and described; or that the object of analysis, automobility, has been constructed through its very naming and describing as that object that thenceforth became available for description and analysis, such that once named, it came into existence. To paraphrase Oscar Wilde, before Sheller and Urry, there was no automobility.

That the ill-named thing is ill-named is not simply a problem of denomination, of a harmless inaccuracy that is a mis-specified signifier. It is *in* the name that is ill—unwell, sick, nauseating—that automobility's truth and secret lies. It *lies* in the double sense that automobility's truth and secret, *there,* in the name, both reposes and tells untruths. Automobility's ill-name is the transcendental signifier for the language that we cannot get outside of, which is repeated to us, inexorably. The picture that holds us captive is the automobility imaginary, to which we now turn. It is an imaginary that is grounded, that lies, in a socio-politically constructed realist ontology.

Chapter Two

The Automobility Imaginary

The focus of the previous chapter was the construction of the conceptual entity "automobility" within the disciplinary context of the academy. In this chapter we turn to the construction of automobility within the world of everyday life, description and analysis of which has been made possible by the very concept of automobility.

In a section of *Being and Time* entitled "Reference and Signs," Heidegger (1962, H78) takes as an example of "sign equipment" an "adjustable red arrow" that some automobiles were then fitted with:

> Motor cars are sometimes fitted with an adjustable red arrow, whose position indicates the direction the vehicle will take—at an intersection, for instance. The position of the arrow is controlled by the driver. This sign is an item of equipment which is ready-to-hand for the driver in his concern with driving, and not for him alone: those who are not travelling with him—and they in particular—also make use of it, either by giving way on the proper side or by stopping. This sign is ready-to-hand within-the-world in the whole equipment context of vehicles and traffic regulations.

Any item of equipment, as Heidegger put it, is "not a mere Thing," but rather all equipment exists within a "manifold" or "totality of equipment." The adjustable red arrow that motor cars were then fitted with, now replaced with a blinking light to indicate change of direction, was an example of a specific type of equipment, namely sign equipment, which, in turn, is one of the many components of the entire equipment context that we today call "automobility."

There is no indication that Heidegger is particularly interested, here or elsewhere, in motor cars or the adjustable red arrow they were fitted with; they were simply convenient examples chosen to illustrate a larger argument.

Whatever the reasons for Heidegger's choice of motor cars to make that argument, it is a serendipitous coincidence. Another instance of *automobilisme avant la lettre*, it points to an alternative description of automobility to those covered in the previous chapter, namely automobility conceptualized as a totality of equipment, each item of which exists within an automobility "equipment-context." Although we now understand automobility to be more than "vehicles and traffic regulations," Heidegger's concept of an entire equipment-context provides an entry point for developing an alternative account of automobility. It is superficially similar to Urry's list of components of which the system of automobility is composed in that many of those components may be described as "equipment."

Conceptualized phenomenologically, automobility is more than the everyday taken-for-granted material reality of an articulated complex of the kinds of equipment Urry (2004, 26) has identified—infrastructure, roads, automobiles and other material objects. Automobility is also the myriad images, visions, accounts, representations and descriptions of automobility we routinely encounter. The latter—images, visions, accounts, representations and descriptions—are the standard components of an "imaginary," a concept that has been employed to describe a variety of phenomena: social institutions (Castoriadis 1997); national communities and the rise of nationalism in the eighteenth century in the work of Benedict Anderson (1991); collective "social imaginaries" (Taylor 2004). The imaginary was a central concept in the psychoanalysis of Jacques Lacan (1977), later incorporated by Louis Althusser (2014) in his theory of ideology. It is a staple concept within anthropology (Strauss 2006), also informing ethnographic work within Science and Technology Studies, most obviously under the concepts of "technoscientific imaginaries" (Marcus 1995; Ihde 2009), "scientific imaginaries" (Fortun and Fortun 2005), and sociotechnical imaginaries as defined by Sheila Jasanoff and Sang-Hyun Kim (2009, 2015). What characterizes these different imaginary concepts is the assumption that imaginaries are separate from some other kind of "stuff" that is assumed to be real as opposed to imaginary. Imaginaries, in other words, are the binary half of a dualist metaphysics.

For the subject at hand, the most obviously relevant of the above imaginary concepts is that of a "sociotechnical imaginary." In the introductory chapter to Jasanoff and Kim's edited book, *Dreamscapes of Modernity: Sociotechnical Imaginaries and the Fabrication of Power*, in a brief aside to the larger argument Jasanoff (2015, 2) observes that "cars as we know them" are the creation of a sociotechnical imaginary:

> [they] would never have taken to the roads without the myriad social roles, institutions, and practices spawned by modernity: scientists, engineers, and designers; patents and trademarks; autoworkers and big corporations; regulators;

dealers and distributors; advertising companies; and users, from commuters to racers, who ultimately gave cars their utility, appeal, and meaning.

In the following section we sketch out Jasanoff and Kim's concept of a sociotechnical imaginary and its relevance for understanding automobility. We then make a case for conceptualizing automobility as a singular and enduring imaginary. This is followed by a brief history of the automobility imaginary, focusing on its origins.

IMAGINARIES OF THE FUTURE

In their comparative study of nuclear energy in the United States and South Korea, Jasanoff and Kim (2009, 123) argued that sociotechnical imaginaries "are instrumental and futuristic: they project visions of what is good, desirable, and worth attaining for a political community; they articulate feasible futures." "Sociotechnical imaginaries as we define them," they wrote, "are associated with active exercises of state power, such as the selection of development priorities, the allocation of funds, the investment in material infrastructures, and the acceptance or suppression of political dissent."

In *Dreamscapes of Modernity*, Jasanoff (2015, 4) remarked that their original definition "needs to be refined and extended in order to do justice to the myriad ways in which scientific and technological visions enter into the assemblages of materiality, meaning, and morality that constitute robust forms of social life." Sociotechnical imaginaries, she adds, "are not limited to nation states as implied in our original formulation but can be articulated and propagated by other organized groups, such as corporations, social movements, and professional societies." In a frequently cited passage, Jasanoff here defines sociotechnical imaginaries as:

> collectively held, institutionally stabilized, and publicly performed visions of desirable futures, animated by shared understandings of forms of social life and social order attainable through, and supportive of, advances in science and technology.

As formally defined by Jasanoff here and by Jasanoff and Kim in their earlier nuclear power essay, sociotechnical imaginaries are entirely future-oriented. Sociotechnical imaginaries are "futuristic," they are "publicly performed visions of desirable futures." Delimiting the sociotechnical imaginary concept to visions of the future has provided a conceptual framework for the empirical investigation of those publicly performed visions and their consequences: what they are; how such visions are disseminated and sustained; by whom; the networks of power; the kinds of sociotechnical entities, material and non-material, that have been brought into being—constructed—in part or wholly, or not at all, from those visions.

Elsewhere in *Dreamscapes of Modernity*, Jasanoff provides, however, examples of sociotechnical imaginaries that are located entirely in the present with no reference to the future. Two examples are her analysis of a James Bond-inspired video created for the 2012 London Olympic Games (Jasanoff 2015, 9–10) and a summary of Donna Haraway's essay on the African Hall of the American Museum of Natural History (Jasanoff 2015, 18–19). The former, she writes,

> blended together memory, technology, the monarchy, and popular culture in a performance designed to play to every register in Britain's happiest imaginations of itself. It reinforced nationhood on many levels at once, and it did so in part by appealing to what we call sociotechnical imaginaries.

Although Jasanoff here emphasizes the sociotechnical, her account contains echoes of Anderson's (1991) study of imagined communities and their relationship to nationalisms in the present—here, the imagined community that is "Britain." Haraway's African exhibit is similarly located not in the future but the present. It "reflects and reinforces," she writes,

> a specific, historically situated, American sociotechnical imaginary in which nature and manliness are simultaneously defended against threats from urbanization. The science of natural history thus ends up speaking truths subservient to the power of a specific cultural imagination (Jasanoff 2015, 19).

In short, Jasanoff and Kim's formal definitions do not cover sociotechnical imaginaries, to paraphrase Jasanoff (2015, 4), that are collectively held, institutionally stabilized, and publicly performed visions of a *desirable present*: utopias not of the future but utopias in the here and now. In defining sociotechnical imaginaries in, as Jasanoff (2015, 1–33) puts it, the future imperfect tense, the sociotechnical objects that are eventually constructed—the design of which, as the case studies in the edited volume suggest, conform more or less to that which was envisaged in the past—are assumed to have moved from the realm of the imaginary to the realm of the material. On Jasanoff and Kim's account, a sociotechnical imaginary is a shared and performed *conceptual* entity that brings into existence a real, material technology. Nor does the formal definition cover the possibility that the sociotechnical objects that are constructed from an antecedent imaginary might themselves not only be inscribed by the meanings attributed to them within that imaginary (Jasanoff 2015, 4) but might, their materiality notwithstanding, be components of the imaginary no less so than the visions that brought the ostensibly material into existence.

AUTOMOBILITY SOCIOTECHNICAL IMAGINARIES

The history of automobility may be read as a history of a succession of sociotechnical imaginaries of the type defined by Jasanoff, each of which predicted a utopic automobile future (Curts 2015; Gundler 2013; Möser 2003; Mladenović et al. 2020), none of which came to pass as envisaged and promised. Two examples from the past are the Futurama exhibit designed by Norman Bel Geddes in the General Motors pavilion at the 1939 New York World's Fair (Jam Handy Organization 1940; Curts 2015) and a 1956 General Motors film, *Key to the Future* (Kidd 1956). The Futurama exhibit contained a display of an automobility future located in 1960, while the 1956 film imagined a future in 1976. Numerous future visions of automobility are also found in science fiction (Braun 2019).

Two contemporary examples are the electric vehicle sociotechnical imaginary and the autonomous vehicle sociotechnical imaginary (Mladenović et al. 2020). Embodied in prototypes and concept cars and disseminated in public visions of a desirable future (Ardente et al. 2019, 60–7), they are imaginaries of a "green" and an accident-free automobility future (Braun and Randell 2020, 2). They are regularly discussed and analysed in the mass media, in newspapers, on television, in trade publications, specialist automotive magazines (Topham 2020; Fraedrich and Lenz 2016), as well as in academic publications (see, for example, Lipson and Kurman 2016; Sumantran, Fine, and Gonsalvez 2017; Wadhwa and Salkever 2017; Pattinson, Chen, and Basu 2020) that extol the wonders and virtues of electric and autonomous vehicles. They are promoted at motor shows (North American International Auto Show 2019; Mercedes-Benz 2020) and museum exhibitions (Victoria and Albert Museum 2019; Braun and Randell 2021). They are institutionally stabilized through the efforts of private and state actors (McKinsey & Company 2013; Bertoncello and Wee 2015; Aptiv Services US LLC et al. 2019). In short, the electric- and autonomous-vehicle sociotechnical imaginaries are represented as significant scientific and technological achievements, thus appealing to shared positive evaluations of science and technology (KPMG 2012). They are exemplary instances of sociotechnical imaginaries as defined by Jasanoff and Kim.

The concept of a sociotechnical imaginary is useful precisely because it allows us to describe this network of institutional power. To identify the diverse agents that are engaged in the task of persuading us that an electric autonomous vehicle future is both superior to existing automobility and a solution to problems that have become no longer possible to ignore or deny. To ask how power is exercised within and across this network (Jasanoff 2015, 4). To ask what makes these sociotechnical imaginaries so persuasive.

On Jasanoff and Kim's definition of a sociotechnical imaginary, there are, at least with respect to automobility, two assumptions that limit its usefulness. The first is that sociotechnical imaginaries are future-oriented. The second, related assumption, which is obscured by this empirical focus on future-directed imaginaries, is the ontological dualism mentioned above. On the one hand, visions, discourses and images, in short, all the elements of the (sociotechnical) imaginary as defined by Jasanoff and Kim; on the other hand, the physical, material objects, the (socio)technologies, that were brought into being by the sociotechnical imaginary, which will conform or diverge to varying degrees to whatever was antecedently envisaged in the sociotechnical imaginary.

What is required is an expanded conception of an imaginary that is: 1) not only an imaginary of a future state but an imaginary in the present; 2) comprised of both the ostensibly material, automobiles and the physical infrastructure of automobility, and the ostensibly representational, its discourses, visions and images. While the many discreet automobility sociotechnical imaginaries of the past and the present are components of the singular automobility imaginary, the latter is not simply the sum total of the former. It is to that enduring, albeit constantly transforming, *singular,* rhizomatic automobility imaginary that we now turn. Unlike sociological imaginaries as defined by Jasanoff, which are temporally located in the future imperfect tense, the automobility imaginary is located in the present continuous tense.

THE AUTOMOBILITY IMAGINARY

The automobility sociotechnical imaginaries of both the past and the present are moments in the history of a larger, singular, hegemonic, enduring automobility imaginary that has continually undergone transformation since the first half of the twentieth century. That imaginary is more than the succession of automobility's sociotechnical imaginaries, and neither is it identical with its temporally synchronous sociotechnical imaginaries. Rather, the automobility imaginary is the background against which individual sociotechnical imaginaries emerge, which background the sociotechnical imaginaries of automobility are reflexively components of. They are sustained by that background at the same time that they contribute to its reproduction. It is an imaginary not of a future technology but is an imaginary that refers to and is operant in the present. It is the background against which a succession of future-oriented automobility sociotechnical imaginaries have emerged.

Automobility studies has provided not only an alternative account of automobility, but it has also defined representations of automobility as themselves intrinsic components of automobility and thus also as objects of inquiry. So defined, automobility is composed not only of its materialities—automobiles, roadside infrastructure and urban and rural spaces that have been transformed by automobility (McShane 1994; Featherstone 2004, 1)—but also the myriad and ubiquitous representations of automobilities that surround us in discourses, images, car magazines, advertising, film, corporate statements, motor shows and so forth. Under Jasanoff and Kim's formal definition, the latter are the typical elements of a sociotechnical imaginary, to be distinguished from the material components of automobility. Across the imaginary literature mentioned above, not just within Jasanoff and Kim's sub-category thereof, imaginaries and the material are assumed to be ontologically distinct, with the latter, the "material," frequently accorded the ontological status of "reality." Here we make a case for defining the ostensibly imaginary components of automobility as well as its ostensibly material components as the equally constitutive components of a singular enduring automobility imaginary.

"The thing itself," Jacques Derrida (2015, 53) once observed, "is a sign." Equally, the "sign itself" is also "a thing." Not only do words—as J. L. Austin (1965), in *How to Do Things with Words*, put it—"do things," so also do images do things (Hook and Glaveanu 2013) as do material objects do things. The ostensible materiality of the world is no less an interconnected, indexical and reflexive collection of signifiers (Wilson and Zimmerman 1979, 57–60) than the ostensible non-material representations, such as verbal and visual images, traditionally taken to be signifiers of an external reality.

Akin epistemologically to speech acts, the components of the automobility imaginary are performative; their ostensible constative meaning is inseparable from their illocutionary force. Like conventional (spoken or written) speech acts, images and material objects possess illocutionary force, have perlocutionary effects, and are performative. They "do things" relationally and mediate between artifacts and people (Verbeek 2005). "Things," human and otherwise, are components of a heterogenous *performative* and *enacted* indexical reality (Law 2009a). Drivers, cars, bicyclists, benches, roads, signs, filling stations, spatial ensembles, socialities, rulebooks and other automobility "stuff," seen and unseen, are entangled, enacted and performed through their semiotic relations within a language game. That language game is the picture Wittgenstein describes in the epigraph to this book.

The ostensibly immaterial and the ostensibly material are the indexically related components of the entire articulated automobility equipment-context outlined by Heidegger (1962, H 79). The automobility imaginary is composed not only of discourses, visions and images but also of artifacts and physical infrastructure inscribed in automobility space. It is an imaginary of semiotic relationality (Law 2009a), elements of which define and shape one another. It is heterogenic, consisting of different kinds of actors, human and non-human, and multistable as meanings depend on use-contexts (such as the mall, the parking lot and the car itself). The car is a variable, fluid object (Law and Mol 2001), and the durability or hegemony of the imaginary is offered by the complex and tightly knit (political) relationality of the rhizomatic network (Law 2009a). This rhizomatic property has rendered it an imaginary with regional and national differences as it has expanded across the planet. These regional differences should not be thought of as distinct and separate imaginaries but as geographic variations within the larger rhizomatic imaginary that possesses both material and strategic durability (Law and Mol 2001). What must be constructed for the durability and hegemony to be sustained is a political ontology of the performative network, a continual promise of a better future inscribed in present reality. That reality is the automobility imaginary. It is the ontology of automobility.

THE ONTOLOGY OF THE AUTOMOBILITY IMAGINARY

"A man who, beyond the age of twenty-six, finds himself on a bus," Margaret Thatcher is reputed to have said in the context of debates over the privatization of public transportation in Britain, "can count himself a failure." There being no reliable attribution for this statement, with some accounts giving the man's age as thirty, it is possibly apocryphal. Of greater significance than whether it was uttered by Thatcher is that many, including many beyond the age of twenty-six and without an automobile, would agree. It may be read as a statement of fact regarding how a man without an automobile might count himself and be counted by others, or as a normative statement regarding how a man without an automobile *should* count himself and be counted by others (Manderscheid 2016, 96). Whichever way it is read, it captures a fundamental characteristic of contemporary automobility: the supremacy of the automobile over other forms of mobility, here specifically public transportation. A man—and it is the masculine gender that is explicitly invoked—who possesses an automobile can count himself a success both as *a person* and as *a man*; he who does not is a failure. Left unsaid is how a woman who finds herself on a bus should count herself.

Whoever its original author, this statement encompasses the central elements of an imaginary. It invokes a collection of visions and images of what such a twenty-six-year-old failure might look like: his demeanor and dress and any contingent combination of features that might be attributed to him. The statement simultaneously invokes an image of *the bus*: crowded, dirty, smelly and populated by similar failures. At the same time, it invokes the image of its binary opposite, the converse of the twenty-six-year-old failure on a bus: a well-dressed, successful *man* in the driver's seat of an automobile appropriate to his station in life. The man, the bus and the automobile each reflexively define the meaning of the other. It is, moreover, the performance of the image of what a (presumably) not numerically insignificant category of women—the gender of the attributed author here being not insignificant (see Charles Moore [2015, 389] on Thatcher's reaction to François Mitterand and Helmut Kohl at a ceremony in Verdun: "Two grown men holding hands!")—presume a successful man would be; conversely, what a failure *is*.

Even for those who possess an automobile, relative success or failure is equally marked: by model of automobile; whether purchased new or secondhand; and its age and state of repair. Otherwise unremarkable, except for its presumed author, the statement provides access to the empirical content of the automobility imaginary at the same time as it serves to reproduce that imaginary. Through a complex of verbal images, articulated through a speech act, the *visual* illocutionary force of which is located in its context, the statement captures how subjectivities, personhood and gender are intertwined within, and inseparable from, the automobile—not least when the automobile is absent, which absence signifies nothing less than personal failure. It is an imaginary, as Jasanoff and Kim argue, that is "collectively held, institutionally stabilized, and . . . animated by shared understandings of forms of social life and social order"—in this instance, through a public performance attributed to a British prime minister.

Turning from these verbal images to our routine encounters with automobiles on the street, while not instances of "language" conventionally understood, the automobile falls equally within the logic of speech act theory. Automobiles are performative, and their meaning is contextual, which is to say they possess illocutionary force and elicit perlocutionary effects (Austin 1965). Luxury automobiles are not meaningless material objects but signify, more obviously but no more so than any other automobile, social class; Italian sports cars and American pickup trucks are distinctly masculine objects; that is, they are gendered objects (Randell 2020a), which is not to suggest that they appeal only to men or that only men drive them (Halberstam 1998). Automobiles are markers of personal and collective memory. Once a symbol of the National Socialist people's community and later an "icon of the early German Federal Republic," the Volkswagen Beetle, Bernhard Rieger (2013, 42–91, 123–87, 257) notes, "conveys distinctive meanings that are widely recognized across the social spectrum." Automobiles are neither amorphous objects nor simply steel and petroleum iron cages (Urry 2006). They are beautiful and desirable not solely because we have been constructed as subjects who desire automobility and thus capable of making aesthetic judgments (Kant 2000) regarding individual automobiles but because automobiles themselves are objects of distinction constructed within the social aesthetic standards of their imaginary (Bourdieu 2014, xv; Wacquant 2016, 66). They are products of specialized engineering and aesthetic design skills for which formal training is typically required, such as that offered by departments of industrial design and fine arts by universities with links to automobile manufacturing.

The automobile is not simply a technological object; it is a semiotic object that signifies more than itself and is saturated with meaning (Barthes 1972; Baudrillard 2005; Flonneau 2012), open to endless interpretation (Rorty 1982b, 94). If shorn of its endlessly iterable significations (Derrida 1988, 7), the automobile is reduced to no more than an engineering abstraction, legible only in the form of design blueprints and technical specifications. That abstraction is no more an automobile than a book is "just" paper and ink, a painting "just" canvas and paint, or a house "just" bricks and mortar. There is no such thing as an automobile that exists in its pure materiality. Such an object would be nothing more than glass, steel, plastic, rubber and other "stuff," as would any of the other components of what Urry has referred to as "the system of automobility," such as road infrastructure or gas stations. It is only through analytically reducing the automobile to the status of what Heidegger (1962, H363) called "presence-at-hand"—namely objects that have been abstracted from their equipmental context—can the materiality of automobility be separated from the automobility imaginary.

That "stuff" is what is emitted through exhaust pipes, and it makes automobiles motile (Kaufmann 2002), and it is why automobiles are dangerous to other road users. It is, of course, real cars that routinely kill and maim real people and that massively contribute to real climate change, amongst other harms; these are not imaginary in the conventional sense of the word "imaginary." But real cars do so and are able to do so precisely because they are components of an imaginary within which death and climate change, if at all possible, are not imagined; or which, whenever they are required to be imagined, are imagined within an economy of acceptable death and environmental damage relative to the numerous ostensible benefits—also part of the imaginary—of automobility or are imagined in the future perfect tense as problems already solved, contemporary cases in point being the electric and autonomous vehicle sociotechnical imaginaries (Fraedrich, Beiker, and Lenz 2015).

What, then, is a "real automobile"? As are other components of the imaginary, it is none other than that which it is constructed as within the imaginary; that which it is understood to be and experienced as within mundane, routine, everyday life. No less a signifier than a spoken or written utterance, the meaning of the automobile is a function of its context, yet the automobile at the same time is a component of the context for any other element within the automobility imaginary. It is a reflexivity to which all language is irremediably subject. As Thomas Wilson and Don Zimmerman (1979, 60) put it in respect to gestures and utterances:

> The meaning of a gesture or utterance depends on the particular context in which it occurs. Moreover, the elements of that context themselves depend on their own contexts for their meanings.... [T]hese latter contexts include the very utterance or gesture with which we began: each element in the situation is reflexively related to the others.

It is an example of an actor network of semiotic relationality, the elements of which "define and shape one another" (Law 2009b, 146). One set of reflexively interconnected components of that imaginary is the succession of automobility sociotechnical imaginaries, which is why a more expansive concept of an imaginary to the Jasanoffian concept of a sociotechnical imaginary is required. That larger, singular automobility imaginary is the background imaginary from which sociotechnical imaginaries emerge and to the reproduction of which they contribute. Although automobility sociotechnical imaginaries are constitutive of the larger automobility imaginary, the latter is more than the sum of those sociotechnical imaginaries.

Böhm et al. (2006, 4–5) have remarked that "the car stands in place of automobility itself." So described, the automobile is simply one component of what it reflexively signifies: "automobility itself." Widening the focus from the automobile to the conceptual entity that is the object of study of automobility studies, namely "automobility," that, we contend, is none other than the imaginary. However, the properties that are attributed to automobiles specifically, and to automobility in general, are held within everyday automobility to exist within the materiality of automobility. It is this realist ontology of everyday life that functions as the foundation of the imaginary. The assumption there is an independently existing automobility—composed of material objects, such as road infrastructure and automobiles—and, in addition, representations of that automobility, such as advertisements and sales brochures, lies at the center of the dualist metaphysic of everyday automobility. It is a realist epistemology that sustains the routine reproduction of automobility (Lindegaard 2016). It is assumed and routinely reproduced in the claims of, for example, automobile advertisements, the performative properties of which are hidden behind the appearance of being simply descriptions of "reality," however inclined or disinclined we might be to believe them.

THE PHENOMENOLOGY OF AUTOMOBILITY

The automobility imaginary encompasses what we understand automobility to be in everyday existence when we encounter automobility as drivers, passengers, pedestrians, bicyclists and any other possible orientation to automobility (McIlvenny 2019). These orientations represent distinct experiences of automobility: driving, passengering, bicycling, walking (Hall and Smith 2013); standing and gazing within the automobility *oikonomia* (Agamben 2009, 9); surveying the autoscapes (Urry 2006: 19; Mate and Pocock 2018) that have been sculptured by automobility—freeways, rural and urban space—as experienced within an automobile. These are not pre-existing spaces through which we travel; they have been transformed by automobility and incorporated into the automobility imaginary with its rhizomatic expansion. (The spatiality of automobility, what we call "the *nomos* of automobility," is the subject of chapter 6.)

It is an imaginary comprised of visions, images, dreams, discourses and ideology. It includes, as Joseph Gusfield (1989, 432–33) in another context has put it, "verbal and visual images, the stuff of newspapers, magazines, books and education, of radio, movies"; the products of "image-making industries," not only mass media and social media but also educational institutions. We would add that the metaphor of an "image" needs to be expanded beyond the verbal and visual to include also the aural, tactile, kinetic and olfactory. Examples are the sound of idling engines, accelerating sports cars, feelings of pleasure and power in driving and the smell of new cars and of gasoline. "The movement, noise, smell, visual intrusion and environmental hazards of the car," as Sheller and Urry (see also 2000, 738; Taylor 2003) have argued, are not "irrelevant to deciphering the nature of city life."

Our sensory experiences of automobility do not, however, occupy some pre-discursive, pre-interpretive moment. "What we first 'hear,'" as Heidegger (1962, H163–64) put it,

> is never noises or complexes of sounds, but the creaking wagon, the motorcycle. We hear the column of the march, the north wind, the woodpecker tapping, the fire crackling. It requires a very artificial and complicated frame of mind to "hear" a "pure noise."

Our "experiences" are those that are possible within the imaginary wherein we dwell in mundane automobility. They are embodied and habituated as well as produced, reproduced and transformed within the imaginary, as was the experience of landscapes analogously transformed with the advent of the railway (Schivelbusch 2014). Indeed, the very concept of a "landscape" is problematic. It suggests something external to us that we either inhabit as if it were a container or perceive from a distance. Conceptualized phenomenologically, "all this" *is* automobility reality; there is no other automobility reality, some other ontological realm composed of the physical and material (which is not to suggest there might not be unknown automobility "things" yet to be discovered). Everyday automobility is neither more nor less than the "collectively held, institutionally stabilized, and publicly performed" visions, images and dreams of automobility.

This imaginary is none other than the reality of routine, everyday automobility existence: "what is 'real' for the members of a society," as Peter Berger and Thomas Luckmann (1990, 15) put it in *The Social Construction of Reality*. It is "the only real world," as Edmund Husserl (1970, 48–49) put it in *The Crisis of European Sciences and Transcendental Phenomenology*, "the one that is actually given through perception, that is ever experienced and experienceable—our everyday life-world" (see also Heidegger 1962, H211–13). Within a phenomenological ontology there is no other "reality," some other "really real reality," hidden or discernible behind or underneath, for the subject at hand, the imagined reality that is the automobility imaginary. The real and the imaginary are not separable binary opposites. There is no space or analytically definable component of automobility that is real and a separate part that is merely imaginary. "The world," as Maurice Merleau-Ponty (2012, lxxx) put it, "is what we perceive." Automobility reality *is* the automobility imaginary; stated conversely, the automobility imaginary *is* automobility reality. It is real not as a materialized set of objects or collection of artifacts (the car, the road, signs, streetlights, etc.) but as the ensemble of artifacts that have been co-produced by and within the imaginary, of which those artifacts are also components.

We need, however, to go beyond this traditional phenomenological understanding of reality. In Heideggerian terms, it is what Being-in-the-world means in the age of automobility, with the proviso that it is Being-in-the-world as it has been constructed within networks of power (Althusser 2014, xiv), the automobility apparatus, which Foucauldian automobility scholarship has brought to our attention. It is an automobility reality that is sustained and reproduced through the continual construction of automobility as desirable, normal and commonsense.

Don Ihde has made the case for a "post-phenomenology," which he describes as a non-foundational phenomenology. Such a post-phenomenology needs to place power at the center of our interest. In this sense automobility as described here is post-phenomenological in that it is a reality constructed by an apparatus of power (cf. Ihde 1993), but phenomenological in that reality remains "what is 'real' for the members of a society."

That, we contend, is the ontology of automobility. It is simultaneously reality and imaginary. It is an "imagined reality." It is also an ontopolitical imaginary in that if we are to understand how it has been constructed, we need to attend to power, the confluence and convergence of agents within a material semiotic network whose activities sustain the imaginary.

Automobility is hegemonic not solely in the sense that we have been convinced of the commonsense truths of automobility, that it affords us freedom, convenience and autonomy. Automobility is a hegemonic ontology because it has been constructed as an imaginary that appears not as an imaginary but as real. The automobility imaginary is a reality that has been constructed, not only in its details but in its very haecceity, as real. "The imaginary," as André Breton (1993, 90) put it in *Earthlight,* "is what tends to become real." Or, as Jean Baudrillard (1994, 12) put it in *Simulacra and Simulation,* "Disneyland is presented as an imaginary in order to make us believe that the rest is real."

It is an imaginary that is ubiquitous and publicly performed across a multitude of locations and through a variety of practices: in the mass media; in popular culture, in movies (Zimmerman 1995; Archer 2017, 512–13) and music; in advertising; in road safety and driver education programs (Elvebakk 2007); in books; in science fiction (Braun 2019); in works of art and in collectibles; in trade magazines and television shows for automobile enthusiasts; in car showrooms and motor shows (Randell 2020a); in articles that regularly appear in the economics section of newspapers and television news that report on the financial circumstances of the automobile industry and individual automobile manufacturers; and routinely on the road (Conley 2012; Randell 2017).

There is a now substantial body of automobility studies literature that has documented various ways automobiles have been represented. It includes the commonsense truths discussed by Böhm, Jones, et al. (2006) above, as well as a now-significant corpus of empirical research. Automobiles are figured as normal, essential, convenient and safe; they represent status, adventure, power, freedom, happiness and autonomy; they are intertwined with race (Pesses 2017; Nicholson 2016; Alam 2020; Sorin 2020) and gender (Jain 2005; Clarsen 2014; Connell and Pearse 2015, 99), identity and social class (Gartman 2004; see also Fish 1994, 273–80). Equally significant is that which is located on the margins of the automobility imaginary, most notably climate change, rural and urban environmental degradation and death and injury. It is under these explicit descriptions, and that which is excluded from those descriptions, that automobility, through diverse public performances, is routinely imagined. "Imagination" here is understood not as whatever might be inside people's heads but, as Jasanoff (2015, 5–10) has correctly argued, as a social practice.

We are not suggesting that automobility is "merely" imaginary and hence not "real"; rather, that automobility reality is none other than the assemblage of discourses, narratives, visions and images and material artifacts of automobility—namely, the automobility imaginary. Our argument has been made in three stages. First, as a critique of an ontology that defines reality in terms of material objects, juxtaposed against which are representations of that reality. Secondly, by substituting this dualist ontology with a phenomenological conception of reality as the everyday, mundane and routinely taken-for-granted. Thirdly, through a redescription of the taken-for-granted as an imaginary.

A HISTORIOGRAPHY AND BRIEF HISTORY OF THE AUTOMOBILITY IMAGINARY

There are many excellent histories of automobility. It is an origin story that typically begins with the invention of the first automobiles and the appropriation and construction of roads for automobile movement. The history of automobiles and roads and the infrastructure without which automobiles cannot move is not, however, coterminous with the history of automobility. Automobility came into existence not with the first automobiles but with the construction of the automobility imaginary. The period in which only the very wealthy owned automobiles existed prior to the emergence of the automobility imaginary. The first automobile was not the product of a sociotechnical imaginary; it was simply a newly invented artifact. The history of the automobility imaginary is neither the history of the development and production of automobiles and roads nor is it temporally synchronous with that history of the material artifacts of automobility.

The absence of critiques of automobility as we now understand the term was not due to a lack of theoretical tools or an inability to "see" automobility during this period but because automobility the entity was at this time only coming into existence. While there were automobiles, there was as yet no automobility. The automobility imaginary can be said to have been brought into existence with the first rhetorically successful public performances that envisioned a utopic automobilized world. Automobiles were only one of the many semiotic components of the automobility imaginary. The history of the imaginary is in part a history of technological and design changes in automobile construction, but to reduce the history of automobility to a history of material artifacts is an example of what Whitehead (1925) called "misplaced concreteness."

The first phase in the construction of the automobility imaginary was Fordism: the mass production and mass consumption of automobiles, above all the Ford Model T, that were in the price range, in the United States, of a significant proportion of the population. Fordism, understood both in terms of mass production and mass consumption, was a central element within a larger vision of a world of cheap and mass automobility. An imaginary of the future, but which already existed *in nuce* in its present, it was a sociotechnical imaginary of the type described by Jasanoff and Kim. It began with a sociotechnical imaginary of a world of cars, yet the sociotechnical imaginary concept is no longer adequate to understand automobility. Out of that first sociotechnical imaginary emerged the singular-enduring, albeit constantly changing, rhizomatic automobility imaginary. It is an imaginary precisely because of its widespread familiarity and acceptance; the acceptance and conviction that automobiles are desirable and the best of all possible forms of transportation, culminating in the building of a world where, for many, access to an automobile is a virtual necessity. Its successful transformation into common sense was the moment in which it was transformed into a hegemonic imaginary. That is the world in which we live. It is not an external collection of objects located in a physical landscape separate from us but is, understood phenomenologically, what Being-in-the-world means in the age of automobility.

It is the world that automobility scholars also inhabit, which we grapple with and try to understand through constructing new metaphors, or what Richard Rorty called new "vocabularies." Under the umbrella category of "automobility," extant conceptual tools have been appropriated to build alternative descriptions to automobility's existential and semiotic hegemony that is the imaginary described in this chapter. In the case of redescriptions of automobility as a system, it is both systems theory and complexity theory that have been deployed; in the case of descriptions of automobility as a regime and an apparatus, it is a Foucauldian conceptual apparatus. In the next four chapters, we outline four different metaphors with the aim not of redescribing automobility but for constructing an alternative object of inquiry to the ill-named thing that goes by the name "automobility."

Part 2

RECONFIGURING THE ILL-NAMED THING

We live in language as in polluted air.
—All the King's Men, *Internationale situationniste*

Chapter Three

Dromos

The Violence of Speed

"There was no 'industrial revolution,'" Paul Virilio (2006, 69) writes in *Speed and Politics,* "but only a 'dromocratic revolution'; there is no democracy, only dromocracy; there is no strategy, only dromology." Dromology was defined by Virilio (2012, 27) as "the science of movement and speed," whereas dromocracy was a form of politics. Each, however, as Benjamin Bratton in the Introduction to the 2006 edition of *Speed and Politics* observes, "become[s] the other" (Virilio 2006, 14).

If dromology is defined as the science of movement and speed, its scientists could be called dromologists. On this definition, Virilio himself would be a dromologist. This is not, however, how he appears to see himself, nor how he should be classified. The science of movement and speed that is dromology is not the reflexive enterprise that Virilio has pioneered. Rather, dromology is the science that aims to enable, expand and increase speed and movement, to invent new technologies of speed and movement. The quintessential dromologist is the engineer.

In both ancient and modern Greek, *dromos* is a road; *cratos* refers to power (Dalakoglou 2017, 5). The English word "road" lacks the semantic and mythic complexity that the Greek word invokes. Dromocracy, like neoliberalism (Brown 2017), is a governing rationality of late modernity. As a metaphor for our epoch, dromocracy is wherein we dwell in everyday life, our shared ordinary experience of our lifeworld. It is not only a general governing rationality of late modernity, but it is also a central characteristic of the automobility imaginary.

Histories of automobility typically begin with the commonsensically obvious: the development, construction and production of the very first automobiles. It is a history that logically follows from placing the physical artifact that is the automobile at the center of analysis. It is an example of what Kuhn called "a way of seeing," wherein automobility—both automobility the conceptual object of automobility studies and automobility as it has been constructed in the imaginary—revolves around the car. In this chapter we trace the emergence of dromocracy to develop an alternative genealogy of automobility.

Dromos was also a passageway leading up to the Temple guarded by the Sphynx. In Egyptian mythology, the Sphynx were dangerous hybrids: women-faced winged animals. In ancient Greece, they were more benevolent man-faced creatures. The Sphynx were not only corporeal hybrids, but they were also conceptual hybrids of both benevolence and ill will. They spatially marked the transition—the passage to the Temple—from the everyday to the transcendental. They represented a secure space in which the visitor to the domain of the Gods passed *(metapherein)* from one world to another. In this metaphoric in-between and closed passage-space between the two worlds that the Sphynx watched over, the earthly subject enters the sovereign province of the Gods.

Dromos in ancient Greece was also the name for the racetrack, mainly for athletic competition but also for chariot and horse races. Like the passage to the Temple, *dromos* was here also a circumscribed space, albeit of a different kind, a competitive arena for running or for chariot races that were provided as spectacle. *Hoplitodromos* was the name for a running race performed in full military armor. Semantically, *dromos* is related to *dremein,* to run. The term exists in modern European languages, such as the French and English "vélodrome," "aerodrome" and "autodrome"; this is a point we will return to later in this chapter.

Cratos, which refers to power or strength, also evokes the mythological figure Kratos, one of the children of Styx, the goddess of the river separating Earth and the Underworld, in Aeschylus's *Prometheus Bound.* In the famous opening scene, the siblings *Kratos* (Power/Might) and *Bia* (Violence), who dwell with Zeus, order Hephaestus to chain Prometheus to a rock as punishment for stealing and giving humans fire. In the scene only Kratos talks, and he is the last to leave the stage. As E. V. Walter (1964, 355) observed:

> If the content of Kratos' speeches is examined, an answer emerges: the persuasive mission of Might is to manage the impression of irresistibility and to diminish resistance, no one can escape obedience and service; only Zeus is free. Resistance is foolish and dangerous. The message of Kratos is that one should learn endurance and resignation in the face of superior strength. Violence, the other instrument of tyrannical power, acts, but has nothing to say.

Zeus is the symbol of sovereign power. Kratos and Bia, agents of Zeus' sovereignty, are inseparably connected. While Kratos/Power is manifest, Bia/

Violence is present but remains silent. A combination of *Dromos* and *Cratos*, dromocracy is a complex spatio-political metaphor. It is an enclosed space wherein dangerous, competitive speed is permitted; additionally, a transitory space between the earthly and the divine wherein power/violence enforce the order of the sovereign.

Power/violence/speed is spatialized in Virilio's *Administration of Fear* (Virilio 2012, 15–16) as "dromosphere," an example of which was Germany's domination of continental Europe, which was enabled by German Blitzkrieg *assault* tactics. Speed, the currency of dromocracy, was invented on the battlefield of modern warfare, the product of the industrial revolution (McNeill 1982). It is the "slot," Virilio (2006, 46) remarked, between the reloading of the moving cannons and the running speed of the infantryman facing death:

> Speed is Time saved in the most absolute sense of the word, since it becomes human Time directly torn from Death—whence those macabre emblems of decimation worn down through history by the Assault troops, in other words the rapid troops.

Ultima Ratio Regum—The Last Argument of Kings—which was engraved on French artillery under Louis XIV, was for Virilio (2006, 43) the central defining metaphor of dromocracy—the final argument of reason that kills instantaneously.

"Dromosphere" is a spatial metaphor for a dromocratic order constructed by technoscientific forms of speed, power, violence and space. Speed lies at its semiotic center. "The violence of speed," as Virilio put it in *Speed and Politics*, "has become both the location and the law, the world's destiny and its destination." "Fast" and "slow" possess meaning only within the material semiotic network (Law 2009) of the dromosphere. In the following section we trace the origins of the politics of the dromosphere to a unique moment in antiquity, an early transformation of our experience of time-space that foreshadowed later developments in the technoscientific age of modernity. This early example points to dromocracy as an entangling of "stuff" in a semiotic network that connects speed, power and violence to form a durable network of human and nonhuman actors (Law 2009). It was a material construct that combined ruts in stone, war vessels and the moving of heavy material from A to B, semiotically entangled as a relational totality. We turn then to three historically recent moments in the construction of the dromosphere of modernity: the railway experience, the construction of capitalist time-space and, finally, the origins of an automobility dromocracy in the Futurist movement.

THE DIOLKOS OF CORINTH

The *Diolkos of Corinth* was immortalized in a poem, *Commemoration of Marcus Antonius' Defeat of Pirates and the Portage of His Fleet*, of unknown authorship, dated sometime before 100 BCE:

> The thing that no one has attempted nor [considered or dared]
> Learn this matter, that we may report the deeds of the man with fame.
> Under the auspices of the proconsul [Marcus Antonius], a fleet was transferred over the Isthmus and sent across the seas.
> The proconsul set sail for Side, the propraetor Hirrus stationed the fleet in Athens because of the time of year.
> This affair was completed within a few days with little confusion, and with great planning and safety.
> The one who is honest praises the man, the one who is contrary [envies].
> Let men envy provided that they [consider] those whom it befits.

Constructed to portage a fleet of war vessels "over the Isthmus and sent across the seas," it marked a significant transformation in the topology of transport as well as how space, technology and speed were *imagined*. It represented a perspectival transformation of the experience of time-space and of technosocial politics, created by networks that held together the components of a dromocratic lifeworld —people, texts and artifacts.

The *diolkos* on the narrow stretch of land that is the isthmus of Corinth was a passageway for people, goods and equipment, and may be considered an early "railroad." It functioned both as an occasional strategic tramway for the portage of war vessels and as a thoroughfare for smaller commercial traffic, also partly by portage, that benefited Corinth through transit tolls and fees. Its construction transformed spatial imaginaries of and between the different regions of the Roman Empire. Although crossing the isthmus was faster, safer and cheaper than sailing around Cape Malea, the portage of large vessels required great effort and was attempted only rarely (Pettegrew 2016). The *diolkos*, whose construction has been dated to the late seventh or early sixth century BCE, was used until the seventh century CE—approximately 1,300 years—following which time the whole of Corinth experienced a period of reduced human activity and the *diolkos* fell into disuse (Lewis 2001). The "tramway," "carriage road," or "portage road," as it is called in archeological literature, then passed into virtual oblivion until a significant part was excavated in the middle of the twentieth century. It was, however, preserved in archeological memory via ancient texts and ceramic evidence.

Since time immemorial in regions including what are now Russia and Canada, small boats were regularly portaged, mainly on river thoroughfares, to skip unmanageable stretches for commercial, exploratory and other purposes. This was typically done by carrying them overhead or by hand. In some instances, wooden rollers were also used. The *diolkos*, stemming from the Greek *dia* (διά–across) and *holkos* (ὁλκός–portage machine), was approximately 8 kilometers long, connecting the Saronic and Corinthian Gulfs (Sanders 1996). It was a limestone road with—at least at one end—rail-like tracks or inlets (ruts) along which vessels were carried through on trolleys. The construction of the road is attributed to the initial aspirations of the Corinthian tyrant Periander to canalize the isthmus of Corinth. However, when its canalization proved to be impossible, in its place a road for portage was imagined.

The problem at hand was that of long-distance control (Law 1986). Previously, to manage the distant lands of Rome beyond the Ionian Sea, fleets had to sail around the Peloponnese peninsula beyond Cape Malea. While the vessels could sail by the coastline and use basic rutters, it was a long, slow and dangerous voyage. Thus, long-distance social and political control required an assemblage of equipment, human and natural, to create an "envelope of durable (military) mobility" for vessels to reach the Aegian Sea (Law 1990). The archeological evidence suggests the problem was addressed by transporting large military vessels and, probably, smaller commercial boats across the isthmus with the help of crew and yokes of oxen or donkeys to avoid the long and costly sail around the peninsula from the Gulf of Corinth towards the Saronic islands and beyond; later, from the Ionian to the Aegian Seas. These required elements of conventional technological innovation, brought together with political and economic vision, as well as familiarity with stories of past heroic deeds, real or invented.

It is an early example of what Law (2009) would call the precarious process of power embedded in semiotic relationality, heterogeneity and materiality, bringing together a network of actors and "stuff," created for mobility and warfare purposes. The regularity of portage for smaller commercial boats is debated (Pettegrew 2016). Although the maneuver was only infrequently attempted by naval forces, it was to great military advantage (Sanders 1996). Historical texts commemorate one unsuccessful and five successful attempts to portage warships over the isthmus between 428 and 30 BCE (Lewis 2001).

The name *diolkos*, "a portage-machine carrying across," suggests that it was understood to be not only as a "road" or a "slipway" but a *technology*. It entangled people, artifacts and their relations into a continuum by carrying vessels and their crews, altering and impacting landscapes, economies, and the power dynamics of the high seas and distant lands, occurring at rare moments of historical contingency exploited by visionary strategists.

While some historians argue that portage on the isthmus did not differ from traditional boat transfer over stretches of land using wooden rollers (Pettegrew 2016, 119, 131), historical evidence suggests that at least on one end of the road ruts were carved into the limestone as "rails" to assist and guide wheeled equipment, onto which vessels were lifted (Sanders 1996). Sailing around Cape Malea was time-consuming and dangerous, and thus a canal would have been preferable. However, it was impossible to cut through the isthmus due to the elevation and the rudimentary nature of the available equipment. Undeterred by previous failures, Emperor Nero began the construction of a canal nonetheless but had to give up (Lewis 2001, 10).

The portage of warships promised speed, comparatively low expense and greater danger for enemies. As Pettegrew (2016, 124) argues, the transfer of ships in the classical and Hellenic period on the Isthmus of Corinth resulted in decisive military victories marked by dramatic, opportune and speedy assaults on surprised enemies. The event commemorated in the poem is unique in being the first and only successful portage in Roman times, but also, significantly for our story, because it originated in an "imaginary of portage" that may be classified as an early sociotechnical imaginary (Jasanoff and Kim 2009), which made the attempt feasible in the first place. Although portages of vessels were remembered in myths—the Argonauts, Semiramis, Dionysios I., Lysander of Sparta, Alexander the Great and Hannibal—in only a few instances (e.g., the Peloponnesians and Philip V of Macedon) is there corroborating historical evidence that they were actually attempted. Nevertheless, portage was preserved in collective memory as something done on a regular basis for both military and commercial purposes. It was remembered as useful and beneficial both in war and peacetime.

When conceived and attempted by Marcus Antonius, in the winter of 102 BCE to wage a surprise attack on the Cilician pirates, and later duly celebrated in Rome when accomplished, portage was probably held in public memory as something that was possible and had been frequently performed. It was canonized in the memory of a heroic past, thus becoming a strategic opportunity for the future: an operation that could be attained by courage and wit and made possible through advances in technology (Jasanoff and Kim 2015, 4). Marcus Antonius would have been familiar with historical accounts of the Greek and Roman past and probably had knowledge of recorded military portage. It was commemorated in books throughout antiquity, such as Polybius' *Histories*, instances of which were described as remarkable and fame-producing political and military deeds (Pettegrew 2016, 125).

The pirates attacked by Marcus Antonius believed the Saronic gulf was a safe haven. From the vantage point of Rome, the gulf was distant, with access hindered by rough seas around the cape. The assault was made possible by an imaginary composed of amphibious war vessels and a land-sea-land continuum. Marcus Antonius would have read stories of past portages, their effects on the enemy, as well as the potential political power that would result from success. Portage was thus part of military and political visions fixed in publicly performed memory, in histories, plays and stories that told of what is technically and strategically possible. It empowered aspiring political leaders to imagine (re)establishing political order and hegemony beyond what previously had been considered achievable (Lewis 2001).

An early example of an imaginary that altered topography, it created a seamless warscape across distant naval battlefields. While little is known of how the Roman fleet actually engaged with the pirates, the speed of the portage was fast and ingenious, the victory great enough to be carved in stone and celebrated on the spot, earning political respect for the victors in Rome. The ruts in the limestone on the Isthmus of Corinth altered the spatiality of the known world. They brought about an "annihilation of space and time" (Schivelbusch 2014, 33), later to be repeated, on a larger scale, by the railways of the nineteenth century. Not only was the space between Corinth and Athens, and later between Rome and Athens, *diminished* by the possibility of avoiding sailing around Cape Malea, Rome as an imagined political community (Anderson 1991) was *extended* by the ability of rulers to spread their power across the isthmus by moving their forces seamlessly across the dual terrains of land and sea.

This story captures many of the elements of how a durable technosocial network (Latour 1990) emerges: material durability (of ruts and vessels) of technology; strategic durability of connecting "stuff" into a network (of the portage entangling different actors, human and nonhuman); the discursive durability of the many logics (of military, of naval, of commercial and of heroic) that were at play in making the portage possible (Law 2009, 148–49).

By changing perceptions of far and near, by connecting Corinth with Athens for economic and military purposes, this early dromological moment created what Virilio (2007, 84) called a dromoscopic illusion. The durability of this unique technosocial network, as the poetic praise of Marcus Antonius that was carved in stone suggested, created and altered the power structures of the seas by enabling the Roman proconsul to defeat the Cilician pirates of the Mediterranean Sea and reestablish Roman rule (Pettegrew 2016) beyond Corinth. The *diolkos* not only "carried across," but it also made the sea and land a fluid continuum seamlessly connecting sea-land-sea. It transformed time-space by making the transport of weapons, goods and people speedier, putting Corinth literally on the map, and it enabled its leaders to charge transit tolls and portage fees for smaller and local cargo vessels.

The *diolkos* transformed time, measured by weeks on the sea to get to the battlefield by the Romans, which provided sufficient leeway for escape for the pirates in case of attack. It also transformed space by eliminating the division between separate seascapes that formed safe havens for pirates, creating a homogeneous powerscape for strategists aiming at long-distance control (Law 1986).

The portage entangled human and nonhuman actors and actants within what Latour (1990) calls a durable network: the boat, the crew, the oxen, the ruts, the strategist, the stories told about heroic pasts, the pirates, the locals fearing them and the law, creating the flow of goods, people and power. It transcended traditionally perceived blockages of flows by transforming Hellenic military ships—*keletes*, *lemboi* and later Antonius's seven-ton Roman vessels—into amphibious vehicles. Fortuitous dromocratic speed—a material-semiotic trope (Haraway 2016b)—was conceived on the isthmus as a slipway connecting two battlefields of the high seas.

Dromology thus first appeared in a political phenomenological sense on this "battlewave" in ancient Greece. It made possible the transportation of vessels, people and arms across previously impassible topographies. The birth of dromology was not located, as a focus on the technology of portage would suggest, in the shipyard to their place of duty in water or in the portage of smaller boats on exploratory missions on rivers but movement across warscapes to get to the enemy faster and in surprise. On the isthmus of Corinth, *attack* connected people and implements in an entangled semiotic network across the seas to rule and control. It was made possible by its material semiotic components: earlier sociotechnical achievements fixed, institutionalized and performed in literary and historical works. Visions of possible political futures made previously impossible social and technological advances possible.

The attack of Marcus Antonius and his fleet not only brought death but, to some, wealth; not only destruction but, by evacuating pirates, peace and rule of law; not only subordination by those who were faster but liberation for those no longer enslaved or killed by the pirates. It brought about a sociotechnically durable social constellation by altering the political ontology of the social and the technological. It brought fame and glory to the leader who devised such a strategy, a desire to copy and repeat (as did Octavian in 30 BCE), becoming part of an imaginary that was a shared vision of potential pasts and desired futures. It was an early instance of the dromoscopic illusion. It allowed for a perspectival intervention in reality in order to govern it (Agamben 2018, 12).

DROMOCRACIES OF MODERNITY

While the origins of dromocracy can be traced to the ancient world, it was in the nineteenth century that dromocracy expanded into everyday life, becoming the dominant spatio-technical order of the twentieth century. Space-time was radically transformed in the nineteenth century by both the railway and, as Max Weber (1925) put it, "the tremendous cosmos of the modern economic order" that was capitalism. In the early twentieth century, a small group of Italian avant-garde artists gained political support for their sociotechnical *visions* that were then realized by engineers. The railway, the capitalist mode of production, and the Futurists each in different ways reordered the spatiality and temporality of the world. These transformations represented the breaking out of the *dromos* from its confines—the enclosed space that was the passage to the temple guarded by the Sphynx, the enclosed track of athletic, chariot and horse races, such that the *dromos* expanded *everywhere*. New dromocratic space-times were created, from which emerged a new, ubiquitous, hegemonic biopolitical constellation that governs our everyday lifeworld.

The Railway Experience

The railroad, one of the primary sociotechnical transformations of the nineteenth century, Max Weber (1925, 255) observed, emerged in the age of steel. It had not only transformed transportation but represented the most revolutionary instrument in economic history. With the invention of the locomotive, "space and time," the historian Stephen Ambrose (2000, 21) observed, were "conquered." Similarly, Wolfgang Schivelbusch, in his cultural history of the railway journey, observed that railroad travel was experienced as the "annihilation of space *and* time." It had effected, Schivelbusch (2014, 33–34) wrote, quoting from an article published in 1839:

> the gradual annihilation, approaching almost to the final extinction, of that space and of those distances which have hitherto been supposed unalterably to separate the various nations of the globe.

This was achieved, Schivelbusch observed, by *speed*: the one-third increase in rapidity by rail-travel as opposed to that of stagecoaches. Any distance travelled by rail had shrunk time to one-third of its former "length." "What was experienced as being annihilated," Schivelbusch (2014, 36) remarked, "was the traditional space-time continuum which characterized the old transport technology," namely the horse-drawn coach. The railway was revolutionary in its alteration of social rhythms. Travel was transformed from a journey between points to a continuum of heterogenous, non-connected experiences. The experience of time and space changed, creating space-time as the unit of experience (May and Thrift 2001).

What Virilio called "human time" (*temps humain*) and Henri Bergson "duration" (*durée*) became in the railway journey a series of disjunct experiences: of interaction with others, of being immersed in reading a book, of eating and drinking, of looking out the window to see a landscape passing by at a speed previously undecodable for human consciousness. Railway journeys are examples of what Bergson (2013, 85–87) called "qualitative multiplicity": layers of continuous, heterogenous flows of experience. They disrupted the social rhythms experienced when travelling by stagecoach, horse-riding, sailing or walking. "Annihilation of time" was the extinction of social rhythms as experienced before the rail journey.

A more accurate description would be not the annihilation of time but the creation of dual-time. One time that is quantitative, countable and measurable by the clock, another time experienced as *durée*. In Britain, already in 1838, Greenwich Time had been established as a standard time for the creation of coordinated railway timetables (Beaumont and Freeman 2007, 19). The duration of journeys and interconnections (Schivelbusch 2014, 43) were measured according to mathematical time and unified for *the entire railroad* journey. In contrast, time, understood as *durée,* was experienced during the railroad journey as freedom, a version of *"élan vital"* (Bergson 2005). "Railway consciousness" was a unique consciousness, the experience of time, space and the multiplicity of human interconnections *in the train on the railroad*.

What was then described as an "assault on time" meant for the railway traveler that time moved not only three times *faster* than for anyone else but that it was qualitatively different. The locomotive-human body hybrid (Thrift 1996; Thrift and Pile 1995) experienced the "conquering of time." The train became a kind of prosthetic that transformed bodily experiences as the locomotive was absorbed into the traveler's living body (Merleau-Ponty 2012). Experienced as "a projectile [. . .] being shot through the landscape" (Schivelbusch 2014, 54), the senses became accustomed to different bodily practices, smells, movements and vistas. The body, as Löfgren (2008) put it, learned to be a rail traveler, habituated of the embodied experience of the journey (Mathieson 2015).

The assault on time was underscored by military images used to describe the train's speed: the locomotive being faster than a "cannon ball," moving with energy twice as great as a "2,000-pound shot fired from a 100-ton Armstrong gun" (Schivelbusch 2014, 54). The railway was one of the "illegitimate offspring[s] of militarism," as Donna Haraway (2016a) put it in "The Cyborg Manifesto." The train-body hybrid acquired the power to be out of pace with human speed; the traveler entering the train in one moment in one place and being in another totally different place in "an instance." The train became a time machine, disembodying and reembodying the traveler at departure and arrival.

The projectile body became a de-individualised, inert commodity: an "atomized parcel of flesh, shunted from place to place just like other goods" (Thrift 1994, 200). The dis-embodiment/re-embodiment experience was a constant series of transformations from the body of the person to parcel, to locomotive-body hybrid and back. The train disrupted not only social rhythms but personal, embodied rhythms as well. "Booming" in darkness and "bursting out" into the sunny day, the train was described by Dickens (1848, 199–200) in *Dombey and Son* as a "triumphant," "indomitable" and "remorseless" harbinger of death, a "power that forced itself upon its iron way—its own—defiant of all paths and roads, piercing through the heart of every obstacle":

> Through the hollow, on the height, by the heath, by the orchard, by the park, by the garden, over the canal, across the river, where the sheep are feeding, where the mill is going, where the barge is floating, where the dead are lying, where the factory is smoking, where the stream is running, where the village clusters, where the great cathedral rises, where the bleak moor lies, and the wild breeze smooths or ruffles it at its inconstant will; away, with a shriek, and a roar, and a rattle, and no trace to leave behind but dust and vapour: like as in the track of the remorseless monster, Death!

The traveler's body was disciplined (Löfgren 2008), power was dissociated from the docile body (Foucault 1995, 138) and transferred to the locomotive-passenger cyborg entity, transcending traditional boundaries of mind-body.

The railway transformed the relationship to the landscape, which was now experienced in and through the window as a "panorama." The landscape diminished by velocity, the railroad led to the disappearance of the "in-between" between the points of departure and arrival, the frequent tunnels switching between light and dark, while the underground train experience created a special spacelessness. As one anonymous author quoted by Schivelbusch (2014, 54) put it:

> The face of nature, the beautiful prospects of hill and dale, are lost or distorted to our view. The alternation of high and low ground, the healthful breeze, and all those exhilarating associations connected with "the road," are lost or changed to doleful cuttings, dismal tunnels, and the noxious effluvia of the screaming engine.

New imaginaries seamlessly incorporated urban and leisure experiences, transforming topographies wherein people's desires merged with reality as they traversed space (Schivelbusch 2014, 39). The railway journey created space as a sphere of multiplicity and power (Massey 2005, 9). The place of departure was present in memory but simultaneously coexisted with a multiplicity of trajectories: the in-between of the cabin and the passageway; the parallel heterogeneities of panoramic vistas seen through relations through the window; in the reading of books; in daydreams and fantasies.

Unusual spatial experiences emerged: "travel fever" (Löfgren 2008), a mix of anxiety and desire created by the materiality of the journey; tensions between the memory of the familiar place of departure and the concerns related to the imagined place of arrival; Freud's (1985, 262, 268) "railway anxiety," a psychological state formed by worries of derailment and by the sexual arousal produced by the pulsating train. As described at the time in the British medical journal *The Lancet*, the traveler was susceptible to the psychological effects of fatigue and deleterious impacts on the brain (Schivelbusch 2014; Beaumont and Freeman 2007) fostered by reading and looking at the passing panoramas. Travel made possible new fantasies. As Agatha Christie and other crime writers learnt, and taught their readers, on the train, "anything could happen."

"For people of our times," as Walter Benjamin put it, "railway stations are true dream factories" (quoted in Ehn and Löfgren 2010). A prominent example of the railway station as in-between of an experiential multiplicity is the Union Station in Cincinnati. Built between 1927 and 1933, it was the largest railway station of its time. A cathedral to locomotion, it is a masterpiece of Art Deco architecture, designed by the architectural firm Fellheimer & Wagner, also the lead architects for Grand Central Terminal (1903–1913) in New York City (Rolfes and Weise 2014). The original design featured Gothic architecture but was later changed and built in an Art Deco modern design. The station featured murals by Winold Reiss and had the largest semi-dome in the western hemisphere (Condit 1977). The station possessed a complex spatial functionality, with an efficient and elaborate vehicular traffic system at its core. It was spatially complex, making the passenger experience intricate and arduous as well as transformative. Not only was Union Station a point of departure and arrival, but it also seamlessly integrated transfers between the railway and private cars, taxicabs, buses and streetcars for travelers arriving from or going to the city and its outskirts.

Like the *dromos* of the Temple, Union Station was a transitory space. The rotunda, with its sheer size, colors, lights and design, was a Benjaminian dream factory. People could enter their dream destinations already before entering the train that actually took them to their desired destination. The feeling of spacelessness was assisted by the different spatial experiences of ups and downs, vestibules, tunnels and open spaces that already foreshadowed the spatial experiences passengers could expect when travelling. The duality of diminishment and expansion was anticipated by the transitions from the small vestibule to the enormous rotunda and then the crowded train concourse. Anticipating the experience of travel itself, desire merged already with reality as people traversed the railway station space. The railway station was a sphere of multiplicity and power. The size of the rotunda, the huge murals and the height of the building all pointed to the humbleness of the human entering railway space. Although Union Station was the largest railway station of its time, it was not atypical; the Helsinki and Kiev railway stations served as examples for the designers in Cincinnati (Solomon 2015).

Space and time not only contracted but expanded, while speed both increased and decreased, not unlike what we have already seen in the case of the *diolkos*. The railway revolution brought dromocracy into the world of everyday life. The steel *dromos* was the railroad expanded beyond the physical space it occupied. It became coterminous with the city, the space of everyday urban life.

The railway journey was, however, only one among many transformations of space-time in the nineteenth century. Time-space was transformed by other technologies with similar effects, including telecommunications, above all the telegraph and telephone, as well as photography. Gas lighting resulted in the "colonization of the night." Developments in the natural sciences led to earlier estimates of the origin of the Earth and the appearance of life on the Earth than had been previously assumed, as well as notions of "glacial time" (Urry 1994). Together, these produced revolutionary changes in the understanding and experience of time and space in the nineteenth century.

One way to assess the degree that space and time were transformed in the nineteenth century is in terms of efforts to instigate a romantic return to some supposedly more natural, humane time-space imagination; a "reality" or Being that invoked non-mechanized mobility, rejecting such "revolutionary" technologies, nostalgically "demanding a return to some prior, seemingly more harmonious and idyllic relations assumed to be possible between nature and culture" (Achterhuis 2001, 6).

Capitalist Space-Time

The annihilation of space *by* time, Marx argued in the *Grundrisse* (1973, 449), resulted from transformations in the physical conditions of exchange created by new forms of communication and transport. Capital and commodities were able to move across spatial barriers creating, David Harvey (1990b) has argued, the social conditions of modernity. While the circulation of capital and commodities radically altered social conditions, this is not our primary concern. Rather it is how perceptions of speed and space were transformed, how the globe as a *unit* emerged as the space of capitalist time, not only as appropriated or occupied land (the subject of chapter 6) but also as a unified socio-economic space, what Immanuel Wallerstein (2004) called "the world system."

The transformation of embodied multiplicities of time-space experience was aided by the newly emerging imaginary of global technoscientific capitalism. It was an early version of social exchange characterized by increasing interdependence between technological innovation, markets and socio-political constructs. These spatio-temporal transformations in the nineteenth century, May and Thrift (2001) note, were both cause and effect of what today we refer to as "technoscience": the emergence and (re)configuration of "things" (e.g., knowledge, infrastructure and bodies) as transformative social agents and as capitalized property. Capitalism was not just a revolutionary mode of production that created a seamless global flow of commodities; it was enabled and empowered by a transformative, disruptive and predatory technoscience. "Capitalism," Wolfgang Streeck (2016, 1) remarks in the introduction to *How Will Capitalism End?*, "promises infinite growth of commodified material wealth in a finite world, by conjoining itself with modern science and technology, making capitalist society the first industrial society." Capitalism, in other words, is a technoscientific society.

As Marx and Engels (1976b, 81), astute observers of the nineteenth century, put it in *The German Ideology*, universal competition had "made natural science subservient to capital." Or as Marx (1977, 104–5) had put it in the 1844 *Paris Manuscripts*, "natural science has invaded and transformed human life all the more *practically* through the medium of industry, although its immediate effect had to be the furthering of the dehumanization of man." Similarly, later in the *Grundrisse,* Marx (1973, 379) wrote that, "The various sciences have been pressed into the service of capital." As a form of alienated human power, "science . . . appears, in the machine, as something alien and exterior to the worker" (Marx 1973, 375).

The emergence of technoscientific capitalism may be described as another Copernican revolution. As Copernicus reimagined the universe as a spatially and not transcendentally conceived order, so technoscientific capitalism created the globe as a single unit in which capital circulated without borders.[*] As Marx and Engels (1976a) put it in a frequently quoted passage from "The Communist Manifesto":

---

[*] In his 1526 *Monetae cudendae ratio,* Copernicus laid the groundwork for the "Quantity Theory of Money," wherein the general price level of goods and services is held to be directly proportional to the amount of money in circulation, which in turn is directly linked to the "velocity of money": the speed (the number of transactions in a given time frame) by which transactions take place in an economy.

The bourgeoisie, by the rapid improvement of all instruments of production, by the immensely facilitated means of communication, draws all, even the most barbarian, nations into civilisation. The cheap prices of commodities are the heavy artillery with which it batters down all Chinese walls, with which it forces the barbarians' intensely obstinate hatred of foreigners to capitulate. It compels all nations, on pain of extinction, to adopt the bourgeois mode of production; it compels them to introduce what it calls civilisation into their midst, i.e., to become bourgeois themselves. In one word, it creates a world after its own image.

These spatial reconfigurations, which Harvey (1990b) calls "time-space compression," were at the same time revolutionary transformations in how the world was represented and imagined. The Copernican spatial reconfiguration of the universe, the importation of the Ptolemaic map from Alexandria to Venice in the early fifteenth century, Giordano Bruno's theory of cosmic pluralism and an infinite universe, the spread of the use of the chronometer and the change of perspective resulting from mathematically based map projections all contributed to the creation of the globe as a single entity. "They allowed," Harvey (1990b) observed, "the whole population of the earth, for the first time in human history, to be located within a single spatial frame," a point we will return to in chapter 6 when we discuss the *nomos* of automobility.

The emergence of the globe as a spatial unit meant that a new form of the spatial, a network for transporting invariant shapes of information, of scientific findings, of technological artifacts, came into existence (Law and Mol 2001). In this network the global is already included in the local as imaginary, as is the local included in the global as a regional variety of technoscientific reality. Time-space compression made it possible to create absences and presences that did not exist in traditional geographies. What occurred in geographically defined other spaces and to other bodies became experiences in the here and now of the emerging new dromocracy.

Coupled with the socio-economic capitalist reorderings of time-space (homogenous and universal time, conceptualizing profit as return on stock of capital over time), these transformations made the compression of time and space a central motif of the nineteenth and twentieth centuries. The spatial frame was the globe, conceptualized as knowable, representable, experienceable and, finally, manageable. The space of the globe was filled with "things" that not only managed but also produced space (Harvey 1990b; Chandler 2019).

The spatial frame was both *real* (i.e., knowable) and *imaginary* in the sense described by Benedict Anderson (1991); *limited* with finite, if pliant (land, high seas, air), frontiers, being part of an infinite and unknowable universe;

sovereign as capitalism and technoscience demolished the legitimacy of the divinely-ordained, hierarchical feudal realm; *inscribed* as a *community* of humans as imagined by philosophers such as Rousseau and Kant; *conceived* as a deep, horizontal and universal comradeship as enshrined in The Declaration of Independence and the *Déclaration des droits de l'homme et du citoyen de 1789*.

The expansion of capitalism across the globe resulted in the increasing assetization of both "things" (Birch and Muniesa 2020) and people, the latter through the transformation of labor power into a commodity (Lukács 1972) and the worker becoming one of the components of technoscientific manufacturing. Capital, as Marx (1976, 375–76) put it,

> steals the time required for the consumption of fresh air and sunlight. It haggles over the meal-times, where possible incorporating them into the production process itself, so that food is added to the worker as to a mere means of production, as coal is supplied to the boiler, and grease and oil to the machinery.

While neither the term nor the concept of a cyborg was available to Marx (see Clynes and Kline 1960), it is precisely a human-machine entity that Marx here describes.

In the twentieth century, these processes were intensified and refined in automobile manufacturing. Diego Rivera's *Detroit Industry Murals* in the Detroit Institute of Arts visually document the new working conditions that were being developed. Painted in 1932 and 1933, its subject matter is the work tasks, the machinery and their interconnections, within the Ford River Rouge factory. The murals are pictorial representations of alienation, exploitation, capitalist class relations and the Fordist production line. Their subject matter is the same as that of Charlie Chaplin's *Modern Times,* released in 1936. Like Rivera's murals, *Modern Times* documents working conditions under the emerging Taylorist regime of scientific management.

Mass production and mass consumption, each symbiotically requiring the other, represented the transformation of nineteenth-century capitalism into the consumerist capitalism of the twentieth century. In parallel with the construction of the cyborg worker described above, an appendage to and component of the machine that is a means of production, what Harvey (2003, 17) calls the "cyborg customer" came into existence, "the insatiable consumer totally hooked into the circulation of capital and its endless output of products" (see also Streeck 2016, 95–112).

Space was not only compressed by the speed of capital and commodity circulation but was created and multiplied. New spaces of consumption sprang up, transforming the socio-spatial arrangements of the previous era. La Belle Jardinière, a store selling multiple pieces of "ready-made" clothing in fixed sizes, was opened in 1824 near the Temple market in Paris. In Newcastle, Grainger Market, a vast structure comprised of four streets housing 243 retail units organized into lanes, pre-dated Haussmann's Paris by twenty years (Lancaster 1995, 8). Kendal Milne & Co.'s "The Bazaar" opened in Manchester in the 1830s with fixed prices and regular sales of remaindered stock.

Haussmannisation, the creation of a novel, consumer-friendly urban space, reconfigured the geographical and social context of lived experience, not only for the Parisian underclasses, artisans and the rentier but also for the feudal aristocracy to whom land ownership had given not only their names and lineage but a physical connection to history. This world was replaced with the bureaucratically sanctioned, privately constructed spaces of the new *Paris geometrique*, created by the rational rule of the straight line and a systematizing vision of a new, modern, bourgeois world. Before Haussmann the chaotic streets of the old city center of Paris were often scenes of barricades and battles. *Paris geometrique* was as much a hygienic measure and construction of a consumer-friendly urban space as it was the production of a politicized disciplinary space ordered along spatial principles of linearity (Bernard 2014, 53).

Capitalist time-space compression and multiplication were accompanied by the appropriation of space-time (Hornborg 2006). Capitalist technoscience was largely an index of accumulation rather than of ingenuity to save local time and space at the expense of (human) time and (natural) space lost elsewhere in the world. In England, by selling £1000 worth of cotton textiles on the world market in 1850, a British factory owner was able to exchange the product of 4,092 hours of British labor for that of 32,619 hours of (mostly slave) labor in overseas cotton plantations. In terms of space, the same market transaction implied the appropriation of the annual yield of 58.6 hectares of agricultural land overseas in exchange for the space occupied by a British textile factory (Hornborg 2006).

The technoscientific management of space, executed through "homogenization," "objectification" and "reification," was inscribed in and made possible through post-Enlightenment maps (De Certeau 1980). A fixed, geometrically spatial construct, the map converted fluid, disorderly, heterogeneous, social, cultural and spatial realities into an ordered static schema. This mathematically constructed objectification and representation of space, which substituted the disorderly reality of social and economic activities with abstract lines showing a functional system of factual ordering, "ran the danger of confining the free flow of human experience and practice to rationalized configurations" (Harvey 1990b). This geometric confinement of human experience and activity enabled the conquest and control of space through transforming the imaginary rational spatial construct of a planetary humanity into a technoscientific discourse of thought and action that conceived of space as an abstract, homogenous universal. This was complemented by the emergence of networks (Law and Mol 2001) and rhizomes (Deleuze and Guattari 1987) of imagined technoscientific space that held time-space together in knowable and manageable configurations. From the local of the map to the global of the imaginary back to the local of the here and now, the production of space was transduced and operationalized: "Builders, engineers, architects, and land managers for their part showed how Euclidean representations of objective space could be converted into a spatially ordered physical landscape" (Harvey 1990b). In addition to the creation of new metropolises through Hausmannisation, roads, turnpikes, canals and tunnels sprang up everywhere in the nineteenth century. New spatial networks were created through the clearing of lands and woods, replacing them first with railways and later with asphalt roads.

As space is also a container of social power, this production of space through new networks of communication and transportation was also a reorganization of frameworks through which social power was expressed and exercised. The global seamless flow of commodities required concrete modes of transportation and communication. Through the assetization of infrastructure, these space-producing assets became both the creators of space as much as the means through which power was rearranged and global flows were made universal. Investments in railways, roads, bridges, canals and urban infrastructures were at the heart of the "annihilation" of space and the further reification of human relations, leading to a total reordering of hierarchies of power. As Harvey (1990b, 258) notes:

> The specific spaces of transport and communication, of human settlement and occupancy, all legitimized under some legal system of rights to spaces (of the body, of land, of home etc.) which guarantees security of place and access to the members of society, form a fixed frame within which the dynamics of a social process must unfold.

The unified space of capital flows annihilated space by making commodity and capital movements transgress speeds enabled by the railway. In the new compressed time-space, commodities travelled from origin to destination "at the speed of light." Goods, artifacts, fruits and vegetables were transformed during the journey. They originated as "raw materials," "ingredients," "bits and pieces" and became commodities at their destination. Consumption is enabled without awareness of the intricate geography of production and the social relationships embedded in the network that enables these flows.

The spaces wherein "the consumer" purchased commodities became detached from the spaces in which commodities are produced. Social, geographical and political information is occluded, resulting in a form of "geographical ignorance" (Harvey 1990a). At the same time, negative externalities—exploitation, slavery, depletion of land—also "traveled," once again eliminating distance. What originated as lower prices, better air quality and a bourgeois lifestyle were transformed into corruption, exhaustion and colonial rule (Birtchnell, Savitzky, and Urry 2015). Commodities increasingly travelled outside of human perception: on the high seas, on railroads and across shipscapes and cargoscapes.

Production and consumption technologies were promoted directly through the creation of the world of what Debord (2014) calls the "spectacle." Technologies of persuasion, mediated through sophisticated machineries of representation and communication, captured, manipulated and promoted desires in ways conducive to endless capital accumulation.

Futurism as Dromocracy

The railway journey transformed the perception of time-space by introducing new vistas, spatial perspectives and the bodily experience of the passenger, who was both inside the train and a component of the locomotive-passenger cyborg entity. Technoscientific capitalism compressed time-space by constructing the globe as a single socio-economic entity, represented on a geometrical map. Analogously to the passenger, the worker/consumer was simultaneously inside and a component of this dromocratic technoscientific apparatus. At the turn of the twentieth century, an artistic movement that emerged in Italy went one step further by making dromocracy its central vision for the future. Inspired by technoscientific advancements, Futurism waged war against everything that was "old." Futurism, Virilio (2006, 84) observed, "comes from a single art—that of war and its essence, speed. Futurism provides the most accomplished vision of the dromological evolutionism of the 1920s, the measure of superspeed!"

The founding document of Futurism, Filippo Tommaso Marinetti's *Manifesto of Futurism*, was first published on February 5, 1909, in the *Gazzetta dell'Emilia* in Bologna. The core of the text, its eleven main points, had already been written in October or November 1908 and circulated in a two-page leaflet among Marinetti's friends in France and in Italy. Later that month Marinetti wrote the narrative preamble that would contextualize the points of the manifesto and sent the document to the *Gazzetta dell'Emilia* and other newspapers. This first version of the manifesto was quickly reprinted in five Italian newspapers and one magazine (*Il Pungolo* of Naples on February 6; *Arena* in Verona on February 9; *Il Piccolo* of Trieste on February 10; *Il Giorno* of Rome on February 16; and the weekly magazine *Tavola Rotonda* of Naples on February 14). On February 20, through a friend of Marinetti's father, the manifesto was published in French under the title "Le Futurisme" on the front page of the leading French newspaper, *Le Figaro*. Later translated into English as *The Founding and Manifesto of Futurism*, the French version established Marinetti's status as a celebrity. *The Manifesto of Futurism*, now published in both Italian and French newspapers, inspired young artists and socialites in both France and in Italy (Rainey, Poggi, and Wittman 2009).

Marinetti describes in the preamble to the manifesto the experiences of the new dromocratic era. These were the *sounds,* the "rumbling" of huge double-decker trams, the "roaring" of "hungry automobiles," the "snorting" of machines; the *vistas,* standing like lighthouses and sentinels in the millennial darkness being stroked through to see the first real sunrise on Earth as the new centaur is born and angels (of the machines) fly. The new era is materialized in a new technology/human cyborg—the person "revived beneath the steering wheel" and rushing in a "great sweep of madness [. . .] through the streets," pushing "[d]eath, tamed, in front of me at each corner offering me his hand nicely, [. . .] sometimes lay[ing] on the ground with a noise of creaking jaws giving me velvet glances from the bottom of puddles" (Marinetti 1909).

It is the eleven main points of the manifesto that fully embrace the dromocratic revolution embodied in the human-machine cyborg:

> We declare that the splendor of the world has been enriched by a new beauty: the beauty of speed. A racing automobile with its bonnet adorned with great tubes like serpents with explosive breath . . . a roaring motor car which seems to run on machine-gun fire, is more beautiful than the Victory of Samothrace (Marinetti 1909).

The manifesto celebrates the machine as the encapsulation of the new era that is to eliminate the millennial darkness, together with its artifacts stored in museums and libraries. The manifesto is not only a sonnet about the human-machine cyborg but an ode to a new social order that is being born:

> We will sing of the great crowds agitated by work, pleasure and revolt; the multi-colored and polyphonic surf of revolutions in modern capitals: the nocturnal vibration of the arsenals and the workshops beneath their violent electric moons: the gluttonous railway stations devouring smoking serpents; factories suspended from the clouds by the thread of their smoke; bridges with the leap of gymnasts flung across the diabolic cutlery of sunny rivers: adventurous steamers sniffing the horizon; great-breasted locomotives, puffing on the rails like enormous steel horses with long tubes for bridle, and the gliding flight of aeroplanes whose propeller sounds like the flapping of a flag and the applause of enthusiastic crowds (Marinetti 1909).

This new social order is the multicolored, polyphonic revolution of the modern metropolis: the interconnected and vibrating network of railways, factories, bridges, steamers and the enthusiastic crowds celebrating the "beauty of speed." For Marinetti this beauty exists only in struggle; its poetry, as violent assault, forces the unknown to bow before man. It is by and through the beauty of speed, embodied in the mobile machine-human cyborgs and their networks that space and time, the manifestation of the old, can finally be annihilated. "Time and Space died yesterday. We are already living in the absolute, since we have already created eternal, omnipresent speed," Marinetti (1909) claimed. It is neither an experiential annihilation as was the experience of the railway journey nor political annihilation as representation of human relations objectified on the map. It was the annihilation of time and space by demolishing memoryscapes (Edensor 1997), such as museums and libraries, the venues where the old time and the old space are stored, visited and adored, which, for Marinetti, described much of Italy.

Marinetti's proclamation was heard by artists in Italy and in France. They issued a number of similar manifestos, all calling for a violent break with the old: in painting, in sculpture, in music, in cinema and in architecture. Antonio Sant'Elia, in a newspaper article published in Florence on August 1, 1914, several days after the official beginning of what is now known as the First World War, declared:

> [w]e must invent and rebuild the Futurist city like an immense and tumultuous shipyard, agile, mobile and dynamic in every detail; and the Futurist house must be like a gigantic machine [. . .] the street will no longer lie like a doormat at ground level, but will plunge many stories down into the earth, embracing the metropolitan traffic, and will be linked up for necessary interconnections by metal gangways and swift-moving pavements (Sant'Elia 1914).

This futurist annihilation of time and space is nowhere more evident than in the *Manifesto of Futurist Painting*, in which Umberto Boccioni, Carlo Carrà and other eminent artists of the movement claim that time is not a fixed moment any more but "dynamic sensation itself," that "space no longer exists: the street pavement, soaked by rain beneath the glare of electric lamps, becomes immensely deep and gapes to the very center of the earth" (Boccioni et al. 1910). In 1913 Boccioni created the human-machine cyborg as artifact, molding one of the most famous works of art by the futurists, *Unique Forms of Continuity in Space*, a figure that is aerodynamically created and deformed by speed. The dynamic sensation is manifested in and on the body, as well as it is represented in the mechanized body or the cyborglike features that is human and nonhuman at the same time.

Inspired by Bergson's philosophy of emotions and the *élan vital,* Auguste Joly, in an article published in 1912 in *La Belgique artistique et littéraire,* argued that the philosophy of futurism follows Bergson in making use of the "symbolic continuities of emotions" (Joly 1912). These revolutionary emotions and time-space experiences formed a call for a new (political) philosophy, for "revolutionary" thinkers and artists to reconceptualize time-space.

This embodiment in Marinetti's *Futurist Manifesto* pointed towards the birth of both a new technoscientific order and a new political ontology. This new technoscientific order, which revolved around the absolutization of dromocracy, was not only a perspectival reconstruction of everyday reality, but it also created a totalizing vision of technoscientific being. At its center, for the first time, was not only the human-machine cyborg—the Futurist automobile/driver hybrid—but a deified *dromos* (speed) combined with the idealized *cratos* (power) as the idyllic human form of life on earth that served as the source of meaning.

Futurism is an early twentieth-century example of what Alain Badiou has called a "poetico-political" group. Such groups, Badiou (2007, 148–49) writes, "assert that they embody the identity between a school of artistic creation and an organization which practices and maintains the intellectual conditions of a political break." Futurism was programmatic in advancing a political vision of an advanced sociotechnical future that would break with the past. At the same time Futurism articulated both in its texts and through art sociotechnical developments that were already present. What the Futurists did was reinscribe their meaning, and here we can more clearly see the political direction of Futurism. Instead of glorifying the human-machine cyborg that is *Unique Forms of Continuity in Space,* Boccioni could have alerted us to what we are becoming, components within a human-machine entity, as, for example, Rivera did.

In the original manifesto, Marinetti (1909) glorified war as the only cure for the world: "militarism, patriotism, the destructive gesture of the anarchists, the beautiful ideas which kill." The war that was deified by the movement eventually came, and the protagonists of the futurist story signed up to serve, with Boccioni and Marinetti joining the "Lombard Battalion Volunteers Cyclists and Motorists." They endured several weeks of fighting in harsh conditions before the cyclist units, deemed inappropriate for mountain warfare, were disbanded. Marinetti spent most of 1916 supporting Italy's war effort with speeches, journalism and theatrical work, then returned to military service as a regular army officer in 1917. In May of that year, he was seriously wounded while serving with an artillery battalion on the Isonzo front. He returned to service after a long recovery and participated in the decisive Italian victory at Vittorio Veneto in October 1918 against the Austro-Hungarian army. Boccioni succumbed to injuries at the age of thirty-three after falling from a horse and then being trampled on during Italian Army cavalry training.

The Futurists who survived the war ultimately aligned themselves, unsurprisingly, with Mussolini and the Fascist movement in the period following World War I. In 1919 Marinetti wrote with Alceste De Ambris a second manifesto, *The Fascist Manifesto*, and spoke alongside Mussolini at a meeting in Milan that marked the foundation of the *Fasci di Combattimento*. However, it was not Marinetti, despite his support of Mussolini, who gave material form to the new social order as described in the Manifesto: the poetic *and* "violent assault on the forces of the unknown, to force them to bow before man." It was an Italian engineer, Piero Puricelli, who invented the *autostrada* that converted the "beauty of speed" to a spatially ordered physical landscape transforming and animating the profound everyday experience of mundane modern life.

The modern highway, a time-space apparatus (Moraglio 2017), completes our story of time-space annihilation and the coming into being of a new political ontology. The first motorway, designed by Puricelli and inaugurated by Mussolini on March 26, 1923, was the foundational moment of the new dromocratic social order that has come to dominate late-modernity. Connecting Milan to Lake Como and Lake Maggiore, it was described by Puricelli as a complex of "several road inspector's houses, which will be home to the road inspectors and will also offer frequent points for shelter and refueling," complete with "distances, the routes, and the obstacles [. . .] carefully indicated with international signs also visible at night," as well as "petrol and oil stations, with automatic dispensers and controlled quantity and quality" and "mechanics" to "patrol the carriageway with flying workshops to carry help wherever it is needed" (Puricelli 1922, quoted in Moraglio 2017, 4–5).* The autostrada catered to petty-bourgeois desires, and the autostrada celebrated the nuclear family, which could now travel by car from the city to the countryside; a patriarchal social order in which decisions were made by the male head of the household; and individualist social aspirations of freedom, affluence and desire inscribed in a rhizomatic topography.

If the symbol of nineteenth-century bourgeois urbanism was the boulevard, the autostrada marked the beginning of a new era of spatio-technical mass commodification. The construction of Puricelli's autostrada was a significant moment in the history of the automobility imaginary. The motorway has come to represent the good life for the people: "a garage in every house; [. . .] distance annihilated; therefore, country life, well-being, pleasure" (Puricelli

---

* The construction of the first German Autobahns began in the 1930s. The first section of the Autobahn network, between Frankfurt am Main to Darmstadt, was opened in 1935. The opening celebration was attended by Adolf Hitler (https://collections.ushmm.org/search/catalog/pa1037717).

1922, quoted in Moraglio 2017, 6). Marinetti's vision of "living in the absolute" became the docile petty-bourgeois social order of the twentieth century, at home within both fascist and liberal social orders. As Hannah Arendt (1958, 338) put it:

> [t]he philistine's retirement into private-life, his single-minded devotion to matters of family and career was the last, and already degenerated, product of the bourgeoisie's belief in the primacy of private interest. The philistine is the bourgeois isolated from his own class, the atomized individual who is produced by the breakdown of the bourgeois class itself. The mass man [. . .] bore the features of the philistine rather than of the mob man, and was the bourgeois who in the midst of the ruins of his world worried about nothing so much as his private security, was ready to sacrifice everything—belief, honor, dignity—on the slightest provocation. Nothing proved easier to destroy than the privacy and private morality of people who thought of nothing but safeguarding their private lives.

The motorway became the technosocial machinery that would provide a "virtuous cycle for mankind: the road, the car and prosperity" (Puricelli 1922).

The autostrada may also be read, ironically, as a direct response to the removing of the obstacles that hindered the free flow of Marinetti's intoxicated vision. His vision was transformed into a utopia in which hunting "death with its black fur dappled with pale crosses, who ran before us in the vast violet sky, palpable and living" was not hindered by the stupid swaying of cyclists. In the new reality of the motorway, this could no longer happen. Those who worship the beauty of speed would no longer have to deal with "drunk cart-drivers, slow bicycle riders, and disrespectful pedestrians" (Moraglio 2017, 4), "the vermin of the street," as Theodor Adorno (2010, 40) was to later describe them. They were forbidden entry into this new space of automobility. However, the converse was permitted. To properly function, the motorway requires the mass production of automobiles capable of achieving high speeds. Yet those vehicles—heavy machinery capable of moving at motorway speeds—are not restricted to motorway travel but are permitted to traverse urban and other spaces inhabited by pedestrians, bicyclists and other non-motorized vehicles.

During the next decades it was "the allure of speed"—namely dromology—which, Illich (1974, 44) argued,

> deceived the passenger into accepting the *promises* made by an industry that produces capital-intensive traffic. He is convinced that high-speed vehicles have allowed him to progress beyond the limited autonomy he enjoyed when moving under his own power [our emphasis].

Those promises are the promises embedded in the sociotechnical imaginaries of automobility that are essential for the reproduction of dromocratic automobility. The automobile is, however, but one element in the materially heterogenous network that forms the dromocratic order. It is an order composed of different types of "stuff": artifacts (cars, gas stations, bicycles), architectures (roads, bridges, buildings), technologies (the engine, the wheel, oil refineries), signs (lights, marks, gestures), language (naming, shouting, shrieking, giving the finger), networks (production lines, supply chains, pipes), people (drivers, policemen, pedestrians, children), rules (laws, economics) and skills (driving, crossing, understanding). It is a semiotic, relational and meaning-producing order. The meaning of the "stuff" of which it is composed, as we argued in chapter 2, is indexically constructed by and within this network. The dromocratic order is an epistemic order.

What is named as automobility may be described as an actor-network, small scale, heterogenous material semiotic network of practice (Law 1986, 2009; Latour 2005). It can also be described as a grand, strategic and relational "epochal episteme" (Foucault 1995), as a dispositif (Manderscheid 2014). Automobility sits in the epistemic meso between small-scale actor-networks and overarching epochal epistemes. Automobility is a heterogeneous and limited form of ordering: more ordered than ANT theorists would define it but less than would Foucauldian STS scholars. Although limited from an epochal and epistemic aspect, it is "reality making." There is no other order, some other "reality" outside the web that is created by the weaved relations holding the network of meaning of automobility together. It is woven together in a specific political constellation that is beyond actual small-scale, heterogenous material semiotic practice. Automobility is a dromocratic order held together by speed, power, and violence.

It is a lifeworld that is not centered around the automobile *qua* technosocial object as it did for the Futurists. This is one of the reasons why "automobility" is an ill-named thing.

THE ONTOPOLITICS OF DROMOCRACY

The annihilation of space *by* time with the development of modern technoscience, the world and the larger universe experienced through implements (Ihde 2009), was accompanied by the annihilation of time-space by speed as a spatio-social construct. The railway journey created the powerful locomotive-body bursting through the landscape: "The gluttonous railway stations devouring smoking serpents . . . great-breasted locomotives, puffing on the rails like enormous steel horses with long tubes for bridle" (Marinetti 1909).

The railroad experience connected those experiencing this new bodily sensation at the same time that it separated them from others. The journey not only produced the locomotive-body hybrid, but it also created its binary opposite, the non-hybrid body: those working on the field as the train passed; people standing and waiting at railway crossings; bicyclists moving slowly about their business.

Transformed from pedestrian to projectile, from docile body to locomotive-body hybrid, animated by Benjamin's "dream factory." Going through the *foyer* of a railway station, the dromos leading up to the cathedral of locomotion, was a rite of passage that prepared the traveler for the uniqueness of the journey that was in part the *angst* of the experience that was to follow.

While commodity fetishism created the consumer cyborg, it also created those who were left out. The proletariat who owned nothing but their labor power; those separated from the newly constructed Haussmannite bourgeois spaces—boulevards, department stores and the housing estates for the middle classes. *Qua* spatial structure, roads—the boulevard and the autostrada—were appropriated spaces comprised of connectors, separators and in-betweens. Divisions were constitutive in the Futurist revolution. Those divisions were marked not only by Marinetti's impatience and anger towards the "slow" bicyclists who forced his automobile-body into the ditch but between those who enjoyed the beauty, the privilege and power of speed and those who did not, against whom Marinetti and his friends revolted: the old, the cowardly and women.

A contemporary example was reported in an Australian newspaper (*The Melbourne Age* 2008):

> About 50 cyclists have been involved in a hit-and-run crash in Sydney this morning. . . . [A] driver, agitated with being held up, accelerated in front of the pack and then slammed on his brakes, giving the riders no time to stop. The resulting smash forced a semitrailer to lock up, jackknife and screech to a halt behind the cyclists while cars had to swerve to avoid them. Several drivers making their way past the aftermath of the accident jeered and taunted the cyclists, despite the fact that a police car and two ambulances were on the scene treating seriously injured people.

The "accident" recounted here was nothing less than a dromocratic spectacle, a *theatron,* replete with a (mobile) audience—spectators—to jeer and taunt those who were vanquished and to applaud the victors.

In Arendtian terms the annihilation of time-space resulted in the depoliticization of technoscience; the elimination of a shared perspectival experience of the "in-between" as the *locus*, in the most literal sense, of the political. The political, Arendt (1958, 57) argued, is the reality rising out of the sum total of aspects presented by one object to a multitude of spectators. Only where things can be seen by many in a variety of aspects without changing their identity, so that those who are gathered around them know they see sameness in utter diversity, can worldly reality truly and reliably appear. Under the conditions of a common world, reality is not guaranteed primarily by the "common nature" of all men who constitute it, but rather by the fact that, differences of position and the resulting variety of perspectives notwithstanding, everybody is always concerned with the same object.

Through the annihilation of space-time, this "object"—"seeing sameness in utter diversity"—was lost. A perspectival "reality rising out of the sum total of aspects" was diminished. A shared political ontology based on freedom and plurality was replaced by, as Arendt (1958, 58) foresaw, "the end of the common world [. . .] seen only under one aspect and . . . permitted to present itself in only one perspective." This one perspective is the automobility imaginary.

In turn this led to Deleuze's "control society," a hegemonic and universal new dromocratic order—the spectacle. As "time and space died" after the devastating experiences of the actual war, Marinetti's absolute was domesticated as a new order of control. The locus of the political moved from the space of the in-between of individuals to the rhizomatic network of augmented human-machine cyborgs. Plurality was submerged in a new order in which differences of position and of perspectives prohibited the possibility that everybody would be concerned with the same object: the political.

The birth of disciplinary biopolitical power has been traced to several origins: to the Roman tradition of bare life and the sovereign exception (Agamben 1998); to pastoral power and secularized practices of confession in early modernity (Foucault 1980); to capitalist alienation and passive spectacular consumption (Debord 2014); to rhizomatic delocalized flows of time, space and capital (Deleuze and Guattari 1987). A political ontology close to these genealogies and biopolitical logics can also be traced.

Annihilation of time and space through speed led to a disruption of social time-space in the dromos: on the railway, within the capitalist ecosystem, on the automobilized road. The railroad and the motorway—speedways—disrupted the realm of the political in multiple ways as a common and shared space of appearances. The railroad became an implement of speed just as much as it became a fence, separating the rich from the poor, the fast from the slow, the docile body from the cyborg body. Dromocratic control disciplined mobility by managing social inequality. Simultaneously, it disciplined inequality by managing mobility. With the destruction of traditional time-space and the production of new spatial forms and orders, a new biopolitical control society emerged. As Deleuze and Lapoujade (2006, 322) put it in reference to, in their view, Foucault's misplaced emphasis on discipline:

> [w]e are entering control societies that are defined very differently than disciplinary societies. Those who are concerned about our welfare no longer need, or will no longer need, places of confinement. [. . .] Control is not discipline. You do not confine people with a highway. But by making highways, you multiply the means of control. I am not saying this is the only aim of highways, but people can travel infinitely and "freely" without being confined while being perfectly controlled.

The new biopolitical control society ushered in a new spatio-social order as well as new forms of bodily control that sublimated discipline, that transformed heterotopic places of discipline into omnitopic places of control. In short, a new technoscientific political ontology has emerged.

Chapter Four

Theatron

The Spectacle

In Homer's *Odyssey*, the *dromos* was not a permanent but a temporary reconfiguration of space, constructed anew for each special event in the *agora* ("meeting/gathering place"). Book VIII recounts an *agones* ("celebration") organized by the Phaeacians to honor Odysseus, which took place on the *agora*. First, a racecourse was prepared for foot races and other competitions. Later, the singer Demodocus, who occupied the *choros* ("center place"), was surrounded by young dancers. *Dromos* and *choros* appear to have been areas within the *agora* prepared for festivals in ancient Greece. Structures were not set up for the audience. Standing on prepared earthen embankments, the crowd spontaneously lined up along the sides of the *dromos,* from where they watched the races (Dubbini 2010, 158–60).

The *orkhêstra* ("dancing place") was an area reserved for artistic performances, for which the spectators occupied the *theatron* ("seeing place"), temporary stands of stone or wood, also erected as required, called *ikria*. The *choros* possessed a strong sacral character, while the *orkhêstra* was used for cultic performances of ritual dramas in the *temenos*, the sacred enclosure around the temple altar, often adjacent to the *choros* as passageway (*dromos*) to the temple. The *agora* was a central space in the urban environment in ancient Greece and beyond. A community without an *agora* was considered lawless; thus the presence of an *agora* signified order and civilization in the city (Lindenlauf 2014). It was a space in which political, social, commercial, religious and cultural activities took place.

Activities did not have fixed places or buildings, at least in the early period of the *Odyssey*, but were set up as required. Some activities were so closely linked to a specific space that the name of the space came to describe the activity. Some are still etymologically recognizable in modern European languages, with examples such as *choros* ("central dance place"), *agon* ("athletic contest place"), *ekklesia* ("popular assembly place") and *theatron* ("viewing place").

The social and political core of the polis, the *agora* was the space where governmental proceedings, archives, religious rites, athletic and dramatic competitions, military activities, trading and shopping, philosophical discussions and chats and eating and drinking took place (Lindenlauf 2014, 69). *Theatron*, the "place of seeing," may be considered both a function (of sporting events, of dramatic activities, of festive or religious events) and as a synonym for the *agora* itself. The *agora* was a spectacle, a place for seeing unity in diversity (of people, of functions, of roles) and the locus and mode of the order that governed this diversity.

As they were temporary structures, there seems to be no archaeological evidence that shows a circular arrangement of *ikria*. Built *theatra* were semicircular structures based on the circular form of the *orkhěstra* (Dubbini 2010, 165). Arendt (1958, 57) has argued that the *theatron/agora* was the locus of the political in the polis. It made possible a shared reality, emerging as the sum total of what was presented to the spectators. This reality, as seen from the *theatron*, was the spectacle of the *agones* (e.g., *dromoi*), that eventually, in the polis, became the shared reality that was the order. The evolving structure of the *theatron*, its eventual semicircular form, offered different vantage points to appreciate the same perspectival object.

The railroad in the nineteenth century and automobility in the twentieth century created new experiences and modes of being. New mobility apparatuses allowed "things," "the world," to be experienced and viewed from multiple vantage points. The *theatron*, like the *dromos*, was for the Greeks fixed, ordered, material and bounded. Like the *dromos* that is no longer enclosed within boundaries, so too has theater exceeded boundaries. *Theatron* is now the space of a generalized *dromocratic spectacle*, dispersed across multiple semiotic spaces characterized by speed, power and violence.

"Spectacle" as order has its origins in the writings of Guy Debord and the situationists in the 1960s. The spectacle, Debord (2014, 2) argued, is "[f]ragmented views of reality" regrouped in "a separate pseudo-world" of "social relation[s] between people . . . mediated by images." The spectacle, in other words, is an imaginary, albeit an imaginary whose defining property is the spectacular. The spectacle, Debord argued, appeared as "fetishistic pure objectivity," concealing and objectifying relations "between people and between classes: a second Nature, with its own inescapable laws" (7–8).

Dromocracy brought into being not only a (new) representation of the world but, as both De Certeau (1980) and Deleuze (2006) later observed, a totalizing machinery of control, comprised of images. Biopolitics, the governance and disciplining of bodies and souls (Foucault), political control through ideological apparatuses occurred in the context of dromocratic changes in time-space perception, represented through Debord's somewhat idiosyncratic name for our condition—"spectacle."

Like Marcel Duchamp's Dadaist urinal that redefined art, Debord may be said to have redefined the theater. Duchamp transformed the urinal into an art object by submitting this ordinary object to an art exhibition competition and subsequently exhibiting it in an art museum, unmasking location as the defining characteristic of art, above all canonical art (Braun and Randell 2021) in the age of museums, Duchamp's urinal being a case in point, having now achieved canonical status. If the traditional theater *qua* architectural artifact is the dramatic equivalent of the art gallery, Debord accomplished the reverse of Duchamp. Instead of locating ordinary activities within the space that is the theater, thereby transforming the artistic event that is a play or dance performance, Debord effectively exploded the confines of the traditional theater. It is everywhere, and its defining characteristic is spectacle. It is the reality in which we live, society "marked by alienation, totalitarian control and passive spectacular consumption—that predominates everywhere" (Debord 2002, 159).

THE SITUATIONISTS

The Situationists were a small group of artists and social theorists, active between 1957 and 1972, whose most important members and exponents were Guy Debord and Raoul Vaneigem (cf. Plant 1992; Trier 2019), both Belgian. The precursor of the Situationists was the Letterist movement, an ensemble of avant-garde artists following the Dadaist and Surrealist tradition around Isadore Isou. Their descriptive name came from their desire to reduce poetry to "the letter." The Letterists engaged in Dadaist cultural and political sabotage, such as the Notre Dame affair in 1950, where they disrupted the Easter Mass with the announcement that "God was dead"; or the disturbance of Chaplin's press conference in Paris in 1952 where they argued that Chaplin is outdated, claiming that "truths which no longer entertain become lies" (Trier 2019, 29–78). Some of the artists and intellectuals aligning themselves with Debord, who had already become one of the key figures of the Letterists, left the group in the late 1950s to do more serious theoretical and political work. The Situationist International was founded at Cosio d'Arroscia in Northern Italy in 1957, mainly out of two avant-garde groups: the radical left-wing Letterists and the Movement for an Imaginist Bauhaus (Trier 2019). The main theoretical texts and visual artistic works of the Situationists were published in the twelve issues of the journal *Internationale situationiste*. In 1967

Debord published *The Society of the Spectacle* and Raoul Vaneigem (1983) published *The Revolution of Everyday Life*. Both works critiqued modern capitalism from a situationist perspective. Over its existence the Situationist International had an average membership of around only ten to twenty people. Altogether thirty-six men and seven women from sixteen different countries were members at one time or another. Their impact, however, was considerably larger than their actual membership would suggest. Their last conference was held in 1969, and the group was officially dissolved in 1972, with only two members remaining: Guy Debord and Gianfranco Sanguinetti.

The focus of Debord's concept of the spectacle is the distorted reality of everyday life. Unlike sociotechnical imaginaries as defined by Jasanoff and Kim, which separates the "real" from the "representational," Debord (2014, 11) argued that the spectacle is "capital accumulated to the point that it becomes images." In this everyday alienated, manipulated, totalizing reality, everyday experience is entangled with and creates "the concrete conditions of present day oppression" (108). The conceptualization of the world as spectacle drew on Marxist analyses of reification (Lukács 1972), on Dadaist and Surrealist practices of automated thinking/writing/painting and on Freudian explorations of the unconscious. The world was a spectacle in which everything was in motion: "Images detached from every aspect of life merge into a common stream, and the former unity of life is lost forever. [. . .] The spectacle in its generality is a concrete inversion of life, and, as such, the *autonomous movement* of nonlife" (5); "it arrogates to itself everything that in human activity exists in a *fluid state*" (10) [our emphasis]. The spectacle is the name for the interconnected "fluid state" of human activities, entrapped in "a common stream" that creates the "conditions of oppression"—the everyday, mundane reality of late capitalism.

The Situationists pointed to the automobile as the "material symbol of the notion of happiness that developed capitalism tends to spread throughout the society" (Debord 1959, 69). The automobile within the spectacle stood for the "supreme good of alienated life" (69), the material embodiment of the spectacle as political imaginary. In the spectacle the car does not "stand in place of automobility itself" (Böhm, Jones, et al. 2006, 4–5) but is one element within the spectacle. That element is the "material symbol" that is a fetishistic objectification within the spectacle. Proceduralized by power, violence and speed, oppression is transformed into happiness. The car thus points to the spectacle as dromocratic.

The Situationists attempted a radical escape from the totalizing production of space as spectacle or, more broadly, a break from what Deleuze and Lapoujade (2006) called the "control society," of reified consumerism. In the method of psychogeography and its practice of *dérive,* inspired by Lefebvre's

Critique of Everyday Life (1991 [1947]) and following the tradition initiated by Benjamin's (1999) flaneur project (who in turn was influenced by Baudelaire), they focused on the lived, temporary experiences of walking, seeing, hearing, imagining and experiencing cityscapes while discovering parts of the city that invoked distinct sentimental value. The humanly experienced city, they believed, offered a discharge from the dromocratic spectacle. Dérive, roughly "drifting," in English, was a method to negate the (capitalist/railway/automobility) annihilation of time and space, to create human time and space in the here and now of the experienced city. It encouraged "getting lost" through aimless wandering or drifting, to "drop their relations, their work and leisure activities, and all their other usual motives for movement and action, and let themselves be drawn by the attractions of the terrain and the encounters they find there" (Knabb 2006, 62). A key concept was "letting-go," a playful interplay between space and psyche, being-in and being-of space, escaping from the dromocratic order of the spectacle not by offering another spectacle or another form of control but by "disorientation"—getting out of spatial, temporal and habitual frames.

Dérive, Vaneigem (1983) wrote, was a "technique of locomotion without a goal" (85). Drifting through the city was to remove oneself from the totalizing dromocratic control of the spectacle. It is an anarchistic orientation similar to what Agamben (2014) calls "destitution," which we will return to in chapter 9.

Although not primarily concerned with the car, the Situationists argued that the automobile should be phased out of the city. "[W]e can envision the banning of auto traffic from the central areas," Debord (1959) wrote in his *Theses on Traffic*, pointing towards a possibility of urban post-automobility. Experiences, not as "totalizing" but contingent, were presented in the form of a map, not as a device but as a guide to "secret" parts of the city that had not been overcome by the forces of capitalism manifested in the spectacle. Such secrets were both spatial—drawing up "hitherto lacking maps of influences"—and temporal, unearthing traumascapes (Tumarkin 2005) that have sank into the status of becoming forgotten by the spatial ontology of the day. What the Situationists called unitary urbanism (Spiteri 2015) broke the "order" of the spectacle by dissolving "separations such as work/leisure or public/private" (Debord 1959, 69). The spectacle united everything that was on the move, both "things" (commodity and capital) and the subject, whose desires, perspectives and actions (in constant motion) were produced and mediated by the qualitative multiplicity of images of everyday reality. Dérive not only attempted to reverse this process but to re-create the experiencing body. Not the techno-human cyborg (the car/driver; the locomotive/human) but the walking person experiencing the city at human speed and in human time. Such experience, Debord argued, could be achieved by "letting-go": dissolving the imaginary unity of "stuff" in the material semiotic network, deactivating the spectacle as "concrete conditions of oppression."

A contemporary example of dérive is the "I am just walking" project (https://imjustwalkin.com/) of Matt Green, who is walking every street in New York City—including sidewalks, private roads, parks, cemeteries, beaches, and abandoned space. His original estimate was that he would cover 8,000 miles, but he had already walked 9,279 miles at the time of writing. Not in a hurry, he wanders and chats with locals, notices intricacies and details most of us would miss, from metal spikes left behind by street cleaners to DIY 9/11 murals and memorials, to the use of the letter "Z" in words like "cutz" on barbershop signs. A recurring theme in a film of his project is Green explaining what he is doing to the people he meets. He's not writing a book, nor is he doing scientific research, nor is he making money. "There's no particular goal other than to just see the whole city," he tells an inquisitive truck driver. "The goal of this walk," Green says in the film, "is not really to finish it; the goal is everything that happens along the way to finishing it." Eloquently articulated in the style of Debord, he asks, "What kind of truth can I hope to find?"

> Every step I take will be deeply colored by many transient factors—the weather, the time of day, my mood, the people around me. I could go back to any given spot the next day and have an entirely different experience. Who knows how many fascinating things I'll totally overlook? Maybe I'll be facing the other way as I pass by, or maybe the fascination lies in some story or context that I won't be aware of. There are countless indoor spaces that I'll never see. My walking experience will be largely confined to street level, even though much of what makes New York "New York" exists above the first floor. If you try to make this quest into a conquest—an attempt to subjugate the bewildering vastness of this metropolis beneath the well-worn heels of my boots—then perhaps it seems dispiriting to contemplate how little of the city I'll have actually seen and experienced after my extensive journey. But why would you ever want to know a place completely? The excitement of New York, and the whole world for that matter, is that there's always something else to see, and something else to learn, no matter how long you've been around. To me it is profoundly encouraging to think how many secrets will still lie undiscovered after I've walked every last one of these goddamned streets. At its core, my walk is an oxymoron: an exhaustive journey through an inexhaustible city (Green 2020).

Although he uses a traditional Euclidean map representation of New York to record his walking, he does not walk "systematically." Nor does he record his experiences in calendar time, only psycho-geographical time: days are numbered continuously from the first step (on the day of writing, he is at day

3,127). Green, like Debord, places his experience on a map that is similar to the Situationists' *Naked Map* collage (McDonough 1994, 59), although it is now a computerized map depicting his route in red, hypertexted and made clickable, allowing one to see what happened on each day of the dérive, what photo he uploaded, what story he unearthed.

The Situationists, Green and others doing similar endeavors in Manchester, London, Ontario and other places (Morris and Morag 2019; Richardson 2015; Taylor and Whalley 2018) are to some degree breaking free of the dromocratic spectacle of late modernity. They are walking, wandering, drifting, floating, experiencing, "looking at things from new angles, radical history, drinking tea and getting lost; having fun," as the *Loiterers' Resistance Movement* explained in their manifesto (Rose 2006). It is an orientation in stark contrast to the automobility experience. Already in the late 1950s, Keats (1958, 144) observed that "it is now possible to drive across the face of the nation without feeling that you've been anywhere or that you've done anything."

THE DROMOCRATIC SPECTACLE

In "The New Mobilities Paradigm," Sheller and Urry (2006, 207) observe that "All the world seems to be on the move": sea, road and air travel; virtual travel in cyberspace; the movement of different categories of people, such as refugees and holidaymakers; the movement of materials, from guns and oil to fresh vegetables and electronic equipment. The thrust of their argument is that these are not single, individual empirical instances or categories of movement but phenomena for which it is possible to provide a general theoretical account (Cresswell 2001, 24). What became known as the "mobility turn" in the social sciences, Sheller and Urry argued, had challenged dominant "a-mobile," (Sheller and Urry 2006, 210) assumptions and had questioned accounts that presumed "sedentary, bounded, and static states and societies" (Sheller and Urry 2016, 11). The mobilities turn, Sheller and Urry (2016, 11–12) argued, had focused on "examining the constitutive role of movement within social institutions and social practices" and "analyzing networks, relations, flows and circulation, and not fixed places."

Elsewhere, Randell (2020b) has argued that what Sheller and Urry call "the new mobilities paradigm" is not a paradigm in any recognizably Kuhnian form. The new mobilities paradigm, Randell argues, is essentially a collection of literature that is in some way "about mobility." Moreover, that literature is comprised of texts that theorize mobility in not only diverse but incompatible ways. The search for an overarching general mobility theory that explains and describes any and all forms of movement is, in our view, both mistaken and destined to failure. This does not mean, however, that there is nothing of a general nature that can be said about contemporary forms of mobility. It is precisely the "constitutive role of movement" that Virilio's dromocracy concept addresses, albeit not in the way Sheller and Urry have formulated the problem.

Dromos and *kratos*, combined under the term "dromocracy," refer respectively to speed and power/violence. It is a space in which Kratos and Bia together appear to reinforce the might of the sovereign. *Dromos*, under its ancient Greek significations, referred to a barriered, safe and/or transitory space, enclosed within which were the sacred or warrior sports enjoyed from the *theatron*. In contrast, what we are living now is the annihilation of human time/space. It is held together as a network by a sovereign that is speed and power/violence in the *dromos*: warscapes of far/near; cityscapes of work/leisure and public/private (Sheller and Urry 2000); traumascapes freezing and inscribing experiences of violence (Tumarkin 2005).

Sheller and Urry are correct in observing that "all the world is on the move." That world on the move that we inhabit is dromocracy. Dromocracy is the expansion of dromos across and throughout the globe. It is the violence of speed that has escaped and exited from the confined space of the metaphorical racetrack and passage leading to the temple. It has spilled beyond "immediate assault," entering the mundane world of everyday life of late modernity. Human time and human space have been compressed, extended and annihilated, reappearing in the imaginary time-space of the dromocratic spectacle. A *theatron/agora*: conflating viewing place, dancing place and the meeting place; coalescing power, order and violence. It is dromocracy, the imaginary reality in which we dwell.

In his 1932 memoir *The Struggle for Berlin*, Joseph Goebbels attributed the growing success of the Nazi party to its innovative use of city streets for propaganda. "The street," Goebbels wrote, "is now the primary feature of modern politics. Whoever can conquer the street can also conquer the masses, and whoever conquers the masses will thereby conquer the state" (Goebbels 1932, quoted in Loberg 2018, 1). With this, a new totalitarian order was born (Esposito 2008). The postmodern equivalent is the streets of social media, and it is Donald Trump who has recognized what Goebbels recognized: Whoever can conquer Twitter can conquer the masses. As Trump once put it: "I find [Twitter] tremendous. It's a modern form of communication. There should be nothing you should be ashamed of. It's—it's where it's at" (Keith 2016).

Dromocratic spectacle is control without confinement, a sublimated Weberian iron-cage (Weber 1925). It is not Urry's steel and petroleum literal iron cage that is "the car" but an *imaginary* in which a new order has become spatially visible that more closely approximates Weber's conceptual *stahlhartes*

Gehäuse: the embodied and materialized speed-power-violence experience of mundane everyday reality in which we dwell. This material semiotic totality, much like the Foucauldian dispositif, orders and controls; not as a theoretical apparatus of discipline but as material and empirical, embodied, habituated, produced and reproduced dual—Euclidean and rhizomatic—technosocial space and biopolitical order.

Automobility is ill-named because its naming identifies it as a discreet entity, whatever its connections and relationship with what is not, within the automobility imaginary, assumed to not be automobility. It is ill-named because it is named after a material entity, the automobile. This ill-named thing—automobility—is the dromocratic spectacle *par excellence* of the "epochal epistemic syntax" that is the political order of late modernity. It is an empirical instance of *homo sacer* as described by Agamben, which we will turn to in chapter 6.

Chapter Five

Hypnos

The Automobility Dreamscape

Hypnos, the God of Sleep, was twin brother to Thanatos, God of Death. As recounted in Hesiod's *Theogony*, Hypnos's mother was Nyx, the God of the Night, daughter to Chaos. Depending on the source, Hypnos was a sibling to Nemesis (Retribution), Eris (Strife), Keres (Violent Death) and other unhappy gods of the netherworld. Hypnos and Thanatos were near-identical twins, sleep closely mirroring the eternal rest of death. Though divinities in their own right, the brothers were not part of the Olympian Pantheon. Homer placed the home of Hypnos on the island of Lemnos, near Troy, while other authors relegated them to the underworld. In a vase by Euphrenios, Hypnos and Thanatos together carry dead warriors to Hades, the underworld. In the *Iliad* they carried the fatally wounded hero Sarpedon, son of Zeus, away from the battlefield of Troy to his homeland of Lycia.

In the *Iliad*, Hypnos famously tricked Zeus twice. Once, on request from Zeus's wife, Hera, Hypnos put the King of Gods to sleep in order to punish Heracles, Zeus's son, for sacking Troy by blasting winds upon the sea while Heracles was sailing home. The second time, on request from Hera again, Hypnos again put Zeus to sleep so that Poseidon was able to assist the Danaans to victory in the Trojan war. In the myth of Endymion, as told by Apollodorus, Endymion, with the help of Hypnos, chose to sleep forever and remain with the immortal goddess he was in love with. His eternal sleep represents the defeat of death, aging and decay. Sleep as cheating death and reaching a different kind of immortality is underscored by Hypnos's powers as savior of those who have been injured or who are in need of a period of rest. Homer, referring to Hypnos, uses adjectives of honey-like sweetness to describe him, while Sophocles, in Philoctetes, refers to him as the healer of suffering and pain. On the vase of Euphrenios, the twin brothers of sleep and death are hard to distinguish. Both are in full armor, carrying the body of

Sarpedon under the auspices of Hermes. Sleep is transitory death, transiting on the river of forgetfulness, one of the rivers surrounding Hades by which Hypnos resides.

THE DREAMSCAPES OF AUTOMOBILITY

Curiously, a central term in the title of Jasanoff and Kim's edited book, *Dreamscapes of Modernity: Sociotechnical Imaginaries and the Fabrication of Power*, namely the term "dreamscape," is mentioned only once by Jasanoff in the concluding chapter to the volume (Jasanoff and Kim 2015, 338), and at that only in passing, and in only one of the chapters by the contributing authors (Miller 2015, 279, 281). It is a term that could be made to do considerably more conceptual, interpretive, empirical and political work. It captures the composite significations of image and vision, as well as that of illusion and fantasy; it also suggests fluidity and interconnectedness between different appropriations of time and space.

The concept of a "scape," originally proposed by Arjun Appadurai (1990) as a topographical metaphor to capture cultural globalization, has been applied in a number of different contexts to designate the interplay of spatial fixes and cultural motion. Appadurai argued that the global cultural economy is a complex, overlapping and disconnected order, and it is highly unpredictable. Capital, goods, information and people occur in and through disjunctures across five dimensions, which he terms "scapes": ethnoscapes, technoscapes, financescapes, mediascapes and ideoscapes. Scapes are not only *imagined*, like national communities as described by Anderson, but they are also *perspectival* constructs of disjunct realities transformed by the historical, linguistic and political situatedness of a multitude of social actors cutting across traditional political and social boundaries. Scapes are interrelated but are not causally ordered, possessing no single organizational principle.

The five scapes described by Appadurai are based on Deleuze's concepts of "deterritorialization" and "flow." They provide a framework for describing transnational cultural flows and the deterritorializing forces of globalization that exist within the situated production of specific local realities. Analogously to landscapes, Appadurai's scapes are social constructs that are given material shape and meaning by human activities. They are descriptive tools to address the consequences of global processes, such as time-space annihilation, but are not the processes themselves. The processes are flows, such as mobility flows, the interconnected "fluid state" of human activities in the everyday spectacles of late capitalism. The speed, scale and volume of these flows are so significant that the disconnections they produce have become central to the politics of global culture. The visual metaphor of "scape" signifies how flows are understood from the perspectives of socio-historically situated groups and individuals. It points to the fluid, irregular relationship between the local and the trans-local, the cultural and the spatial. It is an ethnographic version of the spectacle, albeit absent the Marxism of the Situationists, and is a refrain in Virilio's dromology.

Following Appadurai, Tim Edensor (1997) has conceptualized public monuments as "memoryscapes," comprised of objects in space by which memory is assembled and organized through material iconographic forms. In these memoryscapes social remembering is organized around places and objects built into the landscape. They are archaeological metaphors that construct a relationship with the past. Conforming to different semiotic conventions, memorials articulate sacred, emotional and cosmological meanings. On the other end of the time-horizon, Edward Soja (1996) has described Los Angeles as a "thirdplace," a hybrid real-and-imagined. Soja's version of "futurescapes" (Pordzik 2009) is "pastfutures": intertwined temporal, social and spatial relations that are being constantly inscribed, erased and reinscribed again.

The concept of "scapes" directs our attention to how the referentiality of social constructs is given material shape. Scapes connect the "imaginary" and the "real," such that the very distinction, as we have argued from a different angle, *dissolves*. Theorists embedded in the Anglo-Saxon spatio-political epistemic tradition but inspired by Foucauldian post-structuralism (Thrift 2007) have conceptualized the spatio-cultural dimensions of automobility also in terms of flows and scapes.

The Autoscape

Scapes are spatially anchored, imagined, perspectival constructs wherein social meaning is created through complex, deterritorialized flows embedded in situated local practices. Socialities of work, of consumption, of entertainment are examples of such social meanings. Scapes contain buildings, roads, malls, filling stations, factories and so forth. They are moored in space (Thrift 1996) not as material entities but as perspectival constructs that are both deterritorialized and fluid. One such scape is the scape of automobility, or "autoscape" (Edensor 2004; Kramer 2018).

Edensor (2004) employs the metaphors of "motorscape" and "autoscape" to describe material structures, everyday institutional spatial signifiers distributed across road networks in which objects are fixed and institutional arrangements are embedded. "Autoscapes," Edensor argues, are the familiar things, routes and fixtures, that create habitual engagement with space. Automobility in this rendering is comprised of a fluid matrix of humans, machines, roads and other spaces, representations, regulatory institutions and a host of related businesses and infrastructural features. Autoscapes create the referentiality and connections between the material and the social; they produce habituated practices as well as localized social meanings that are anchored in and animated by the materialities inscribed in space. In doing so they also *create* these materialities.

"Autoscape" should be read as a dromocratic metaphor evoking flows: the rapid and ceremonial movement of people and goods, the situated experiences of the locally anchored perspectival realities of the road, the vista and buildings. Automobility conceptualized as a "scape" allows us to attend to the reorderings and inflections of space and time. It allows us to re-politicize technosocial reality by creating a new perspectival experience of the "in-between," the locus of the political.

The basis of this new shared material semiotic world was the adoration of speed, of motorized power and the *political* disjuncture that followed. The locus of the political moved from the common space in-between individuals to the dromocratic in-between of the road, of the human-machine hybrid named "the car." Annihilation of time and space shattered a previously shared common social reality. Automobility created a new, shared imaginary of submerged differences of position and of perspectives. The spatial construct of the autoscape, as a hegemonic and universal perspectival totality, collected disconnected fluidities into a single domesticated order. The new dromocratic production of space not only managed, surveilled and ordered bodily movement, but it also did the same to embodied imagination. Deleuze's "control society" was as much the product of the highway, discussed in the previous chapter, as it was the making of the autoscape. Reality was constructed, experienced and lived "infinitely" and "freely" without being confined by the road but restricted by the perspectival totality that is dromocracy (Deleuze and Lapoujade 2006, 322). The autoscape represented the transformation of *material* heterotopic spaces of discipline, as suggested earlier, into imaginary omnitopic spaces of control.

The term autoscape describes the intertwined production of meaning of the mobile and the stationary; social realities that are created through culturally constructed and spatially anchored perspectives. Scapes are always perspectival totalities. Dromocracy is such a perspectival totality: things make sense only by looking at them from within the spectacle. Looked at with an "anthropological eye" (Appadurai 1998, 11), these perspectival constructs appear as lived, embodied and situated actualities that create subjectivities and moral economies. Specific objects materialize these actualities by assembling them in specific forms built into or moving through the landscape. The autoscape does not link objects and social meanings into one interconnected relationship ("a system"); it is the name of the perspectival totality by which such social meanings are created and objects are named. Automobility is a metaphor that entangles both what is called the "real" and what is termed as "representational," articulating the present and the future within semiotic conventions that are moral economies. Dromocracy is one such moral economy in which subjectivities are created and experienced as well as controlled (Latimer 2006; Bonham 2006). We will return to the politics of this moral economy in the next chapter.

The Dromoscape of Automobility

The dreamscape metaphor suggests illusion—a term we have so far intentionally avoided. "Illusion" suggests something "not real," which is not the argument we have wished to make, except in so far as we argue that automobility is not real in the sense realists understand reality to be (see, for example, Bhaskar 1978; 2015). Materialities are no more real or unreal than socialities: all are elements of a lifeworld and equipmental totality. Nor is our argument that automobility is composed of falsehoods. Within the imaginary, commonsense truths are nothing less than what they appear to be. Imaginaries are epistemologically analogous to scientific paradigms, as described by Thomas Kuhn (1970). Within any paradigm, "truth" is that which appears to be true, that which is obviously the case and not otherwise.

The concept of a dreamscape suggests a different ontological order to that of the ostensibly "real." The social and the material, we argued in chapter 2, are ontologically inseparable. Urry's "automobility as system" concept, in contrast, to avoid falling into the relativist trap, separates the representational and the real, the social interactions and the technologies that enable them. Urry describes the car as "the literal 'iron cage' of modernity, motorized, moving and domestic" (Urry 2004, 28) that people "inhabit." This transforms Weber's iron-cage from metaphor to an ostensible *literal* description of the car.

Automobiles, roads, maps and filling stations do not exist in an ontological void; they are "real" only in-as-much as they are seen, understood and endowed with meaning from within the material semiotic network, which is "the system." It is not the car that is the iron-cage but "the system." It is within "the system of automobility" that individuals are trapped in the bureaucratized automobility imaginary of rational efficiency and bodily control. Although Urry does not make this connection, a "system" is not so different from what Foucault called a *dispositif*—in English, an "apparatus." The name "system," moreover, has diverse registers. Within sociology, system is an analytic and descriptive concept. Within social systems theory as understood both by Talcott Parsons and Niklas Luhmann, that "the system" is a system is simply the fact of the matter. An alternative orientation is to start from the assumption that what is existentially problematic is the very fact that we are components of a system.

Dromocracy is the perspectival totality that endows meaning to these artifacts from within. Analogously to Wittgenstein's account of language, this perspectival totality is performative: meaning depends on contexts of use. There is no direct link between social meaning as an entity in language and as an artifact embedded in space. Language is woven into the fabric of human activity or, put another way, the meaning of words and objects is inscribed in use-contexts (Wittgenstein 1953; see also Heidegger 1962, 74). Dromocracy is not a separate realm of signs, symbols and social meanings, signifiers of the signified materiality: the "things" (artifacts, technologies, infrastructures) of the world. Dromocracy as "scape" is a fluid matrix of humans, machines, roads, other spaces, representations, discourses, rulebooks and other *meanings*, entangled in a referential circle of social constructs and given material shape.

Referentiality is a mode of sense-making, knowing how to "do certain things." For the subject at hand, it is *knowing* how to *do* automobility. It is a "*knowing-to-do*" of language and of space (Law 2009). Doing automobility is not "doing or experiencing things" on the move or being stationary, nor is it related to the artifact of the automobile. Nor is it simply "transport" or "mobility" as theorized under the moniker "the new mobilities paradigm," automobility being one more case thereof, similar to all the other "mobilities." Doing automobility is the performance of routine practices, reproducing subjectivities (Manderscheid 2014), constructing connections, "in-betweens," social and material meanings and relations. It is dwelling in the world of automobility, the perspectival totality of dromocracy.

Automobility is a "form-of-life," a temporal and spatial (language) game (Wittgenstein 1953, §19) of habituated (dromocratic) practices that go beyond driving, passengering and other forms of bodily movement with or by the automobile. It is doing things with others, a dromocratically ordered form-of-life and mode of Being. Dromocracy is an "instrument of social cooperation and mutual participation" (Dewey 1929, vi). It is a rule-governed language game that is also a "technology game" (Coeckelbergh 2018). It is how we live in and experience the world around us. It is more than a "system" or "regime" (Böhm, Campbell, et al. 2006). It is the local and global politics of this "form-of-life" in late-modernity across nothing less than the entire planet.

AUTOMOBILE DREAMS

Freud claimed, in opposition to the accepted wisdom of the medical profession of the time, that dreams are not meaningless, somatically determined impressions stemming from the body but that dreaming is a complex psychological process that propels concealed and distorted unconscious representations of the real into the patient's consciousness. Freud (1999, 7–9) begins *The Interpretation of Dreams* by contrasting his own analysis and understanding of dreams with earlier understandings of dreams, as being of supernatural origin, for example. These differences notwithstanding, what was not in doubt, neither for Freud nor for his predecessors, is that a dream is something that occurs during sleep. It is these dreams that are held to be *real dreams*. On this realist ontology of dreams, the dreams that are the subject of this chapter would be not real dreams but unreal dreams. Indeed, Jasanoff and Kim's, and our, very use of the term "dream" is suspect, a term that is parasitic on real dreams. This opposition invokes two sets of binaries: sleep/wake and real dream/unreal dream.

The inverse of this real/unreal binary is equally plausible. First, that the dreams we dream while awake are real dreams, while those of sleep are the unreal dreams. Second, that what we take to be wakefulness is sleep, the sleep of *Hypnos*, which, for us, is inseparable from hypnotism. While the dreams that visit us in sleep are immediately recognizable as dreams, our dreams while awake are not so easily identifiable. The first task is to identify the dreams of automobility. They are the publicly performed visions of the imaginary, discussed in chapter 2.

Dreamscapes—the space of dreams—are not dual realities, one part dream and one part scape, but an ontological entanglement of the real and the illusionary. Dreams evoke sleep and, as Lefebvre intimates, in sleep, one enters the "poetic moment" with its own truth, its own beauty and its own worth. The "space of dream" is:

> [a]t once imaginary and real, this space is different from the space of language, though of the same order, and the faithful guardian of sleep rather than of social learning. Is this then the space of "drives"? It would be better described as a space where dispersed and broken rhythms are reconstituted, a space for the poetic reconstruction of situations in which wishes are present—but wishes which are not so much fulfilled as simply proclaimed. It is a space of enjoyment, indeed it establishes a virtual reign of pleasure, though erotic dreams break up on the reefs of the dreamer's pleasure and disillusion. The space of the dream is strange and alien, yet at the same time as close to us as is possible. Rarely coloured, even more rarely animated by music, it still has a sensual-sensory

character. It is a theatrical space even more than a quotidian or poetic one: a putting into images of oneself, for oneself. (Lefebvre 1992, 209)

It is in the dream, Lefebvre (1992, 353) suggests, where desire appears. It has no particular object "except for a space where it has full play: a beach, a place of festivity, the space of the dream." Desire is central to automobility, and it is in automobility's dreams, which are the publicly performed visions of its sociotechnical imaginaries, where desire is both visible and constructed.

Foucauldian scholarship has questioned the assumption that the automobile is a natural object of desire that embodies within itself beauty, class, status and other social instruments of power, pointing instead to technologies of automobility governmentality that produce subjects who desire the form of life that is automobility (Randell 2020a). For Lefebvre, dream is a space where desire has "full play" to (re)construct situations in which wishes are present. Such is the space of automobility. It is a "virtual reign of pleasure" manifested in feelings of autonomy, freedom and power, constructed by and for the automobility subjects who are, in turn, produced as subjects by automobility itself. Puricelli inscribed the poetry of the automobile into space through the design and construction of the autostrada, making the good life available to "everyone." The autostrada was dromocracy as petty-bourgeois social order, a (re)constructed futurist utopia of "living in the absolute" that is the automobility dreamscape.

A central concept in Freud's *The Interpretation of Dreams* is that of "dreamwork." Dreamwork refers to processes occurring during sleep by which the dream is constructed. Dreams that visit us in sleep are recognizable when we awake as dreams. The dreams we dream while awake are frequently not taken to be dreams. Even less identifiable as dreams are the dreams that are fabricated for us within what Raoul Vaneigem called "the factories of collective illusion"—the automobility dreams, within the dreamscapes of modernity.

The dreamscape is a topography, albeit a topography not spatially homologous to the topographies of physical space (Ricoeur 1970, 107). For Freud dreams are the main speculative tools of the unconscious; psychologically deterritorialized flows of meanings that hold the hermeneutic key to understanding the visible and invisible workings of the mind. They point to experiences of childhood and adolescence, sexuality, the Oedipal complex, what Appadurai (2015, 481) in a different context calls the "libidinal physics" of desire and wish fulfillment.

In *Freud and Philosophy: An Essay on Interpretation,* Paul Ricoeur (1970, 91) notes that "the realm of dream-fantasy is a realm of desire." This realm of desire is the space where the transition from pleasure to reality takes place. The libidinal physics at work in the dreamscape point to another ontological dualism: a space that is magical, a reign of pleasure, but also calculable, traceable to the origins of the wish for pleasure. This "magical proceduralism" transforms the realm of desire into a predictable social order (Appadurai 2015, 483). Freud, as Wittgenstein (1967, 48) put it,

> wanted to find the essence of dreaming. And he would have rejected any suggestion that he might be partly right but not altogether so. If he was partly wrong, that would have meant for him that he was wrong altogether—that he had not really found the essence of dreaming.

The dreamscape of dromocracy has its "own truth, its own beauty and its own worth." It is a truth created at motor shows, in automobility advertisements, Hollywood movies and the ubiquitous platforms of industries of desire (Randell 2020a). In the context of dreamwork, the dreamscape (as opposed to the "essence of dreams") projects a vision, in Freudian language, of a transition from the pleasure principle to the reality principle that is effortless and simple. Serendipitously, pleasure and reality coincide in the dreamscape. Dromocratic pleasure has none of the characteristics described by Freud: neither the Oedipal drama nor the lost and missed, mourned objects; no disappointed and wounded desires. Desire transduces into the utility and usefulness of the reality principle effortlessly. The "magical proceduralism" of the dromocratic dreamscape brings together fantasy, desire and imagination as libidinal manifestations of status, freedom and power, coupled with manageable risk, governable order and bracketed violence.

The beauty of the dreamscape is manifested in the utmost object of desire: the automobile. An object of desire, the automobile is a substitution for the lost objects, a prosthesis that enhances the self. Utility and beauty are intertwined, as are the bodies of the driver and of the automobile intertwined. The car-driver hybrid becomes the autoself (Randell 2017) in the dreamwork. The dreamwork is disciplined dreaming, playful movement and governable speed—the governmentality of dromocracy. The magic of and in the dreamscape, similar to the capitalist dreamwork described by Appadurai (2015), is a series of "coercive and divinatory performative procedures" by which uncertainty and risk are managed.

The explanatory value of the dreamscape as metaphor lies in the interplay between the unconscious and the conscious in producing the dream as object of psychoanalytic study, of *analysis*, through the method of interpreting dreams developed by Freud. The interpretation of dreams (Freud 2010) as method is a process in which the dream is first constructed as a readable narrative assumed to represent the "real" mental processes of the patient to be analyzed. This text—the dream as territory between the imaginary conscious and the imaginary unconscious: the dreamscape (Rogoff 2018)—becomes "the real" that stands in place of the "concealed thoughts lying behind it" (Freud 2010, 142). The original idea of the interpretation of dreams, contradicting the accepted logic of the profession in the late nineteenth century, was this change in ontological status. In contradistinction to everyday use, the dream in Freudian terms is the "real" as opposed to the experienced behavior or physical symptoms the patient displays that are interpreted as "imaginary." Dreamscape is a hermeneutic construct, a boundary object occupying the space between the somatic and the psychic in which the interpretation finds the link between body and mind. The "poetic reconstruction" of Lefebvre is not a reconstruction; it is the *production of space* as dreamscape, the creation of a narrative territory, legible and open for analysis.

Dreamscapes are located at the imaginary intersection of the psychical and the mental. They are of the same order, Lefebvre argues, as language: "real" as revealing, through analysis, the distorted imprints of patients' life experiences, and "imaginary" as narrative constructs that come into being only by and in analysis. Interpreting dreams is the producing and appropriating of this space. Impressions of lifeworlds are "collected into a single group of ideas" (Freud 2010, 144), creating a narrative mapping of the "thoughts that played a part in the dream" (Freud 2010, 144). The narrative and its analysis, as the geometrical construct of the map, *make* the dreamscape a "totalizing production" (De Certeau 1980) by converting fluid and messy human interactions, feelings, emotions and impressions into legible and scientifically objectified constructs of narrative ordering.

The analysis of dreams as method creates dreamscapes as sites of contestation between analyst, patient, medical institutions, discourses and the social norms governing the private and the public. By designing the legible and politicized dream-text, the analysis colonizes the territory of the dreamscape, evoking the practice of nineteenth-century European imperialism (Rogoff 2018). This imperialism is reinforced by Freud's reference to the sexual life of adult women as a "dark continent" (Freud 1959, quoted in Rogoff 2018): dreamscapes present a territory to be conquered and controlled by the analyst. The colonized dreamscape as dark continent is, at the moment it is produced, already an appropriated space in and through which the authority of the analyst is established and practiced. This authoritarian process of creating and appropriating the dreamscape politicizes the space of the dream. By constructing it as the *locus* of psychic etiology, Freud makes his key theoretical intervention into medical discourse precisely at this point. The dreamscape is placed beyond the "gaze" of clinical medicine (Rogoff 2018, 61; Foucault 2009). This locus is the place of the political: a colonized dreamscape. Dreamscape befits dromocracy: it is a perspectival totality that both creates and endows the material and the social with meaning. The automobile, the road, the shopping mall and the other "elements" of the "system" are of dromocracy's making, as are the habituated practices and localized social meanings that occupy the "space" of social interactions.

The automobile is similar to the Portuguese vessel (Law 1986a), a bunch of materialities (chassis, tire, seats, windshields, etc.) inscribed into a heterogenous web of relations, actor-actant rhizomes of the road, the filling station, the driver, the passenger, the car manufacturer, the policeman, the road signs, the advertisement, the mall, the parking lot, the speedometer, the family dinner, the bicyclist plus all else we can think of; all of which holds this together as a stable network. As Law and Mol remark, a dual spatiality is here at work: the dreamscape is both Euclidean and network/rhizomatic. As dromocracy is inscribed in both spaces, there is a dual production of space: Euclidean by way of geometries and topographies on the map that objectifies social relations, that imagines and turns the Earth into a version of the map, filled with roads, highways and other objects (Harvey 1990a); network/rhizomatic in that it is held together by the actor-actant network that is the scape of dromocracy (Law 2009). The metaphor of dreamscape does the *Latourian trick* of making automobility artifacts immutable mobiles: they simultaneously participate in both the network and the Euclidean space of dromocracy (Law and Mol 2001, 613).

This dreamscape is fluid, not only because it enables the flow of people, of commodities, of raw materials, of capital, of signs and of information (Urry 2000), but also because its objects, the car included, are also "mutable mobiles," showing configurational variance (Mol and Law 1994). All objects within the network have local varieties in size, in speed, in design and purpose, as have other actants of the network. All artifacts are variable to fit the rhizome that works.

Mutable mobility is key to the hegemony of the dreamscape: not only do its objects allow for variability of shape or size, but it also is open to changes in the politics of the imaginary. "Sustainability" requires the propellent be changed, and instead of the petroleum-and-steel car, a new version must be built that is lighter and propelled by electricity. This does not change the dreamscape. Or when the driver-car hybrid is separated, as the human is found to be all too human and often "responsible" for the accidents on the road, the driver of the hybrid is replaced by a "self-driving" algorithmic technology (Braun and Randell 2020). This variability assists the dreamscape, allowing the spatio-imaginary container to prevail and hold the rhizomatic network of dromocracy together. The fluid spatiality (Law and Mol 2001) of the dreamscape again evokes the Wittgensteinian family resemblance: the car, the filling station, the automobile in the advertisement, the endless road in the Hollywood movie and all other objects within dromocracy, both in time and space, Euclidean and network, display a sameness, a meaning consistency that does not depend on any particular feature of the automobile or other objects, or a particular relationship of the scape, but rather on the presence of some features of meaning that intersect with one another. We will revisit the concept of mutable mobility and the hegemony of automobility in light of technological and social innovation, from electric to self-driving, connected mobility, in the final chapter on post-automobility.

The dreamscape is not only a disjuncture of deterritorialized flows of meanings and objects; it is also held together by the *conjoined alterity* of all "Others" that are not present or are not visible (Lee and Brown 1994). The dreamscape is a plenitude of denials: of accidents, of guilts and of pleasures that are neither present nor visible. To paraphrase Virilio, it is the invention of the dreamscape of automobility that invented the automobile accident, not the invention of the automobile that invented the accident (Virilio 2007b). The accident is denied (Beckmann 2004) in dromocracy. It is removed and displaced from the visible dreamscape to the hospital where the injured are treated, to the cemetery where the accident victims are buried or the laboratory (Latour and Woolgar 2013) where accidents are analyzed and new meanings of risks and safety as universal but purified scientific facts are created. These sites are also part of the dreamscape, even if they are rarely thought of as being part of automobility. "Accident workers" (Beckmann 2004, 95), people who clean the road and repair the car that thus make the displacement possible, are part of the network as creators of absence that in turn gives the dreamscape its stable and determinate shape. They displace "rematerialized objects" that are not immutable mobiles: the wreck, the separated driver-car hybrid, the barred road. No longer held together in the network, they are "fixed" and made ready to re-enter the network as immutable once again. In a reversal of traditional causation, fixing is not repairing the materiality of the car but remaking its place and fit within the material semiotic network. Their immutability is the guarantor of them being mobile once again; otherwise they are just a bunch of metal and glass "stuff." The Other of the dreamscape is not only the unseen or absent but also a Freudian "unconscious-scape," where lost and missed objects and wounded desires are suppressed.

Having been purged from the dreamscape, they need to be reinscribed within the dreamscape. First, by providing alternative interpretations of the dream that is the automobility imaginary, analyzing the contents of the dream, the agents and processes that have brought it into existence, that sustain and reproduce the dream. As Wolfgang Streeck (2016, 212) has observed,

> A rising share of the goods that make today's capitalist economies grow would not sell if people dreamed other dreams than they do—which makes

understanding, developing and controlling their dreams a fundamental concern of political economy in advanced-capitalist society.

Providing alternative interpretations of the publicly performed collective dream that is not simply automobiles—one of the goods Streeck presumably has in mind—but automobility has been one of the most significant achievements of the critical automobility studies community. The challenge is not to demonstrate that the automobility is not real but is a dream; rather it is to demonstrate that what is real *is* simultaneously a dream. Put another way, what is real, what is imaginary and what is a dream are indistinguishable.

It is here that we enter into the realm of the ontopolitical. It is ontopolitics on the part of a diverse network, a *dispositif* of automobility interests, who have brought the automobility imaginary into existence and ensure its continued reproduction. To challenge those activities, but more so to point out that those activities are a politics of ontology, is equally to enter the fray of the ontopolitical. This is the politics that a transition to a post-automobility world requires.

The oscillation between present-presence and absent-present in dromocracy is created by automobile manufacturers, policymakers and other agents within the automobility imaginary. This is the imagined speed of fifty kilometers per hour in the city or 130 kilometers per hour on the highway, or even the potential speed of the automobile made possible by its engine beyond these legally permitted speeds, created and justifiable in the dromocratic actor-actant network of the dreamscape. Also present as absence in the dreamscape are pollution, deforestation, the abolished, removed and exploited habitats of people, animals and plants. The dreamscape is held together by the imaginary speed, the destroyed habitats. The list of conjoined Others includes the manufacturers, the policymakers, the advertisers and the dead accident victims as well as the "accident workers" and the desire workers—of Hollywood, of advertising, of motor shows (Randell 2020a)—that make all this absent and present at the same time. This is the dream in and of late modernity: colonized, appropriated, dromocratic dark continent of actors and actants. The automobility dreamscape is the scape composed of those dreams.

In Peter Weir's movie *The Last Wave*, there is the following dialogue between a white European lawyer and his client, an indigenous inhabitant of the land that is now called "Australia." The dialogue begins with the lawyer trying to impress upon his client the direness of his legal situation:

"You're in desperate trouble."

"No! You in trouble! You!"

"Why do you say that?"

"You don't know what the dreams are anymore."

It is a dialogue between two individuals but may be taken as an exchange not only between two cultures but between indigenous peoples across the planet and those of us who inhabit the dreamscapes of modernity. We—all of us, not just humans but all terrestrials, the inhabitants of this planet—are in desperate trouble because we—us who are components of the sociotechnical apparatus that is late-modernity—don't know what the dreams are anymore.

Chapter Six

Nomos

*The Appropriation of Space**

The first recorded automobile-related death occurred in 1869 (National Trust No Date), the first death of a pedestrian, Bridget Driscoll, outside Crystal Palace in London in 1896 (*The Manchester Guardian* 1896). In September 1899 Henry Bliss became the first American to be killed by an automobile (Nader 1965, 295). At the trial following Driscoll's death, the coroner remarked that he hoped "such a thing would never happen again."

In New York, already by 1905, "death in the streets had become," as Clay McShane (1994, 129) put it, "a routine part of metropolitan life." Since these first automobile deaths, approximately eighty-five million people have been killed in what are commonly referred to as "accidents": roughly sixty million in the twentieth century and a further twenty-five million in only the first two decades of the twenty-first century. To provide some comparison, around sixty-six million people were killed in World War II. Globally, more people are killed in road crashes than from any other form of violent death, wars included. Annually, approximately 1,350,000 people are killed and fifty million are seriously injured (World Health Organization 2018, vii), an increase of 100,000 deaths since 2015 (World Health Organization 2015, vii). Someone dies through direct impact with an automobile every twenty-three seconds, approximately 3,700 individuals every day. Automobility death and injury is a cause of immeasurable physical and emotional suffering, not just of those killed and injured, but also those left behind (World Health Organization 2004, 50). What was believed to be the exception at the trial of the driver who killed Bridget Driscoll has become realized as a permanent state of normality. There is no other area of social or political life where such a

---

* An extended version of this chapter was published in the journal *Mobilities* (Braun, Robert, and Richard Randell. 2022. "The Vermin of The Street: The Politics of Violence and the Nomos of Automobility." *Mobilities* 17(1): 53–68).

constant, routine, violent attrition of human life and destruction of the human body, now over a time span of more than a century, is considered normal and acceptable (Paterson 2007, 41).

The ancient *dromos* was the enclosed space that was the sacred passageway or competitive racetrack. The *dromos* at the conceptual center, dromocracy is an entirely different *dromos* to the *dromos* of ancient Greece. It is a *dromos* that is neither defined by boundaries nor limited in its spatial extension but a *dromos* that has expanded and exceeded its boundaries, becoming a fluid technoscientific space of power and violence (Law and Mol 2001). In this chapter we examine spatiality in the light of our prior discussion of dromocracy.

Reflecting on "what 'spatiality' could possibly mean," Virilio, in *Open Sky* (2007a), remarks that "we are forced to re-examine not only the classic notion of materiality, but also those of spatiality and temporality." The accident, he adds, "now conditions our apprehension of reality" (130). It is "apprehension" in two senses: apprehension in the sense of understanding and comprehension; and apprehension in the sense of fear and dread. It is apprehension in the face of the violence that is constitutive of dromocracy. The street is a place of apprehension, of fear. It is an apprehension we are aware of every time we cross a street or ride a bicycle. We can forget it, we have learnt to live with it, but the collective repression that is collective forgetting that the automobility dreamscape enables does not mean it has been banished. As Virilio (2006, 71) observes, when "power-knowledge is eliminated to the benefit of moving-power" this means that power-knowledge is replaced by power-violence as the key to our apprehension of reality.

Engaging with Michel Foucault's (1986, 22) observation that "the present epoch [is] above all the epoch of space," during the latter part of the twentieth-century "space" became an object of increasing theoretical and empirical interest (Thrift 1996; Soja 1989; Massey 1994). Within the field of geography, mobility scholars turned their attention to the spatial properties of automobility (Pearce 2012; Merriman 2009; Cresswell 2010; Walks 2015; Böhm, Jones, et al. 2006). However, as Gregg Culver (2018, 146) has noted, "the violence of the car arguably constitutes something of a blind spot even within much of mobilities and transport scholarship, let alone within much of the rest of human geographical scholarship, where the issue has been left largely unaddressed," calling for "greater attention to (auto)mobility in general, and for deeper engagement with violence and justice in (auto)mobility in particular." While Culver directs his call to geographers, it is a call that could well be heeded in other disciplines. Culver's focus is automobile violence and the injustices of that violence, which do not randomly and equally fall across class, race, gender and other already existing social inequalities. As John

Rennie Short and Luis Pinet-Peralta (2010, 43) observe, "The young and the vulnerable and the poor and the marginal are more likely to be hit by a car than the rich and the powerful. While road deaths have declined among rich countries, they have increased among poor countries." Automobile violence, consequently, can be seen as a special instance of environmental injustice (Bullard 1990; Pellow and Brulle 2007; Cottrill and Thakuriah 2010). These are important topics that deserve further research and attention. Our focus is not, however, the injustices Culver, Short and Pinet-Peralta rightly point to but the constituent characteristics—juridical, material, political and social—of the space within which automobile violence occurs.

To describe automobile death and injury as "violence" is to take a specific stance in respect to automobile death and injury. Such a description of "accidents" as violence is a description and conclusion largely absent in traditional "road safety" discourses and research where, rather than conclude that automobility is irremediably violent, road safety publications hold out the continual promise that it is remediable; that automobility is intrinsically safe but contingently hazardous (Noland 2013; Schepers et al. 2014; Elvik 2005). As Culver (2018, 145) has put it, "car deaths have always been in principle entirely preventable: cars could be banned, and the problem of car deaths would simply disappear." Yet this is a conclusion and recommendation that one will, in vain, search for in traditional road safety reports and publications.

Safety is theorized in road safety models as exposure to risk (Schepers et al. 2014). Neither dromocracy nor its more immediately visible manifestation, automobility, is held to be responsible for the majority of crashes. It is "the driver" who is held to be responsible. A standard and frequently cited statistic is that 93 percent of accidents are due to driver error (Singh 2018). The other two causal factors are assumed to be "the environment" and "the vehicle" (Treat et al. 1979; United States National Highway Traffic Safety Administration 2008). The *prima facie* evidence, summarized above, is that dromocracy is not "safe" but an intrinsically, not contingently, risk-based, violent spatial order; that this violence cannot be adequately conceptualized by statistical models that attribute death and injury to one of these three causal factors (Braun and Randell 2020).

A "fundamental stuff of geography" (Thrift 1994), not only is space inherently political (Harvey 2001) but also how we conceptualize and represent space is political. Attending to space requires attending to topographies of power, the "complex web of relations of domination and subordination, of solidarity and co-operation" (Massey 1994, 265; 2009). In respect to automobility, it is the distribution of power as "constellations" comprised of the interchange of reasons, speed, route, the feelings and the frictions of mobility (Cresswell 2010). One of the *loci* of those constellations of power is the automobilized body. That body is not the automobile *simpliciter* or the physical car-driver hybrid (Beckmann 2004) but a human-car cyborg assemblage entity, comprised of both a self and a body (Randell 2017, 663). It is, as John Urry (2004) put it, the "metallic and glass shell," which "provides an extension of the human body, surrounding the fragile, soft and vulnerable human skin with a new steel skin." It is a body in which enormous resources are invested in: to make it safe and protective for those "enframed" (Heidegger 1977) within that body; to render it beautiful and desirable through the technical and aesthetic design skills of car manufacturers and the efforts of the factories of illusion that are advertising and marketing firms (Randell 2020a, 45). Within the spatiality of the road, that body routinely confronts what Agamben (1998) called "bare life" (*nuda vita*): docile bodies that are repressed and, frequently, maimed and killed.

Automobility has brought about, and is a consequence of, nothing less than what Carl Schmitt (2015, 47) called a "global spatial revolution." In *The Nomos of the Earth in the International Law of the Jus Publicum Europaeum* (hereafter, *Nomos of the Earth*), Schmitt (2003, 70) described *nomos* as "the immediate form in which the political and social order of a people becomes *spatially visible*" [our emphasis]. What we will refer to as "the *nomos* of automobility" or "automobility *nomos*" is one such spatially visible form. It is a global *nomos* in that not only roads but automobility (Böhm, Jones, et al. 2006, 3–4) has come to envelop much of the planet through its rhizomatic expansion (Manderscheid 2014, 616). The *nomos* concept allows us to expand the *dromos* concept. Autospace is not only a space of dromocratic speed and violence; it is a space whose existence and expansion have required massive appropriation and the juridical transformation of space.

In the following section the themes within *Nomos of the Earth* that are relevant to our own concerns are briefly summarized. We then outline the basic spatial contours of the automobility *nomos* and its genealogy. Like the European *nomos* that is the focus of Schmitt's monograph, automobility is founded upon the appropriation of land and space. We then examine the political and juridical properties of the automobilized space that is the road. It is a space wherein the state of exception has become normalized, wherein human life is reduced to what Agamben (2017, 56), in *Homo Sacer*, calls "bare life," life that may be killed without homicide having been committed. Road violence and the ubiquitous threat of violence (Taylor 2003, 1621–22)—the proximate cause of which is the automobile—is, we argue, constitutive violence in that it ensures the reproduction of the automobility *nomos*.

Although the focus of much of this chapter is the internal, bracketed space of the road, it is a space that is spatially intertwined and inseparable from public and private life. Automobility's global extension has changed the very spatiality of the planet, which warrants describing it as a global *nomos*. Automobility violence is not limited to the internal space of the road but is the violence of disease and the appropriation of the global commons through automobility's contribution to the environmental crisis. With respect to automobility, the entire planet has become a space of exception wherein we are all reduced to bare life.

NOMOS AS ORDERING AND APPROPRIATION OF SPACE

Although the Greek term *nomos* is frequently translated as "law," its primary reference, Schmitt (2003, 70) argued, is space:

> one should not translate *nomos* as law (in German, *Gesetz*), regulation, norm, or any similar expression. *Nomos* comes from *nemein*—a [Greek] word that means both "to divide" and "to pasture." Thus, *nomos* is the immediate form in which the political and social order of a people becomes spatially visible. . . . In Kant's words, it is the "distributive law of mine and thine". . . . *Nomos* is the measure by which the land in a particular order is divided and situated; it is also the form of political, social, and religious order determined by this process. Here, measure, order, and form constitute a spatially concrete unity.

First published in German in 1950, *Nomos of the Earth* covers three periods in the history of the Earth. First, the period before the rise of a hegemonic European *nomos* when, Schmitt (2003, 50–51; see also Schmitt 2001, 58–59) argued, there "was no spatial ordering of the earth as a whole, no *nomos* of the earth in the true sense." There were, he writes,

> A variety of great power complexes—the Egyptian, the Asiatic, the Hellenistic empires, the Roman Empire, perhaps even Negro empires in Africa and Incan empires in America—in no sense were disconnected and totally isolated from one another. But their interconnections lacked a global character. Each considered itself to be the *world* [Schmitt's emphasis].

Second, the history of the European *nomos,* from its rise in the sixteenth century to its demise in 1919 with the Treaty of Versailles. Third, the post-Versailles period, which, in Schmitt's view, lacked a single hegemonic *nomos.*

The central subject matter of *Nomos of the Earth* is the genealogy and characteristics of the global *nomos* constructed by European powers in the sixteenth century. A hegemonic balance and complex of laws, treaties, customs and traditions, the *nomos* of the *jus publicum Europaeum* (European public law) mediated relations between sovereign (European) states. It was a social order that divided and situated the entire Earth, wherein oceans and landmasses were marked and divided by the colonial powers, with the landmasses of the "New World" inscribed as available for land-appropriation by the European powers, primarily Portugal, Spain, Holland, Britain and France (Schmitt 2001, 76).

At the center of Schmitt's concept of *nomos* lies land appropriation (*Landnahme*). "The European peoples to whom the new, apparently infinite spaces opened and who swarmed out into these expansive spaces," Schmitt (2015, 60) wrote in *Land and Sea,* "treated the non-European and non-Christian lands and peoples that they discovered like ownerless property, belonging to the first Europeans who took it in possession." The indigenous inhabitants were not recognized as subjects but were inscribed as objects within international law (Schmitt 2001, 73). "Neither Columbus nor any other discoverer," as Schmitt (2003, 132) put it, "appeared with an entry visa issued by the discovered princes. Discoveries were made without prior permission of the discovered"—a process and project that continues to this day (Kopenawa 2013, 352). "Settler colonialism," as Patrick Wolfe (2006, 388; see also Ostler 2019) has argued, "destroys to replace": "the primary motive for elimination is . . . access to territory."

The elements of the spatial order of the *nomos* of the *jus publicum Europaeum* were land and sea, amity lines and lines of longitude and latitude, Europe, the New World, and with its dissolution, the appearance of areas Schmitt called *Großräume* (Great Spaces), such as the Western hemisphere under the Monroe Doctrine and later an imagined National Socialist *Großraum* (Barnes and Minca 2013; Minca and Rowan 2015, 153–86). Similarly, it is the global spatial order that is the focus of the critical secondary Schmitt literature in the fields of international law (Koskenniemi 2004, 2005), international relations (Chandler 2008) and geopolitics (Odysseos and Petito 2007; Rowan 2011; Minca and Rowan 2015; Maier 2016, 251–56). In particular, Stephen Legg and Alexander Vasudevan (2011, 1) note that post-September 11, 2001, Schmitt has been turned to, "to understand the enmity of a new century of conflict characterized by the emergence of spaces of exception placed outside the law *by and through* the law" (see also Dean 2010, 463–65), such as Afghanistan under US occupation and the Guantánamo Bay prison camp (Gregory 2006; Chambers 2018, 146–49). Whatever the differences between Schmitt and his critics, including the usefulness, or otherwise, of Schmitt's thought for understanding the contemporary world (Galli 2015, 97–134), across much of this literature the terrain of debate concerns what Rory Rowan (2011, 145) has called the "macro-spatial," the macro spaces of the geopolitical order.

While the automobility *nomos* is articulated with and located within these geopolitical macro spaces, it also exists on a micro-spatial level, the internal space of the road. It is a micro-spatial realm that has transformed the macro space that is the globe, a point we will return to later.

Carlo Galli (2015, 117) has argued that Schmitt's thought, not just in respect to his Nazi period (see Bendersky 1979; Koskenniemi 2012; Barnes and Minca 2013; Sitze 2015), is highly ideological and "must therefore be handled carefully: it's never neutral, and it's always oriented to some or another political position." Two of the central elements of Schmitt's thought in *Nomos of the Earth* are land appropriation and the ordering of space. It is these basic concepts—not the orientation of these concepts to some or another political position by Schmitt (which is the focus of much of the secondary literature)—that offer a path for reconceptualizing the genealogy and spatiality of automobility.

AUTOMOBILITY SPATIALITIES: THE APPROPRIATION OF LAND AND SPACE

The history of automobility is a history of the appropriation and subsequent transformation and reordering of space that previously was external to automobility. At the turn of the twentieth century, urban space was shared by different sociotechnical artifacts and by humans moving, selling and playing on the streets. "Before road traffic became so dominant, hectic and dangerous" (Taylor 2003, 1611), city streets, Clay McShane (1994; see also Holzapfel 2000) notes, were a "recreational space where urban children had amused themselves since the invention of cities." Motorists were initially seen and defined as invaders of the existing social and spatial order (Norton 2008, 1–46), and limits were imposed on drivers both in terms of speed and the use of space. That order was disrupted when automobility entered with deadly force. Roads were transformed into thoroughfares where road and roadside activities became subordinated to automobility (Bonham 2006).

Already in the decade between 1920 and 1929, more than 200,000 people were killed on the streets of the United States, four times more than in the previous decade (Norton 2007, 21). In New York City at the beginning of the twentieth century, "Cars hitting pedestrians, especially children," McShane (1994, 176) observed,

> became a major new form of accidents, and over the next dozen years a war raged between automobiles and youngsters for the control of New York's streets. Not surprisingly, the cars would win the hostilities. . . . Probably three quarters of the auto's victims were pedestrians, mostly children playing in the street, inattentive to the new vehicles.

Read from a Schmittian perspective, Norton's and McShane's accounts of the early history of automobility document the originary violence (Galli 2015, 107) by which space was, first, appropriated and then constituted as automobilized space. While largely forgotten in the global north, this originary violence continues unabated with the expansion of automobility across the Earth (Lamont 2012).

Cars unsurprisingly won the hostilities not only because automobiles are "item[s] of heavy machinery designed to travel at speeds significantly in excess of the limits of lethal injury to the human body" (Randell 2017, 671) or because car travel "cut[s] mercilessly through [the] slower-moving pathways and dwellings . . . inhabited by pedestrians, children going to school, postmen, garbage collectors, farmers, animals and so on" (Urry 2004, 29). While "the car" is the proximate physical object through which space was appropriated, what was also required was the social, political and juridical transformation of road space. "Cars"—i.e., machinery designed to travel at high speed—won the hostilities because they were permitted and encouraged to move within and through the legally transformed space that is the road.

Roads—it is routinely assumed both within the law and within everyday life—are intended and built primarily for automobile use. It is an intention that is legible—spatially visible—within the very artifact that is the road: in its markings and signings (Heidegger 1962, H 76–83); in its divisions of and within space; in the very materials of which it is constructed; in the size, speed and weight of the sociotechnical machines that traverse its surface. It is an assumption that is not just a recognition of fact but an ethical and normative judgment, that this spatial arrangement is just and proper. Like the *nomos* of the *jus publicum Europaeum*, automobility is founded both on an array of laws regulating space, not just those relating to the rules of the road, and on "tradition" and "custom" (Schmitt 2003, 72).

THE ROAD AS BRACKETED SPACE

The *nomos* of the *jus publicum Europaeum*, Schmitt argued, had "bracketed" the conduct of war between sovereign European states. The bracketing referred not to the abolition of war but to the containment, or fencing in (*Hegung*), of war, not only spatially but also in terms of what was permissible (Jacques 2015). Conflict and violence were contained through the "rationalization, humanization, and legalization" of war (Schmitt 2003, 100). Within this *nomos* "just enemies" (*justi hostes*) with specific political rights were recognized within international law, both in victory and defeat. That recognition was not, however, extended to all enemies. Armed conflict with those defined as criminals, such as pirates, was defined not as war but as a police operation. Similarly, the indigenous inhabitants of the New World were not recognized as *justi hostes*.

Schmitt's description of the bracketing of war and of the differing legal status of enemies within the *nomos* of the *jus publicum Europaeum* cannot be transposed in a straightforward manner onto automobility. It provides, however, a starting point for reconceptualizing the spatialities of automobility. First, in respect to bracketing, the history of automobility is a history of the construction of a distinct—bracketed, fenced—socio-juridical space, namely the road. Although there are differences across legal jurisdictions, the road is a space wherein death and injury routinely occur under conditions of relative impunity. Within that bracketed space, violence that is neither permitted nor tolerated within spaces external to automobility is both permitted and tolerated. Discursively, it is represented under the designation "accident." Secondly, it is a space, entry into which results in the transformation of one's juridical status. To enter that space is to cross a border, and as Charles Maier (2016, 277) has remarked in respect to national borders, "crossing a border can radically change our rights and security." This bracketed spatial realm is the micro-space of the *nomos* of automobility.

THE ROAD AS SPACE OF PERMANENT EXCEPTION

In *Political Theology* Schmitt (2005, 5; see also Schmitt 1923, 5) famously defined the sovereign as "he who decides on the exception." In *Nomos of the Earth,* Schmitt (2003, 98–99, 209) only in passing explicitly mentions spaces within the *nomos* of the *jus publicum Europaeum* wherein law has been suspended. Yet as Agamben (2017, 34) has pointed out, a careful reading of *Nomos of the Earth* reveals that the New World was "a designated zone of free and empty space," wherein "everything required by the situation was permitted" (Schmitt 2003, 98–99). Those spaces of exception within the *nomos* of the *jus publicum Europaeum*, as well as the principal space with which *Political Theology* was concerned, namely the territory of a nation-state, are geopolitical macro spaces of the type discussed above. To consider the juridical properties of the micro space that is the road, it is to Agamben that we now turn.

For Agamben, the paradigmatic space of the contemporary political order is the concentration camp (cf. Ojakangas 2005). It is the site in which the state of exception is given a permanent spatial arrangement, where the state of exception has become the rule. "The camp" is the site wherein those who enter it are "stripped of every political status" and reduced to what Agamben has called *nuda vita*, or "bare life," as it has been translated into English.* The camp, Agamben (2017, 140–41) argued, "was . . . the most absolute biopolitical space ever to have been realized, in which power confronts nothing but pure life, without any mediation."

In describing the camp, above all the Nazi concentration camp, as paradigmatic, Agamben's point was that the camp was not a singular, unique historical space or event. "The essence of the camp," Agamben (2017, 143) argued, "consists in the materialization of the state of exception and in the subsequent creation of *a space* in which bare life and the juridical rule enter into a threshold of indistinction" [our emphasis]. We are in the presence of such a camp, Agamben argued, whenever we are confronted with such a structure, "independent of the kinds of crime that are committed there and whatever its denomination and specific topography." It is:

> a space in which the normal order is de facto suspended and in which whether or not atrocities are committed depends not on law but on the civility and ethical sense of the police who temporarily act as sovereign (for example, in the four days during which foreigners can be held in the *zone d'attente* [in French international airports] before the intervention of the judicial authority).

Bare life is he who Agamben (2017, 61, 150) has identified as *homo sacer*, an "enigmatic figure" within Roman criminal law whose "entire existence is reduced to a bare life stripped of every right by virtue of the fact that *anyone can kill him without committing homicide*" [our emphasis]. Exposed unconditionally to potential killing, *homo sacer* is reduced to a continuous relationship with the power that banishes her precisely because she is at any instant exposed to an unconditional threat of death. Banned from the domain of political being, *homo sacer* is life reduced to *zoē*, biological existence. *Zoē* is thus separated from *bios,* qualified (political or public) life.

The camp, Agamben (2017, 144) argued, "is the hidden matrix of the politics in which we are still living, and it is this structure of the camp that *we must learn to recognize in all its metamorphoses*" [our emphasis]. Automobility, we are suggesting, is one such metamorphosis.

Within the *nomos* of automobility spaces have been delineated wherein a constant threat of automobility violence has become a permanent state of normality. It is a "structure in which the state of exception . . . is realized

---

* The Italian *nuda vita* is Agamben's translation of *bloßes Leben,* which appears in Walter Benjamin's (1991, 179, 203) *Zur Kritik der Gewalt* (Agamben 2017, 56). *Bloßes Leben* in the English translation (Benjamin 1996) of *Zur Kritik der Gewalt* is rendered not as "bare life" but as "mere life." Although neither more nor less satisfactory than "bare life," "mere life" suggests a different form of reduction and abandonment of "life" (Agamben 2017, 51–52). See Carlo Salzani's (2015) "From Benjamin's *bloßes Leben* to Agamben's *Nuda Vita*: A Genealogy" for a discussion of the differences between these terms.

normally" (Agamben 2017, 140). The *homines sacri* of the automobility *nomos* are all who enter that space. Although a "micro space" relative to the macro spaces that are the focus of much of the Schmitt literature, it is a spatiality that is everywhere, that cannot be circumvented. As pedestrians, cyclists, drivers or passengers, it is a space that must be entered and crossed to engage in the most basic and routine activities of daily life: going to and from work, purchasing food, socializing, attending school and so forth.

THE MORAL ECONOMY OF AUTOMOBILITY

McShane's reference to cars as the victor of the hostilities on the streets of New York is not entirely accurate. It is not *cars* that won the hostilities but a car-driver entity (Katz 1999; Lupton 1999; Beckmann 2004; Dant 2004; Randell 2017). It is the presence and movement of this cyborg entity possessed of, as Urry has put it, a "steel skin" that is the proximate reason why roads are dangerous spaces of violence. This cyborg entity capable of dangerous, competitive *speed* is a key artifact within the dromocratic order that is automobility. Within the spatiality of the road, the automobile body routinely confronts bare life, docile bodies that are repressed and, frequently, killed and injured. Speed and rhythm, as well as dwelling, consequently, are spatially ordered.

It is, however, too simplistic to suggest that the road is a space occupied solely by two distinct and unequal entities that confront each other: the human-machine entity and those who Adorno (2010, 40) called "the vermin of the street," the latter being the *homines sacri* of automobility. The car-driver assemblage is a dual entity, not just in that it is a hybrid human-machine entity, but also because bare life is simultaneously enclosed within and a component of that entity. Those enclosed within the human-machine entity—drivers and passengers—are equally subject to the violence of automobility (see, for example, Furnas 1935; Watkins-Hughes 2009); they also may be, and routinely are killed without homicide having been committed; they also are the *homines sacri* of automobility. Their deaths and injuries equally occur within the space of exception.

Once the road has been established as a space of exception, the sociotechnical dominance of the car-driver hybrid serves as the "guarantor" of the spatial order (Schmitt 2003, 352). Space becomes ordered in the *nomos* in complex ways: by permitted and forbidden access, speeds and rhythms (Cresswell 2010; Pearce 2012); visible and non-visible (technologically black-boxed) connections and relations created in and by spatial appropriation (Latour 1990). Non-automobile bodies are confined to the pavement and, if they enter the space of the road by, for instance, crossing it, are ordered to do so in specific spaces, at specific speeds and in specific rhythms (Sheller and Urry 2000). Speed and rhythm, as well as dwelling, consequently, are spatially ordered (Lefebvre 2013). Action as social existence of any sort occurs within this topographically and politically constructed spatial order.

The term "jaywalker," for example, already by 1924 had entered into a standard American dictionary as "one who crosses a street without observing the traffic regulations for pedestrians" (Norton 2007, 358). The rulebooks of automobility originating in the *nomos* adjudicate conflicts between automobilized and non-automobilized bodies. The Schmittian "*occupatio bellica*" applies (Schmitt 2003, 207): the temporary reordering of space in which "unintended" violence happens is the state of exception that upholds the original "constitutional" order of the *nomos*. Death is accepted as collateral damage within the *nomos* of automobility. Within the moral economy of automobility, the exception—a constitutive force in Agamben's description of the *nomos*—is inscribed as human error and rationalized as technosocial necessity.

Simultaneously threats and reminders of the intrinsic violence of automobility (Taylor 2003, 1611), the most obvious and frequently encountered examples of the proximate causes of death and injury are tailgating, cutting off bicyclists, accelerating at pedestrians deemed to be crossing the road too slowly or at non-specified points. Automobiles driven by, as Joanna Latimer and Rolland Munro (2006, 45) have put it, "the kind of guy that comes 'right up your arse' . . . flashing his lights, and thrusting his way forward regardless of others' safety or sensibilities." Yet atrocities occur not only because of egregious driving. Braun and Randell (2020, 7) note that "perusing the codebooks of [road safety] studies . . . what is striking is the extraordinary number of things that can go wrong on the road." As Agamben (2017, 95) remarks in respect to the banality of road violence:

> What confronts us today is a life that as such is exposed to a violence without precedent precisely in the most profane and banal ways. Our age is the one in which a holiday weekend produces more victims on Europe's highways than a war campaign.

ROAD SAFETY RESEARCH: THE STATISTICAL CONSTRUCTION OF CAUSALITY

The examples above, ranging from the driver Latimer and Munro describe to momentary lapses of attention, would seem to confirm the claims of traditional "road safety" research, which attributes automobility violence primarily to human agency. A frequently cited figure and attribution of responsibility is that 93 percent of road accidents are the result of human error (Singh 2015). It is an attribution of cause and responsibility in accord with how "accidents" are understood within the automobility *nomos*, wherein responsibility for automobile violence is located primarily within individuals *qua* "drivers."

Except in the limiting case of the intentional targeting of victims (see, for example, Chambers and Andrews 2019),* road deaths, in most circumstances—and there are 1,350,000 each year—are not understood to constitute either homicide or manslaughter, neither legally nor in routine everyday accountings of automobile death. In everyday life we take it as given that someone involved in a "car accident" should not be charged with homicide; that it is, after all, "something that could happen to anyone." It is because automobile deaths occur within the bracketed space of the road that they are tolerated and permitted. While the degree of impunity—both juridical and in respect to social ostracism (custom and tradition)—of drivers varies across legal systems and cultures, everywhere road death and injury are treated differently from death and injury in other spaces.

In locating violence within the individual driver, not the spatial ordering, automobility violence is rationalized and rendered acceptable. Quantified as a statistic—93 percent—violence forms one side of a moral equation, on the other side of which are located the freedom, speed, autonomy, efficiency, pleasure, convenience, comfort and safety of the human bodies enclosed within the automobile body (Böhm, Jones, et al. 2006, 7). Impunity, however, extends beyond drivers. To think of impunity, either total or partial impunity, *solely* in terms of something the driver might or might not be afforded, is to accept that responsibility—ethically, causally and legally—lies entirely with drivers. It is an automobility version of the analogous argument that "it is not guns, but people, who kill people." Although present in 100 percent of car crashes, with the exception of defective vehicles, vehicles (and by extension automobile manufacturers) are relieved of responsibility. As Mark Lamont (2012) has put it, "drivers or victims [are] blamed for negligence, but vehicles almost always exonerated and considered inert, speechless witnesses to crime."

In locating both causality and moral responsibility in the driver, not only vehicles and automobile manufacturers but also, more importantly, *automobility in its entirety* is relieved of causality and responsibility (Beckmann 2004; Braun and Randell 2020). In short, it is automobility that is afforded complete impunity. Both in the aggregate and in each individual accident, *who*, or *what*, is responsible and how impunity is to be distributed fade into

---

* An exception is Florida, where drivers who intentionally strike street protesters are afforded legal immunity (Epstein and Mazzei 2021) on the grounds that protesters are illegally blocking traffic.

indistinction. The most significant property of the road is that it is a site of Schmittian exception.

DROMOCRATIC VIOLENCE: THE CONSTITUTIVE CENTER OF AUTOMOBILITY

Within the philosophical literature (Bufacchi 2013), violence has traditionally been conceptualized either in terms of intentionality (Finlay 2017; Burgess-Jackson 2003) or in terms of consequences (Coady 1986; Murphy 2012). With respect to automobility violence, neither of these approaches is adequate. The English word "violence," as well as cognates in other European languages, originate from the Greek βiá—force and rush—which captures the combined meanings of power, mobility and speed. With respect to automobility, it is "power-knowledge . . . eliminated to the benefit of moving-power" (Virilio 2006, 71).

In her seminal essay on violence, Arendt (1970) separates violence from power. Following Walter Benjamin (1996), she argues that while power is absolute, violence is not; it is merely instrumental and is justified by the end it pursues. Power, according to Arendt, needs no justification as it is inherent to the very essence of political communities, whereas "violence needs justification and it can be justifiable, but its justification loses plausibility the farther away its intended end recedes into the future" (Arendt 1970, 52).

Automobility violence is not, however, a means to any end that might or might not justify it. It is the constitutive property of the spatially visible political and social order that is the automobility *nomos*. It is constitutive in the same sense as are constitutive rules as described by John Searle (2018), which he differentiates from regulative rules. Constitutive rules are world-making, whereas regulative rules order already-existing behaviors. In respect to automobility, "drive on the right" is a regulative rule that establishes ways of driving while the activity of driving exists independently of it. Violence is constitutive of automobility as it creates and sustains the spatial reality in which existence is experienced in automobilized societies. You cannot dwell within the realm of automobility without following the political and social order made spatially visible within the automobility *nomos*. If you do not, you have a very high and contingent chance of not being able to live in this world at all. It is precisely because not following, acceding to or recognizing this political and social order is likely to result in death or injury that small children are taught about this order—the automobility *nomos*—and instructed in how to navigate the spatialities of a world dominated by automobility.

Power "springs up," Arendt (1970, 31) argued, whenever people congregate and act in concert. This is the realm of the political; people acting and speaking together (Arendt 1958, 179). In the *nomos* of automobility, power and violence also "spring up" together; both are constitutive of the order that makes acting/moving in concert possible. Violence *is* power, and power *is* violence; neither one is a means to another end, nor are they in need of justification in the Arendtian sense. Automobility power/violence is the political order made spatially visible and topographically operable, which is why power/violence is spatially "bracketed": neither are a means to the other; both are ends in themselves through which the automobility *nomos* is constituted and reproduced. This is the essence of the automobility order. It is within this spatial order that many of the planet's inhabitants, not only humans (Davenport and Davenport 2006), dwell, move and act.

In the *nomos* of automobility, violence "does not depend on implements" (Arendt 1970, 3). Automobility violence transgresses traditional conceptualizations of violence as being either in need of implements or intentional to inflict harm. Power/violence is constitutive of automobility because human agents are neither in need of implements of violence; they are one of the components of "the implement" that is the car-driver entity. Nor do they have specific and direct foresight of the consequences of their actions beyond being actors in a complex interconnectedness of human agents and "things" (Latour 2005a). Intentionality (Jacquette 2013) or foreseeability (Bufacchi 2007, 66) thus become blurred and evaporate in the actor-actant sociotechnical setup (Latour 1990) that is "automobility."

THE RHIZOMATIC SPATIAL REORDERING OF THE WORLD

Politically, automobility has required massive public investment and the building of vast infrastructures (Paterson 2007). Like the great land appropriations of the New World by European powers beginning in the sixteenth century, the success of which required the use and threat of force and violence, so too has the expansion of automobility required the appropriation of land and space. As Lewis Mumford (1963, 220) observed in an essay first published in 1959 in *The New Yorker*, the US federal highways project required "slashing through old neighborhoods, stealing land from public parks, dumping traffic in urban centers."

Since the beginning of the twentieth century, automobility has spread across the globe in extension, density and intensity. It is a process of massive land appropriation. Existing roads have been transformed into thoroughfares for dromocratic movement (i.e., appropriated for automobile traffic); new roads are built primarily, often solely, to enable such movement. This has rearranged the spatial order beyond automobile movement. Not only roads but also the contiguous and surrounding spaces have been appropriated and transformed within the economy of automobility. Bicycle lanes, walkable pavements designated for other types of movement were appropriated, as were spots for stationary use, parking lots, public benches, filling stations and drive-through facilities. These materialized, privatized dwelling-and-movement road and car spaces constitute the spatial order of dromocracy.

Approximately thirty-six million kilometers of roads have been constructed across the surface of the planet (United States Central Intelligence Agency No date). The vast majority of road construction has been for access by mechanized vehicles. Rhizomes, Gilles Deleuze and Félix Guattari (1987b, 1–27) point out, are plants that expand and grow horizontally, spreading new growth with the rhizomatic expansion of their root system. Blackberry plants are a domesticated example. "Rhizome" serves as an appropriate metaphor for the expansion of automobility across the surface of the planet. From its original habitus in Europe and North America, automobility has now expanded across much of the global south, becoming a spatially visible *global* political and social order. There are increasingly fewer parts of the planet that are not accessible by road. Through the global expansion of automobility—roads, infrastructure and all the components of that which John Urry (2004, 26) called "the system of automobility" is composed—much of the planet has been transformed into an automobilized world. In central Europe there are two kilometers of road per square kilometer of land (Grilo et al. 2020).

Total kilometers of road that have been constructed provides, however, only an abstract measure of the transformation of the space that has been brought into the realm of automobility. Examples are the destruction of rainforests in Papua New Guinea (Gabbatiss 2018) and of the Amazon, neither of which would be possible without road construction and, in these cases, not cars, but trucks and heavy land-moving equipment, the success of which equally requires violence and the threat of violence: against indigenous inhabitants, non-human species and the very "environment" itself.

Automobility is the most violent sociopolitical order on Earth, not only for humans but for many other species, whose existence depends increasingly on what we humans do or refrain from doing. Automobility impedes and redirects the mobility of animals (Castellano 2018; Chambers 2018, 33–38; Hodgetts and Lorimer 2020); hundreds of millions of animals are killed each year through collisions with vehicles (89). Across Europe, 194 million birds and twenty-nine million mammals are killed annually on roads (Grilo et al. 2020). We could think of them not as *other* but as "terrestrials, just like us" (Rorty 1989, 189–98; Latour 2018; see also Derrida 2008), who also suffer and feel pain. It is a term that opens up the possibility of solidarities not only with other humans but also a post-human solidarity with our fellow terrestrials (Ferrando 2020; Haraway 2015); they also have been reduced to bare life.

Beyond the abstract physicality of roads and their mathematically measurable extension, automobility has transformed, as did train travel, our mode of Being-in-the-world. For those outside the automobile, it is a world of constantly moving automobiles; for those within the automobile, it is a world as experienced and perceived from within the vehicle (Böhm, Jones, et al. 2006b; Merriman 2009; Katz 1999; Taylor 2003). In the guise of the attached garage, through television, in advertisements, through social media, music and film, automobility is intertwined with and ever-present, existing beyond the physical space of the road. Automobility intrudes upon and reorders what we take to be private spaces outside of the public space occupied by physically visible automobility. It has receded into the perceptual background of much of social life (Goffman 1963, 21; Taylor 2003), yet that background is everywhere. Automobility is not separate from us but, understood phenomenologically, is what Being-in-the-world has come to mean in the age of automobility.

THE GLOBAL NOMOS OF AUTOMOBILITY

Though one of many sources of greenhouse gas emissions, automobility is one of the central technologies responsible for climate change. The consequences are well known and include the disappearance of land with rising sea levels, desertification, droughts, bushfires, hurricanes and other extreme weather events, species extinction and the death of coral reefs resulting from increased water temperatures. Like the *nomos* of the *jus publicum Europaeum*, it is appropriation of the global commons (Harvey 2007, 35), albeit through climate change caused by greenhouse gas emissions, not plunder and settlement. In addition to land and sea, it represents, as Schmitt (2001, 103–7) conjectured in the concluding pages to *Land and Sea*, the conquering of the space that is the air.

The *homines sacri* of automobility are not only those who enter the space of the road but all of us. In addition to automobility's contribution to global warming (Bonneuil and Fressoz 2016), automobile pollutants result in disease and death. Automobility, as David Pellow and Robert Brulle (2007, 41) put it, is one of the "institutions that routinely poison the earth and its people." In the European Union alone, four hundred thousand people die every year from respiratory diseases caused by automobility-induced pollution (European Commission 2017; see Vohra et al. 2021 for global estimates). They also are killed under conditions of impunity. Not only do all who enter the space of the road become *homines sacri,* so also are those exposed to automobility pollution and subject to the effects of greenhouse gas emissions. Automobility's global extension has, in effect, contributed to the transformation of the entire globe as a space of exception. *Homo sacer* has become virtually indistinguishable not only from the citizen (Agamben 2017, 141) but everyone. Bare life, as Agamben (2017, 116) has put it, "is no longer confined to a particular place or a definite category. It now dwells in the biological body of every living being."

The *nomos* of automobility, in other words, is everywhere. It stretches across much of the land surface of the planet. However, its constituent elements are not the macro geopolitical spaces of nations, continents, land and sea. Its constituent elements are the myriad micro spaces that are the road. Yet those micro spaces have reordered the spatiality of the entire planet. Earlier we noted that the automobility *nomos* is articulated with, and located within, the geopolitical macro spaces that are the focus of much of the secondary Schmitt literature. That is not subject of this book, but we would here note that supply chains (Cowen 2014), the extraction and transportation of oil (Campbell 2005) and raw materials required in the manufacturing of automobiles, the protection of shipping routes by naval forces, the importance of automobile manufacturing in national economies (Paterson 2007, 91–121), are points at which automobility is articulated with these geopolitical macro spaces; the spatially visible "political and social order of a people" (Schmitt 2003, 70)—container ports and shipping lanes, for example—that is the political economy of the planet (Mitchell 2013).

While there are significant regional, national and other geographic variations within the automobility *nomos*—namely differences in respect to law, custom and tradition—it is appropriate to describe the automobility *nomos* as a singular global *nomos*, evidence for which is that automobility death and injury occurs wherever there are roads and automobiles. More importantly, automobility death and injury are normalized and not punished, as are death and injury in spaces external to automobility. That death and injury rates vary across countries speaks neither to the absence or presence of the automobility *nomos* nor to there being many separate automobility *nomoi* but to variations within the global, singular, automobility *nomos.*

One of those variations is degrees to which the state of exception prevails, the degree to which the spaces within the automobility *nomos* are void of law. In arguing that "the camp" was "the most absolute biopolitical space ever to have been realized, in which power confronts nothing but pure life, without any mediation" Agamben (2017, 140–41) has in mind above all the concentration camps of Nazi Germany. Clearly, Agamben was not of the view that all metamorphoses of the camp are equivalent, indistinct, *absolute* biopolitical spaces.

The *nomos* of automobility is not everywhere a space wherein an *absolute* state of exception void of *all* law pertains. It is a bracketed space wherein all are subject to the possibility of being killed under circumstances wherein homicide has not been committed and where responsibility is dispersed and indistinct. To the degree this juridical situation is mitigated it is primarily due to efforts to reduce legal impunity in respect to drivers. Penalties for driving under the influence of alcohol in some jurisdictions, mainly within the Global North, are a case in point. It remains, however, that the spaces that have been appropriated by and for automobility are spaces of exception. In which ways they differ, which we here can no more than gloss, are important potential areas of research.

SPATIAL VIOLENCE

The violent wars of land appropriation of the *jus publicum Europaeum* were bracketed and tragic, although increasingly recognized. In contrast, death and injury in the *nomos* of automobility are not considered even to be sacrifice; rarely can they be described as heroic, one of the few exceptions being the death of motorsports drivers (Williams 2020; see also Möser 2003, 240). Automobility deaths are rationalized and dehumanized by being purged from public memory, remembered only by friends and family. As opposed to the casualties of wars between nations, with the exception of private makeshift flowers, white ghost bikes or religious symbols such as crosses placed on roadsides (Reid 2015; Bednar 2020), there are few public commemorative memorials or statues of either the unknown or known automobility casualties (Neiman 2019, 261–307). Among the few exceptions are public memorials in Budapest and in Prague (see Norton 2008, 21–46 for past examples) and the designation of an annual world day of remembrance, November 15, for road traffic victims.

Violence, we have argued, is the constitutive element of the socio-spatial order of automobility, the dominant system of land transportation and mobility across much of the planet. Automobility violence is not limited to actually occurring violence on the road but includes epistemic violence (Spivak 1988): the describing of violence not as violence but as "accidents," investigation of which is referred to as "road safety" research, thereby transforming epistemic violence into epistemic injustice (Fricker 2011). Bracketed and made to disappear from the location in which they occurred, the detritus and markings of accidents are routinely effaced (Virilio 2007b): the road is cleaned; automobiles are removed and repaired or junked; victims are transported to hospitals; accident reports are completed (United States Department of Transportation 2008), each a new data point available for statistical analysis (Beckmann 2004). Not automobility, but "the driver," is held to be responsible for the majority of automobility crashes.

The few examples of metamorphoses, of "the camp" that Agamben has identified, are all temporally or spatially delimited. The automobility *nomos*, in contrast, is an example of an enduring, permanent global space wherein the state of exception has become normalized. It is precisely the kind of paradigmatic space identified by Agamben, one in which almost 100 million people have been killed and more than one billion, perhaps many more, have been seriously injured. Automobility's spatial extension has resulted in the creation of a global space within which all are reduced to *homo sacer*, who is not only she who may be killed but also she who may be injured without a crime having been committed.

Qua nomos, automobility is one of the metamorphoses Agamben has warned us of. The signs and traces of its violence routinely removed and cleared away, automobility has become so unremarkable and taken for granted that we are unable to recognize it as such a space.

Part 3

FUTURE AUTOMOBILITIES AND POST-AUTOMOBILITY

I destytute, I forsake or leave a thyng or persone, *je destitue.*
 —John Palsgrave, 1530, *Lesclarcissement de la langue françoyse*

Destitution & delaissement, Destituting or disappointing.
 —Claudius Hollyband, 1580. *The treasurie of the French tong teaching the waye to varie all sortes of verbes: enriched so plentifully with wordes and phrases (for the benefit of the studious in that language) as the like hath before bin published*

Chapter Seven

Ker

The Political Religion of Nomocracy

Chapter 3 began with a discussion of the multiple significations of *dromos* in Ancient Greece. Dromos referred to both the running track and the road leading to Temple, the protected space through which the visitor transited or was carried from one world over to another. This book is the story of how, in the twentieth century, a new, hegemonic, violent and totalitarian dromocratic order spread throughout cities, rural spaces and across the entire planet. That order is not just an assemblage of components within a system that can be identified, placed in relations with each other, their empirical properties described, as Urry has done; it is an ontology. It is an ontology not in the traditional sense of metaphysics but a political ontology, held together and sustained within and by a network of multiple actors and actants.

It is an ontology of realism that is grounded in material objects and artifacts. It is a realism which, we have argued, needs to be placed under erasure. First, in respect to the dualist epistemology such a realism entails, wherein the ostensibly real of automobility is detached from its ostensible representations. Second, with respect to the very notion that automobility is the appropriate name for an already constituted object "out there." Deconstructing *that* requires interrogating the name, entertaining the possibility that automobility is an instance of an "ill-named 'thing.'" What was further required was to show what it named and what it did not. From there to construct not alternative names in place of automobility's signifier, which has the same name as that which it signifies, but to construct new signifiers, new metaphors, with which to displace the ostensibly signified that is "automobility." To show why automobility is ill-named. We have done this through a series of alternative metaphors: imaginary, dromos, spectacle, dreamscape and nomos.

In this chapter we collect these metaphors together with three goals in mind. First, to revisit the central question this book has addressed: How does a critique of automobility get us to post-automobility? Second, to expand the phenomenological analysis of chapter 2, where we argued that this order is the taken-for-granted reality of everyday life. Third, to address the following questions: What is the political ontology of automobility? What kind of onto-political imaginary is this ill-named thing that is "automobility"? Put another way: What is the philosophical meaning of automobility? What kind of order is it? Is there something about this order, the ill-name of which is "automobility," that is existentially unbearable? Our performative aim has been to bring the reader into this existentially unbearable order. Not to simply see differently a world that is presumed to independently exist but, as we put it in the introduction, to inhabit a different world in the sense articulated by Thomas Kuhn. A post-automobility world, however, is not something that is sufficient to just imagine; the challenge is how to get there.

Beyond the deconstruction of the metaphysics of automobility, we suggest in the final chapter strategies of destitution. Our project is philosophical, interrogating what Roberto Esposito (2008) has referred to as philosophical powers struggling to control and dominate the world and determine its ultimate meaning. What goes under the name of "automobility" is one such philosophical power. It is a philosophy that has constructed a world and an ontology, and it has done so without us, or it, realizing this has been done. Who, after all, would think that automobility—and here the colloquial term "the automobile" is more appropriate—is a philosophy? Marx made both a political and a philosophical point in the Eleventh Thesis on Feuerbach: "The philosophers have only interpreted the world, the point is to change it." Automobility has done precisely that, only not in the direction Marx had in mind. It is a philosophy of happiness, of the good life, a eudemonics; it has constructed an aesthetic, a set of standards of the beautiful, an automobilized critique of judgment; it is a utilitarian ethics, a moral economy, wherein the greatest happiness of the greatest number outweighs the misery and grief of automobility's victims.

In respect to the question "what is automobility?" the very term "automobility," we have argued, requires re-examination. We have used the term frequently throughout the book. It is an unavoidable term, but it obfuscates as much as it enlightens. That, however, is what needs to be foregrounded. Although the automobility studies literature has displaced "the automobile" from the center of analytic attention, those attempts have been only partially successful, as of necessity also has ours. We all are held captive within Wittgenstein's picture.

Sheller and Urry decentered the automobile by representing automobility as a "system," which system was composed of components that the automobile was either dependent on or that were interconnected with the automobile.

Similarly, Foucauldian analyses have displaced the automobile from the center of attention. Yet it is "automobile" that is the root term in the noun "automobility"; the very term subverts attempts to decenter the automobile; the artifact in its physicality and materiality remains at the very center of the object of analysis.

We have tried to further decenter the automobile, locating it as one component of what we have described under the metaphors of an order, an imaginary, spectacle, dromos, nomos and dreamscape. These are neither layers nor versions of reality, nor can they be arranged in a causal chain or hierarchy that could be operationalized for quantitative analysis. They are, in the Derridean sense of *écriture*, automobility's "inscriptions in conflictual and differentiated contexts" (Derrida 1998, 141). They highlight a specific aspect or shed light on an experience of this constructed ontology that is everyday automobility, a multistable and multiple reality, multidimensional *and* singular, coexisting in the experiences of different vantage points as performed in different human-non-human entanglements.

Alternative possible terms are "dromocracy" and "nomocracy." Dromocracy on Virilio's (2006, 167) account is "the violence of speed" that is both the "location and the law, the world's destiny and its destination." This makes the problem political, raising two questions: What mechanics of power are at work (the political maintenance operation managing the threat of invention)? How can the distribution of power be managed? While Virilio's focus is the politics of speed mobilized and machinated by speed, our focus is the political ontology of violence, political existence or being in automobility space. What is this being-in or political existence that is located at the threshold of the law and destiny?

THE STATE OF EXCEPTION

In respect to the phenomenology of automobility, the ontology of everyday existence, we here take up what was previously discussed separately by bringing together imaginary, nomos, dromos, and dreamscape in order to construct that larger "thing" that automobility may be a case of. Our focus is the aesthetic, understood in its broadest signification, of automobility: the quality and texture of Being-in-the-world in the age of automobility.

One of our aims, following Agamben, is to see "politics returned to its ontological position." Agamben (1998, 31) argues that:

> [t]he problem of constituting power [. . .] becomes the problem of the "constitution of potentiality," and the unresolved dialectic between constituting power and constituted power opens the way for a new articulation of the relation

between potentiality and actuality, which requires nothing less than a rethinking of the ontological categories of modality in their totality.

While our aim is more modest than that of Agamben's, we argued in the previous chapter that the nomos of automobility is one of the metamorphoses of "the camp": the state of exception where *homines sacri*, automobilized cyborgs and docile bodies, dwell. It is a space where bracketed violence reigns, albeit a violence that is denied and exonerated, where power, in the form of bracketed violence, confronts biological life without mediation. It is a space of speed and exception.

It is not bare biological life, *homo sacer*, that moves from the threshold to the city, but it is the threshold that becomes the nomocratic city where automobilized cyborgs and docile bodies dwell. Automobility, discipline and control of and by biopolitics, the Foucauldian "to make live and to let die," is a manifestation of the form of political being of late-modernity. The essential politico-ontological condition of biopolitical sovereignty in automobility is transformed into a technoscientific being: the sovereign subject as the car-driver cyborg. As the automobility subject that is the cyborg becomes the bearer of sovereignty, biopolitical control—to make live and to let die—is dissolved in a delocalized, multidimensional material semantic entanglement, a spatio-temporal performed reality that is the automobility imaginary.

As we saw in chapter 4 in reference to Deleuze, the highway where people could "travel infinitely and 'freely' without being confined while being perfectly controlled" was a means to give permanent, material, biopolitical form to performed reality. The State, the mechanics of the body politics of the nation-state, that is the biopolitical sovereign, eventually transformed itself into material semiotic entanglements imagined *and* real. It is a dispositif, an apparatus (Manderscheid 2014), that provides the biopolitical control of Being within automobility.

What Schmitt (2003, 71) called "nomocracy" is this sociotechnical apparatus. It is dissolved, bracketed violence and dislocated power, the imagined and real biopolitical sovereign, inscribed in "stuff" that offers imaginary *and* real stability to the performed realities but also exercises biopolitical control. Automobility is a displacement and gradual expansion of the limits of the decision on bare life. As Agamben (1998, 72) has put it:

> If there is a line in every modern state marking the point at which the decision on life becomes a decision on death, and biopolitics can turn into thanatopolitics, this line no longer appears today as a stable border dividing two clearly distinct zones. This line is now in motion and gradually moving into areas other than that of political life, areas in which the sovereign is entering into an ever more

intimate symbiosis not only with the jurist but also with the doctor, the scientist, the expert, and the priest.

To Agamben's list of the jurist, the doctor, the scientist, the expert and the priest, we would add the engineer, the road safety expert, the corporation, the advertiser and the state. The nomocratic in automobility is the transformation of biopolitics into thanatopolitics, where the decision on life becomes inseparable from the decision on death. The body of the cyborg serves as a prosthetic to save biological life at the same time as it endangers life. That body, as Urry (2004) has put it, is the "metallic and glass shell," the "steel and petroleum iron cage" that "provides an extension of the human body, surrounding the fragile, soft and vulnerable human skin with a new steel skin."

In Greek mythology *Thanatos* had several sisters, the *Keres (Ker* in the singular). Dark, hovering beings with sharp teeth and a voracious taste for blood, the Keres represented violent death. They flew above battlefields and plague withered cities. Hearts glutted with human blood, portrayed as shaggy, blood-bespattered demons and grim-faced beings with fangs and talons dressed in bloody ripped garments, the Keres were associated with death, famine, hate and violence. Keres hover over the nomos of automobility. The Keres suggest an alternative and more appropriate term than "thanatopolitics" to designate automobility's relationship to death and injury: keropolitics. Automobility death and injury are not death and injury *simpliciter* but violent death and injury.

Schmitt argued not only that the sovereign is he who decides on the exception but that it is the sovereign who decides on whether a normal situation exists. Agamben has taken Schmitt's observation a step further in arguing that the exception has become the normal situation. The spaces of exception within automobility have not been decided by a singular sovereign but by a dispersed and delegated sovereign (Dean 2010). One of those dispersed and delegated sovereigns is the car-driver cyborg entity, who decides on life and death and, in so doing, exercises the power to recreate its human subject arbitrarily by breaking the technoscientific entanglement of car-driver. It is a sovereign that enters into symbiosis with the police officer as well as their bureaucratically organized body, the Police, the violent and limitless executive organ of the State that is afforded legal impunity, the bearer of, as Weber observed, the monopoly of the legitimate use of violence.

It is, as Sarah Seo (2019) has argued, a blueprint for totalitarianism. The violence of fascism, we need to remember, does not fall equally over entire populations. In fascism's past and present nation-state manifestations, many not only were able to live their lives as they did before, but it also was the fascistic order that sustained and made possible that continuity. It was "the others" who were harassed, molested, imprisoned, tortured and murdered, whose lives did not continue as they did before.

This space of exception gradually expanded, and its political ontology—normalized exception as a state of emergency, wherein life may be killed without homicide being committed—became generalized. The totalitarianisms of the twentieth century are the extreme examples of this expansion, the appearance of the permanent state of sovereign emergency. Fascism, as Virilio put it, "never died, it doesn't need to be reborn. It represented one of the most accomplished cultural, political and social revolutions of the dromocratic West." In this sphere the religious by way of the sacred and the political by way of the sovereign are united. It is, therefore, not by chance that automobility possesses a family resemblance with totalitarian orders that constitute themselves as political religions (Maier 2007). It is a sphere of exception where legal demarcations that balance civil liberties and manageable biopower are suspended. The state of exception is the collapsing of the legislative, the executive and the judicial within the apparatus of the state (Seo 2019).

"Othering," the process of representing some social group as different and, typically, as inferior to one's own, is at the center of automobility (Dawson, Day and Ashmore 2020). The road that is the space of normalized violence is also one of the spaces where conflicts of identity and Othering are performed. Others include ethnic groups (Alam 2020) and different technosocial hybrids. Automobility identities are often related to the affordances of vehicles and are modally contrived: "bus driver," "car driver," "cyclist," "scooter," "pedestrian." Automobility Othering also entails producing hierarchies legitimized by claiming a right to the road. Stereotypes create relational identities such as "inefficient," "leisurely," "unpredictable," "entitled" and "unregulated" others when drivers talk about bicycle-rider hybrids and, in exchange, "unsustainable," "inactive," "undiscerning," "impeded" and "inconsiderate" others when bikers write about car-drivers (Dawson, Day and Ashmore 2020, 218–21). In the "multi-auto-cultural" space of the road, violence is the keropolitical operator of Othering. The Othering of drivers and cyclists is typically embedded in a neoliberal discourse of efficiency and privatized space.

Such spatiopolitical conflicts are inherent to nomocracy, not only because space is scarce or limited but also because it is appropriated by violence. Automobility's intersectional Othering combines traditional social identity constructs such as gender, race, class or religion with technosocial hybrid identities as car-drivers, cyclists or pedestrians. While violence has a chaotic, disruptive and obtruding quality, rationalization by accident causation discourse and dehumanization by purging from memory, private and public alike, renders road violence as probable, predictable and unremediable (Thornton

2002). Violence contributes to the production, reproduction and contestation of automobility intersectionalities, including power hierarchies (Balkmar 2018). Automobility and nomocracy are closely tied to power, embodiment, movement, space and representation (Balkmar 2019). Nomocracy narratively fixes such intersectional automobility identities in a political hierarchy that renders car-driver cyborgs as "normal" and other vehicular identities as aberrant (Dawson, Day and Ashmore 2020). The political hierarchy of automobility intersectionality masks the fact that, in the keropolitical order, every citizen is bare life: dislocated and dissolved material semiotic power which, in the form of bracketed violence, confronts life without conciliation.

AUTOMOBILITY AS POLITICAL RELIGION

This order represents the transformation of a secular object into a political myth and mode of absolute control that is a political religion. Nineteenth- and twentieth-century political religions exist on both the left and right. In their extreme forms, when power was successfully seized, they became the totalitarian terrors of the twentieth century.

Franz Werfel, in a series of lectures given in Germany in 1932, referred to the need of the typical "man-on-the-street," shattered by world war, despairing of reason or science to search for a higher order falling to "systems of belief acting as religious surrogates and by no means just political ideologies" (Werfel 1946; quoted in Maier 2007, 9). Eric Voegelin (2000 [1938]) developed the concept of "political religions" in his 1938 book, arguing that emerging totalitarian regimes seek to achieve political cohesion through mass ideologies with a quasi-religious dimension.

On the right, one of the most impressive accounts of a totalitarian regime as political religion is Emilio Gentile's (1990) description of Italian fascism. He defines political religion as:

> a type of religion which sacralizes an ideology, a movement or a political regime through the deification of a secular entity transfigured into myth, considering it the primary and indisputable source of the meaning and the ultimate aim of human existence on earth (Gentile 2004, 328).

He argues that the concept of political religion does not refer solely to the institution of a system of beliefs, rites or symbols but also relates to the conquest of society, the homogenization of societies formed by the governed and to the ambitious expansion and construction of a new supranational civilization. It is totalitarian in as much as its ideology is based on a myth, is virile and anti-hedonistic, affirming the absolute primacy of the community understood as a homogenous organic entity with the bellicose mission to achieve grandeur, power and conquest. At its core lies the politicization of existence, to shape the individual and the masses through an anthropological revolution in order to regenerate the human being and create a new man, who is dedicated in body and soul to the realization of revolutionary and imperialistic policies with the ultimate aim of creating a new order (Gentile 2004).

We have made the case for describing automobility as an imaginary, a collectively held, institutionally stabilized assemblage of publicly performed visions of a desirable present. It is a system of beliefs, rites and symbols, publicly performed and iterated through verbal, visual, aural, tactile, kinetic and olfactory images in newspapers, magazines, books, in the mass media and social media and also by educational institutions. We have shown, in our discussion of dromocracy, that the foundational myth of automobility is the conquering and annihilating of space and time. More than the railway, automobility brought rational, geometric order to the world, experienced as autonomy and freedom of movement.

Automobility has rearranged hierarchies of power by creating the primacy of a community of drivers as opposed to non-automobilized docile bodies. By furthering and supporting geographical ignorance (McCright and Dunlap 2003), it has contributed to the exploitation and conquering of the entire planet. In this sense it is central to the construction of what Schmitt called "the nomos of the Earth." Its bellicose mission was discussed via Marinetti and the Futurists and the method of dreamwork which, in disguise, lies at the heart of automobility as dreamscape. The new human was represented as the human-machine cyborg created by the Futurists, most notably Boccioni.

The anthropological evolution of Futurism was, not ironically, imagined in one of the canonical museums of the world at a recent exhibition celebrating automobility history at the Victoria and Albert Museum (Cormier and Bisley 2019; Braun and Randell 2021). In that exhibition a new type of human, Graham, was on display. Graham was created by the artist Patricia Piccini and commissioned by the Transport Accident Commission of Victoria to show what a human might look like if this human evolved naturally to withstand crashes. In contradistinction to Bocconi's futurist man, Graham's face is flattened to absorb impact, his enlarged skull contains extra fluid to protect his brain, and the numerous nipples on his chest act as a kind of airbag to protect him in a crash. The new human is more like Marinetti's driver in body and soul, dedicated to the realization of the dromocratic revolution and the imperialism of creating the new order by and for the beauty of speed. Political power was monopolized by interpreting the automobility dream as wish fulfilment but without its traumas.

Political religions such as fascism and Soviet and Chinese communism base their identity on a sense of comradeship, another facet of automobility as imaginary (Muniz Jr. and O'Guinn 2001). Marinetti and other Futurists turned fascists waged war not only against their obvious political adversaries but also bicyclists and pedestrians—the vermin of the street (Adorno 2010, 40). Automobility has created a "mystic union" of national touring clubs and of automobile enthusiasts, mostly men, who share a passion for the artifact, for speed and power endowed by dromocracy, another aspect of a political religion. It has also produced a moral community, a righteous bracketing of violence, of the car-driver cyborgs.

An institutional dimension of political religions such as fascism, Gentile argues, is the corporate organization of the economy in order to reach its goal of power while preserving private property and class divisions. Automobility as spectacle is grandeur. As the central order of the fascist "New Civilization," it permeated, captured and colonized Earth. Fascism is a political system ordered in a hierarchy of functions, nominated from above and dominated by the figure of the "capo." This "capo" is the automobile that stands in place of and acts as sovereign in automobility. It is invested with charismatic sacristy, is entangled with humans to command, direct and coordinate the actions of the regime by subjectifying its members. In short, automobility resembles a political religion with fascist traits.

AUTOMOBILITY AS POLICE STATE

Automobiles have been constructed within the automobility imaginary as artifacts that contribute to liberal society's promises of autonomy, freedom and equality, democratizing the benefits of personal independence through wider housing location options, the expansion of consumption choices, freedom to take pleasure in high-speed private travel or to cruise through the city. In *Policing the Open Road: How Cars Transformed American Freedom,* Seo (2019) argues that automobility effectively ushered in a police state in the United States. The freedoms enshrined in the Fourth Amendment of the US Constitution, she argues, have been dismantled. What is called "discretionary policing" is none other than the collapsing into each other of the legislative, the executive and the judicial. It is the state of exception.

Not only in the United States, driving or being in a car has become the most policed aspect of everyday life across much of the globe. Automobility has wreaked disorder by "slicing through space like a great knife" (Lefebvre 1992, 165). It has transformed existing institutions that were meant to maintain order (Seo 2019). It first dislodged one of the raisons d'être of the police by transforming "reputable citizens" into offenders who regularly disobeyed the law. As a New York newspaper rhyme as early as the 1920s put it, "traffic violations were committed 'up town, down town, all around town.'" From protecting those defined as "law-abiding citizens" from "criminals, loiterers and vagrants," "modern policing begun with the need to police upstanding citizens." This continued when the increasingly penal nature of traffic laws required managing traffic under the full control of a modern, proactive and increasingly lethally armed police force. The police were modernized by and for controlling and disciplining automobility. Police officers were put on bicycles, motorcycles and, later, Ford cars and provided with two-way radios to manage the new time-space compression automobility had created. Berkeley police chief August Vollmer, considered the father of modern policing, declared that "traffic was the police problem of the day," echoed by other police chiefs throughout America in the 1920s and 1930s (Seo 2019).

Automobility not only required the controlling of traffic but the disciplining of society as a whole. In the United States, 75 percent of all documented crimes involve an automobile. Patrolling by the police has spilled over to other areas of policing. During prohibition, suspected bootleggers were subject to stop and search. This posed, however, a legal problem as cars were private property but *sui generis* as they were mobile and their use was on public roads, the state regulated their operation. When used for bootlegging purposes, the automobile was transformed, in legalese, into an "inanimate outlaw." This, however, did not exclude drivers and passengers from being protected by the law. The last step in the making of the "automobility police state" was the progressive transformation of the interpretation of the law to provide exclusions to protecting people's right to privacy and freedom from unreasonable intrusions by the government. The Fourth Amendment of the US Constitution affirms:

> [t]he right of the people to be secure in their persons, houses, papers, and effects, against unreasonable searches and seizures, shall not be violated, and no Warrants shall issue, but upon probable cause, supported by Oath or affirmation, and particularly describing the place to be searched, and the persons or things to be seized.

Through a series of rulings, the US Supreme Court interpreted the Fourth Amendment so as to dispense with the requirement of issuing a warrant. First, *time* was introduced as the measure of reasonableness, suggesting that issuing was often not practicable as the vehicle and its drivers may quickly move out of the jurisdiction in question. Next, in the landmark decision of *Carrol v. United States* in 1925 about a bootlegging case in which the police stopped a vehicle without probable cause and found illegal liqueur in it, the court held that a warrantless search and seizure was lawful if "the officer shall have reasonable or probable cause for *believing* that the automobile which he stops and seized has contraband liquor therein which is being illegally transported" (our emphasis).

The *Carrol* rule established the automobile exception to the Fourth Amendment as it relaxed the standard for probable cause from knowledge to belief. This was significant as the relaxed rules for probable cause authorized police officers to take action, search and seize (later to become known as "stop and frisk"), if they *believed* the situation at hand called for it. Courts have further permitted an extension to search the entire motor vehicle, as immediate surroundings of the arrestee, for precautionary safety. This led not only to the right to search the glove compartment and the trunk but also, in a later case, a jacket on the back seat that was suspected of having drugs in it. The policing of traffic provided an opportunity for the police officer, via the relaxing of Fourth Amendment criteria for permitting search and seizure, to police anyone on the road. Minor traffic law breaches, busted stoplights, missed lane-change signals, minor speeding all allowed the police to stop, search and seize. Discretionary policing became the law. Discretionary policing was soon complemented by discriminatory policing: no one was exempt from disciplinary control, but people of color even less so, resulting in systematic, racist injustice (Sorin 2020). Martin Luther King Jr. was arrested four times, one of which was for speeding, while George Floyd was forcibly taken from his car before being murdered by four policemen.

Not only did the car become an inanimate outlaw, so did the driver-passenger-car hybrid. The law granted to the police officer, based on his "belief" that a crime might be committed, the right to breach the basic liberties of privacy and personal freedom. "Belief" was granted a privileged epistemological status within the law. Agency was reassessed, and the car was transformed from a "dangerous instrumentality," an object delineated in the law requiring a higher standard of care regardless of intent or negligence by the owner or user, to an "inanimate outlaw," deemed capable of committing crimes and being subject to legal consequences as a person. In the material semiotic interpretation of the law, the automobile was an animate-inanimate outlaw, an entangled human/non-human complex, its presentation and condition becoming a probable cause for suspicion that a crime might be committed. The driver-car cyborg became "criminal bare life" in the state of inclusive-exclusion at the (material semiotic) threshold.

Beginning with these legal decisions, the legislative, the executive and judicial, separation of which are considered central to the liberal, democratic state, were handed over to police departments. Incorporated in police codes of conduct, the decision of whether to stop, search and seize became entirely contingent on the "belief" of the police officer. Not only did the law offer the opportunity and requirement as part of the day's work tasks to arbitrarily exercise the power to search and seize, stop and frisk, but it also granted virtual impunity to police officers.

CONSTRUCTING THE FACTS OF ROAD SAFETY RESEARCH

The police had another important function on the road: to determine the cause and collect data related to actual cases of road violence—namely "accidents." The statistic that 93 percent of road crashes are due to "human error" (or "driver error") is regularly cited in academic publications (Salmon et al. 2010; Stanton and Salmon 2009; Petridou and Moustaki 2000), in governmental and intergovernmental reports (NHTSA 2015; IRTU 2007), in the mass media (India 2019), in reports (Walker-Smith 2013) and at automobile industry events. The first of several studies to conclude that 93 percent of road crashes are due to "human error" was conducted by the Institute for Research in Public Safety at Indiana University Bloomington, the *Tri-Level Study of the Causes of Traffic Accidents* (Treat et al. 1977a, b; Treat et al. 1979). In the body of the report, there is some qualification regarding the contribution of "human error" as a causal factor (Treat et al. 1977a, 28): "conservatively stated, the study indicates human errors and deficiencies were a cause in at least 64% of accidents, and were probably causes in about 90–93% of accidents investigated." In the "Abstract to the Executive Summary" (Treat et al. 1979, Technical Report Documentation Page), it is stated that "Human factors were cited as probable causes in 92.6% of accidents investigated.... Environmental factors were cited as probable causes in 33.8% of these accidents, while vehicular factors were identified as probable causes in 12.6%." Rounded up to 93 percent in the "Capsule Summary" to the "Executive Summary," it is this latter figure from the *Tri-Level Study* that is regularly cited.

Although critical of some aspects of the earlier *Tri-Level Study*, a second study by the US National Highway Traffic Safety Administration (NHTSA) employed a virtually identical empirical and theoretical framework, with causality assumed to lie within "the vehicle, the roadway, the environmental conditions, and the human behavioral factors" (United States National Highway Traffic Safety Administration 2008, 2). Crashes were investigated by the police at the crash scene to collect driver, vehicle and environment-related information pertaining to crash occurrence, with a focus on the role of the driver. The targeted information was captured mainly through four data elements: movement prior to critical pre-crash event; critical pre-crash event; critical reason for the critical pre-crash event; and the crash associated factors. While this latter US report is more sophisticated in respect to the data analysis and, unlike the *Tri-Level Study*, is based on a representative sample of the United States, it arrives at similar estimates (Singh 2018).

From the early 1970s, parallel to the Indiana University accident causation study, several institutions in Europe began to investigate the causes and consequences of road crashes. In the late 1990s the European Automobile Manufacturers Association (ACEA) initiated a "European Accident Causation Survey" with the support of the European Commission and under the auspices of the European Road Safety Federation (ERSF). Five partners from Germany, Italy, Finland and France collaborated in the development of a data bank containing information on accident causes. The methodology follows the traditional assessment of accidents, locating causality in "human, road and environmental factors as well as traffic conditions" (Chenisbest, Jähn and Le Coz 1998). Although the study does not provide a summary statistic, a parallel study, the European Truck Accident Causation Study, funded by the European Commission (EC) and the International Road Transport Union concluded that "the main accident cause is linked to human error in 85.2% of all cases [while] other factors play a minor role" (IRTU 2007, 4).

The ERSF paper begins with the observation that "Sufficient information on the causes of accidents is still lacking, although it is well known that more than 90% are related to human errors" (Chenisbest, Jähn and Le Coz 1998, 415), while the *Handbook of Traffic Psychology* claims that "it is widely accepted that driver error contributes to more than 90% of all automobile crashes" (Porter 2012, 73). That it is reported as "well known" and "widely accepted" is evidence of the performative success of the statistic, achieved through its recurrent citation, even in the face of a lack of "sufficient information on the causes of accidents."

To make someone or something the "cause," a specific theory of accidents was required in which the accident is defined as "an unsuccessful interaction between the person, technology and organisation" and a "probable cause" as a critical event that is "the single immediate precursor to the accident defined to describe an action of a person" (Thomas et al., 2013, 14). When an accident and a probable cause are so defined, it is unsurprising that automobile crash studies using such a methodology find precisely what they are looking for and identify the human as the probable cause in the overwhelming majority of crashes.

Aristotle remarked in his *Metaphysics* (Aristotle and Ross 1981, VI) that "there is no science" of the accident. With the emergence of "vehicle accident causation theory" (Thomas et al. 2013), such a science for automobility has been developed, wherein what are held to be the root causes of road accidents are identified. Their identification, it is assumed, will open possibilities for their alleviation through improved technologies. The "natural science of accidents" has its history in the twentieth century. The first accident-causation model, the domino theory, was developed in the context of a search for the cause of industrial accidents (Heinrich 1931). The model accounted for accidents via a simple linear sequential model: an accident is a misstep in a sequential chain of events, each of which is dependent on the preceding event. By removing one of the events, the consequences may be avoided and the accident prevented. Amongst the categories, one is "the fault of the person," thus early theories of accident causality focused on human culpability. Since the 1930s, accident causation models have modified the original linear sequential model. The Haddon matrix employed a modified sequential epidemiological model to capture the complexity of accidents, assumed to be caused by a combination of driver, vehicle and infrastructure, for each of which a pre-crash, crash and post-crash phase can be identified (Haddon 1968).

Later models conceptualized accidents as possible outcomes within tightly coupled sociotechnical systems in which humans are assumed to have control and thus the opportunity to adapt their behavior, and therefore the system is able to accommodate adverse conditions. Addressing road accidents specifically, James Reason (2000) pointed to the different types of "unsafe acts" that are committed by persons *qua* components of the system, with human errors and latent system conditions being identified as root causes. Adding further complexity to the systems approach, Hollnagel (1998) developed the Cognitive Reliability and Error Analysis Method (CREAM), in which an accident is conceptualized as a failed interaction between person, technology and organization.

Applying the CREAM method to road safety but substituting "Cognitive" with "Driver," M. Ljung (Ljung 2002) developed a Driver Reliability and Error Analysis Method (DREAM). Between 2004 and 2008 the European Commission (Thomas et al. 2008) supported the establishment of a European Road Safety Observatory (ERSO) that involved the development of a new approach to investigate crash causation for policymaking purposes (Paulsson 2005). DREAM, in its 3.0 version (Warner et al. 2008), was adapted and specified as appropriate for traffic safety analysis. Referred to as "SafetyNet Accident Causation System" (SNACS), it follows the traditional DVE (driver-vehicle-environment) schema: "DREAM method has a Human-Technology-Organization perspective, which implies that accidents happen when the dynamic interaction between people, technologies and organizations fails in one way or another, and that there are a variety of interacting causes creating the accident" (Paulsson 2005, 9–10).

Identifying what is revealed in automobility accidents requires more than detemining what "causes" them. The "virtual speed of the catastrophic surprise," Virilio (2007, 12) argues, lies at the heart of every accident and suggests looking at "what lies beneath the engineer's awareness as producer" (Virilio 2007, 12). What lies there is the police officer and traffic safety researcher, using the "science" of accident causation to determine cause and responsibility and, later, the coder working with codebooks and a model that creates an abstraction composed of discreet variables, which mathematical abstraction is not only substituted for the phenomenological reality of the accident, it is assumed *to be* reality (Husserl 1970, 48–49). It is not only the cause that is determined but the ontology of space. In its police construct it is a place of potential failures of dynamic interaction between people, technologies and organizations, which require discipline and control. From a material semiotic interpretation it is spatial and temporal control (Law 1986). The human becomes an animate outlaw entangled in a human/non-human complex, assumed to be potentially committing a crime—causing an accident—which it always did when an accident actually occurred. The driver of the cyborg becomes again "culpable bare life" in a state of inclusive-exclusion at the (material semiotic) threshold.

THE NOMOCRATIC REVOLUTION

Traveling in a space of disciplinary control, subject to arbitrary search and seizure by the police, the driver was constituted as a potential criminal. The exercise of power by the police replaced the regular operation of legislative, executive, and judicial bodies through publicly visible legal and administrative procedures. This is a textbook definition of a police state.

The sacralized ideology of the human-machine cyborg entity, living in a permanent state and space of inclusive-exclusion, mobilized by the political religion of dromocracy was complemented by the repressive control of a police state. Combined, dromocracy and nomocracy produced a spatio-political totality that resubjectifies the human within the cyborg entity as a potential criminal created by the police state: barely alive, partly dead, disowned of her political body who migrates from camp to the city. Bare life not in transition to death but in a new state of being/non-being, as Primo Levi (1991) described the muselmann in the camp, but bare life as an ontological double: biologically alive, politically victim, witness and even collaborator in the totalitarian automobility order s/he imagines and dwells in (Oster 2014).

We now are in a position to return to our original question: What is automobility? We have followed a path from automobility as Urry's autopoietic system to a socio-spatial construct based on movement, speed, power and violence. By doing so we proposed moving beyond automobility in any of its current adjectival versions. When thinking of automobility, we should not think of "the automobile" but rather the deployment of power in the space we inhabit. The automobile is but one element but is *imagined* to be the central operator. The automobile, a complex signifier of a multitude of material, semiotic fluid signifieds, is only one of the agents that have constructed the spatial reality we live in. It is an indexical space inside which people and technological artifacts move; simultaneously, that space is constructed and sustained by those moving entities, above all the car-driver entity, by which and around which the space is defined as automobility space.

This space is *politically* ordered by our activities. It is hierarchical and complex, fluid and entangled. This complexity involves material and non-material semiotic operators, with power, violence and speed at its core. The space is mobile and dangerous, wherein cyborgs and non-cyborgs cross paths. Technology and people may be entangled, but *real people* die alarmingly often. Danger and death are, however, *operationalized* as remediable and *bracketed* as proper and just within the moral economy of the imaginary. Operationalization and bracketing mark a biopolitical shift in the political ontology of automobility.

This operationalization and bracketing, in our view, must be challenged. We have followed Agamben (1998, 97) in focusing on:

> the juridical procedures and deployments of power by which human beings could be so completely deprived of their rights and prerogatives that no [violent] act committed against them could appear any longer as a crime. (At this point, in fact, everything had truly become possible.)

The entangled, multiple, performed realities that coexist in the automobility imaginary, the weaving together of human and non-human stuff, are mediated by meanings that reflect an inexorable subjugation of the human as qualified or political life. Juridical procedures, statistical codebooks and rulebooks of movement, as well as other deployments of power, were created by which human beings—dwelling in the space that gradually opened up from a delimited dromos to include the whole of the Earth—were deprived of their rights and prerogatives to an extent that arbitrary violence, control and discipline appeared as normality. In the nomocracy of automobility, power/violence was politicized by being normalized and constructed as technosocially desirable. The human became the potential criminal, occupying a nomocratic threshold: a multidimensional space, a constituted political, material semiotic order of near-total control, of depoliticized being—bare life. It is existence at a keropolitical threshold.

SOCIOLOGIES OF MOBILITY

In *Sociology Beyond Societies*, Urry (2000) argued that mobility systems operate within a triangle of "networks, scapes, and flows," composed of socio-material structures and networks based on "scapes" (road, rail, water, airways, cables, GPS connections, wireless connections of various kinds, etc.) in which people, commodities, raw materials, capital, signs and information flow. Following Castells (1996), Urry (2000, 34) argued that networks are the "material basis" of social processes and social structures; they are "in and of space, they are temporal and spatial." Scapes, Urry argued, are special networks—of machines, of technologies, of organisations, of texts and actors—that constitute interconnected nodes along which flows move.

As the title—"Metaphors of the Global"—of one of the chapters of *Sociology Beyond Societies* suggests, Urry considers networks, scapes and flows to be linguistic operators; semiotic devices to describe technoscientific social processes *in* and *of* space. Suspicious of what he takes to be technosocial "relativism," Urry takes metaphors literally. Metaphors *represent* the social, their appropriateness and fit to be evaluated and implemented on the basis of empirical data derived from "situated contexts." Yet situated context is another metaphor, that of the material basis of the social. He anchors scapes in what he takes as the "real": physical networks that enable mobility. Flows are also "real" (peoples, images, information, money and waste) but belong to the social. Urry does not mention the origins of the concept "-scapes" (Appadurai's original piece does not appear in the bibliography) and translates deterritorialized flows as spatially inscribed material constructs. On Urry's account they are neither imagined nor perspectival realities but instead the signifieds of the metaphors that operate in the social. Urry's goal is to create order in the metaphors of global fluids. One way to do this is by reference to appropriateness and fit, by differentiating between clusters of meaning and approximations of realism. Fearing falling into the relativist trap, Urry's point of scientific reference, in line with the Anglo-Saxon empiricist tradition, is the techno-scientifically understood "real": material technologies of space that are entangled with the spatial fluids of the social.

Urry's perspectival and epistemological location is a realist sociology. He argues that sociology has barely noticed the complex, systemic aspects of automobility: how the mass production of cars has transformed social life; how democratized car ownership, made possible via Fordism, has altered patterns of socialities; and how consumption patterns have brought about a unique culture of desire and status. Much of Urry's automobility-related work has been an attempt to remedy this theoretical and empirical *lacuna* through providing a sociologically informed account of automobility (Hannam,

Sheller and Urry 2006, 6). Urry is correct in observing that there was a dearth of sociological accounts of mobility, understood as physical movement, although there is a long and established research tradition of social class and occupational mobility within sociology and of migration within demography. What is problematic is the distinction he makes between a "social" and a "technical" system in describing automobility as a "hybrid social and technical system."

Although it is a different context, it echoes Arendt's (1973) criticism in *The Origins of Totalitarianism* of sociology, that sociology had systematically misunderstood totalitarianism. The problem, as Peter Baehr (2002, 805) has put it, is "the extent to which sociology is disabled from recognizing and comprehending radically new political phenomena." The question is whether "sociology's terms, methods, and domain assumptions impede the recognition of political novelty by absorbing it within ideal types, reducing it to a manifestation of structural causes and, ultimately, making it functionally interchangeable with grossly dissimilar phenomena." Urry's question was, *mutatis mutandis*, what is automobility a case of? From the toolkit of sociological theories, Urry chose social systems theory. His answer was that automobility is a "system," one of the central paradigms of mid-twentieth-century sociology. Automobility was simply one of many mobility systems, such as the "pedestrian-system," the "rail-system" and the "aeromobility" system (Bogard 2009, 51). To rectify sociology's failure in not having even recognized that "automobility" was an object of paramount sociological significance, required showing that what is called "automobility" is similar to something that is already known within sociology.

Sociology's failure, for Urry, was not only to have not realized that automobility is a system but that it is a hybrid system, an interconnected *social* and *technical* system. The problem is not that Urry takes automobility to be an interconnected network of socialities and materialities but that the two *elements* of the hybrid system are assumed to be ontologically different. On the one hand, Urry defines "the car," "the road," "the filling station," among other technological artifacts, as "real." On the other hand, there are the deterritorialized social flows, defined as representational, linguistic constructs. As we have argued in previous chapters, automobility is a material semiotic totality: a material and empirical, embodied, habituated, produced and reproduced dual—Euclidean and rhizomatic—technosocial space and biopolitical order. The problem is that in his attempt to avoid the relativist trap, Urry falls into the realist empirical trap: he creates the real (artifacts, networks and materialities) in contradistinction to the social (linguistic constructs of meaning production, such as images, information and money).

It is symptomatic of a disciplinary division of labor whereby the subject matter of sociology is "the social," combined with the assumption that the social sciences and the natural sciences operate within two different ontologies. The latter has been the central point made by critics of naturalism, the view that the social sciences can be modelled on the natural sciences. Just because, for certain *scientific* purposes, primarily methodological, it makes sense to distinguish between the ontologies that the natural sciences and the social sciences each construct when engaged in inquiry and research, does not mean that we actually live in a two-ontology world.

Louis Everuss, in "The New Mobilities Paradigm and Social Theory" (Everuss 2020), has argued that the distinguishing feature of the new mobilities paradigm is that it is grounded in a "mobile ontology." His paper provides an outline of that ontology which, he argues, is identifiable in the mobilities literature. We have here argued the case for conceptualizing automobility as an ontology. If we accept Everuss's reading of the mobilities literature in respect to having accurately identified what is indeed a shared understanding of a new ontology, namely a new "mobilities ontology" that is none other than the ontology of "the new mobilities paradigm," there are several points of difference between the ontology of the new mobilities paradigm and what we have argued.

First, as described by Everuss, this mobile ontology is an ontology that has been specified by mobilities researchers. Whatever its differences from the supposed sedentary ontology of traditional social science, it is an ontology that has been arrived at through theoretical reasoning. Our argument is that ontologies, which we take to be referring to what is understood to be "reality," are political. While it is not the main point we have made throughout this book, arguments such as Everuss's are equally political in the sense that one of the things that makes them persuasive is their appeal to metaphysical reasoning.

We have argued that within automobility studies—a subfield of the new mobilities paradigm for those who subscribe to the new mobilities paradigm thesis—automobility reality at an ontological level, as an object of theoretical and empirical inquiry, has been constructed by the discourses of what we have called "automobility studies." We have also argued that everyday automobility reality is a constructed ontology.

It can, of course, be countered that we have equally relied on "metaphysical" arguments to make this point, that we have simply replaced one ontology with another, one that is comprised of actors, actants and practices who are continually engaged in the activities of reality construction. We assume, it can be further argued, that these are real, that they exist. We do indeed assume that they exist, but here we enter the question of what is "reality." Is it simply the things that exist, what Heidegger called the "present-at-hand," or is it the equipmental totality discussed in chapter 1? Our argument is that "reality" should be considered the latter, what we take to be reality in everyday life. As Heidegger (2002, 23) put it,

> [the w]orld is not a mere collection of the things—countable and uncountable, known and unknown—that are present at hand. Neither is world a merely imaginary framework added by our representation to the sum of things that are present. World worlds, and is more fully in being than all those tangible and perceptible things in the midst of which we take ourselves to be at home. World is never an object that stands before us and can be looked at. [. . .] By the opening of a world, all things gain their lingering and hastening, their distance and proximity, their breadth and their limits. In worlding there gathers that spaciousness from out of which the protective grace of the gods is gifted or is refused. Even the doom of the absence of the god is a way in which world worlds.

Following up on the concept of worlding—which was introduced into political discourse with a somewhat different "orientalist" meaning by Gayatri Spivak (1988)—"reality" is always immediately material, as embodied and embedded in material practices, and—as a material practice—it participates in the ontological networks or assemblages that make up worlds. Thus, we are always faced with many different practical metaphysics, many different practical ontologies (Latour 2000). From a worlding perspective ontology is always an ontology of acting: pragmatic and performative. Realities are understood as *performative* worlding; the performative construction of ontologies. The new mobilities paradigm is one such performative worlding and, in this sense, as is any other "opening of the world"—academic or otherwise—an ontology. Any (political) ontology operates on the presumption that divergent worldings are constantly being constructed through negotiations, enmeshments, crossings and interruptions, that is to say by discourses that rework an imaginary and by a modality of analysis and critique that is permanently concerned with its own effects as a worlding practice (Cadena and Blaser 2018).

Our criticism of a "mobile ontology" is akin to Mario Blaser's work highlighting the connections between European foundationalist, hegemonic discourses and the ontopolitics of indigeneity (Blaser 2013). Blaser argues that culture as a key concept in anthropology suffers from ontologized "Sameing." Even in its most critical "thin" interpretation, "the possibility of seeing all difference as relative depends on an omniscient vantage from which all difference is visible to a detached perspective that is not relative. The coordinates of such an omniscient epistemological vantage point that distinguishes the culture that uses the concept of culture to conceive otherness" (Blaser 2013,

550). This leads to "culture" (or, in Everuss' case, paradigm) being used interchangeably with "ontology" serving the purpose emerging from the suspicion that difference is not different enough, or cultural difference has been reduced by critics to a mere effect of political instrumentality.

This is the case with the assumption that "paradigm," even if one subscribed to such a paradigm, may be inadequate to describe the object of study properly, let alone to "explain" or "interpret" the data that emerges from research done within the mobilities paradigm. In search of locating the inadequacies of the paradigm, a turn to "ontology" is offered to argue that "social relations and phenomena need to take account of the mobilities that at least partially constitute them" (Everuss 2020). It is not clear how the mobile ontology differs from the mobilities paradigm or how a mobile ontology would highlight modes of being beyond the relational epistemologies that endow mobile formations with meaning. The mobilities paradigm, even if there were one (Randell 2020b), is already a mobile ontology, as Kuhn's very concept of a "paradigm" emerged from reflecting on Galileo's investigations into the unreliability of our senses and the "worlding" they provided. Earth, he realized, must move through space with tremendous speed. In this mobile ontology any observation we make, any scientific inquiry we perform, is always the observing of relative motion; what is seen as in stasis is actually in motion. This led him to the abstract world of mathematics, the language in which the book of the universe was written and which could help overcome distorted observations of an outdated geocentric paradigm.

The mobile ontology that Everuss describes is, of course, also a reality constructed within a network of power. The difference is that, for Everuss, the ontology, reality, is the space where power is exercised. Our argument is that the ontology—any ontology that is worlding—is constructed by power, for which reason it may be described as a political ontology—a point to which we will soon return.

Kuhnian paradigms are disciplinary apparatuses which, their ostensible revolutionary origins notwithstanding, are normalizing hermeneutic apparatuses. Their purpose is to create the conditions for, and to require, the practicing of normal science. Mimi Sheller and John Urry, in "Mobilizing the New Mobilities Paradigm," not only make the case for the existence of a mobilities paradigm (cf. Randell 2020), they also argue that "the new mobilities paradigm should be the new normal science" (Sheller and Urry 2016, 21). To the degree this book might be read as a contribution to debates regarding the new mobilities paradigm, about which we have little to say beyond these brief observations here, it is to question the very project of "normal science."

THE ONTOPOLITICS OF AUTOMOBILITY

An ontopolitical analysis of automobility as both a dromocracy and a nomocracy points to four facets of automobility. First, automobility is an imagined world open to subject-centered human control based on and politicized as a cartographic projection of diverse imaginary appropriations of land on a horizontal plane (Chandler 2019). Second, that imaginary is the universal reality that is the dreamscape. Third, forms of collective life in which what is called "the market" were dis-embedded from the dense connections and constraints of life as previously lived, creating new rules, norms and deployments of power in human interactions (Mitchell 2020, 50), made manifest in the alienated spectacle. Fourth, space, the product of inter-relationality and coexisting heterogeneities (Massey 2005), was ontologically simplified into a politics of power/violence repressing contingent relations and simultaneous multiplicities and occluding their potential keropolitics. In such an ontopolitical framing, automobility reveals to us how modern biopolitics has successfully suppressed the key facets of a material semiotic order: the iconic, the indexical and the symbolic (Chandler 2019).

The automobility imaginary, embedded in a realist ontology and a purified politics, governed reality by acting upon the effects of previous actions, on their seen and unseen unintended consequences by mapping and tracing path dependencies and lock-ins. This eliminated the "iconic aspects" of a multiple reality; events, actions, challenges potentially visible as sign complexes that bring into being more complex meanings and interconnections. Cities, as imagined by the Situationists, are prime examples. They are available for exploration as a complex of signs of multitude relations, instead of as frozen social connections placed on a map and produced as cityscapes to be lived in and through a car. The "coerced flexibility" of the automobile urbanscape (Urry 2004, 36; Sheller and Urry 2000) flattened the larger ensemble of relations and transformed reality so that it would fit in the coerced modes of problem-solving visible in its engineering, its artifacts, rulebooks and technologies of governance, managing its policing and imagining its order. By excluding a more complex reality of deeper and multiple relationalities, humans have become subjected to life at a permanent threshold in a keropolitical regime of discipline and control that has become accepted as normal, unremarkable and proper. It is the apprehension we confront whenever it is necessary to cross a street.

Automobility's co-temporalities have been eliminated by the automobility nomos. Space has been appropriated, creating the order, bracketing and making violence invisible within the imaginary, displacing it to "the driver." Co-temporal, small impacts have been suppressed by producing space through governance in and of mobility, devising control via roads. Real-time responsiveness was eradicated by totalitarian policing, which assumes crimes *before* they have happened, by accident causation methods assessing impacts based on assumed pre-existing causal relations *after* tragic events have occurred. Ignoring automobility's violence, the dromocratic revolution pressed on with dromological solutions, technological and engineering fixes: redesigned cars, roads, signs, fences, barriers and limitations—i.e., deterministic technological solutionism (Dewandre 2018; Mladenović et al. 2020).

The biopolitical reality of totalitarian control suppressed the symbolic aspects of the ontopolitical. It forged causal relations between discreet entities, created in and by flat realities that simplified automobility's significations. The Driver-Vehicle-Environment (DVE) system of the accident causation framework established relations between the ostensibly physical entities of the road, focusing on agency as a final cause and concluding that the driver is responsible. In this rendering, as in DVE, meaning is human-as-subject centered, human-dependent and technologically mediated in a causal and simple universe. This order is the automobility nomos. It is an order that masks power/violence within the network. On the road the driver may easily be seen as separable from the environment and the vehicle as in "accident science."

Virilio remarked that there was no industrial revolution, only a dromocratic revolution. Yet dromos/speed is not the only operator in an entangled material semiotic universe. The dromocratic revolution, as described by Virilio, invented the shipwreck together with the ship, the pile-up alongside the automobile. Such modernist binaries mask the multiplicities of coexisting heterogeneities in technosocial lifeworlds. Automobility, the "ill-named thing," is endowed here with other (ill)names: imaginary, dromos, spectacle, dreamscape and nomos. Bare life on the move, bracketed power/violence, roads of control, the religious politicization of existence, together with a multitude of other power deployment strategies, served to flatten, simplify and sanctify meaning-production. These power deployment strategies led to the emergence of a political totalitarianism that, as Levinas (1990, 289; quoted in Eskin 1999) has argued, rests on ontological totalitarianism.

The fascist totalitarian political regime, inscribed in the autostrada, producing a new space of control (Deleuze and Lapoujade 2006), rests on the political ontology of Futurism: to "live in the absolute, because we have created eternal, omnipresent speed" (Marinetti 1909). The futurist vision unleashed dromos/race/speed from its place near the Temple and meshed it with a dreamscape mesmerized by the spectacle. By bracketing violence as normalcy and creating the city as a camp in which bare life dwells, automobilized power/violence became the new nomos of the Earth. The nomocratic revolution killed, (re)produced and colonized Euclidean and rhizomatic, network meaning-space/time. *That* is the ill-named thing.

With others we share the hope that another kind of ontology, thus another type of politics, another world, is imaginable (Esposito and Campbell 2008, 644).

Chapter Eight

Metron

Electric and Autonomous Automobility Dreams[*]

In this and the final chapter, we consider possible trajectories for our shared futures. The focus of both chapters is the ontological properties of utopias, the "embedded idea of what it means to be human, what is good for us and makes us happy" (Levitas 2017, 8). As does Ruth Levitas, we consider utopias to imply not an "unrealistic idealism"—Moore's sphere or place that can never exist—but a holistic approach to describe potential shared social futures as political arrangements, ways of life and their accompanying ethics (see also Wright 2010). Levitas's (2013) concept of the "imaginary reconstitution of society"—utopia understood as method—is a mode of thinking that takes (imaginary) distance from the present to address the existing state of affairs from a future vantage point. It proposes examining what we are actually doing as opposed to what we *could* or *should* do. It is a version of Daniel Kahneman's (2011) "pre-mortem"—running ahead in time and looking back on what could go wrong.

The automobility imaginary that we inhabit is a space of embedded, commonsense ideas and visions regarding what it means to be human, what is good for us and what makes us happy. It is a utopia of the present, whose sociotechnical imaginaries offer serial promises of an always-better future. That is the subject of this chapter. Our utopia focuses on possibilities for a biopolitical shift and the imagining of a different, non-keropolitical ontology, the subject of chapter 9.

One of the audiences to which this book is addressed includes those convinced that automobility is remediable, that a post-automobility world

---

[*] Parts of this chapter appeared in the journal *Humanities and Social Sciences Communications* (Braun, Robert, and Richard Randell. 2020. "Futuramas of the Present: The 'Driver Problem' in the Autonomous Vehicle Sociotechnical Imaginary." *Humanities and Social Sciences Communications* 7 (1):163).

would not be a better world. What we might understand "a better world" to be is an unavoidably existential question, the answer to which depends on what we mean by "better" and what we understand "the world" to be. The world when experienced and analytically circumscribed under the ill-name of "automobility," we have argued, is an imaginary that is, at the same time, reality, the reality of everyday existence, what Heidegger called Being-in-the-world or Husserl called the lifeworld. That reality, we have argued, is a constructed reality, both in respect to its ontic details and in respect to the ontology of commonsense realism within which automobility is experienced and lived. Our approach may be characterized as both ontopolitical and post-phenomenological.

As Kahneman has pointed out, for any imagined future, much can go wrong. In this chapter we examine new technologies that are being proposed as solutions to the lifeworld problems of existing automobility. Proponents of these sociotechnical imaginaries argue that a different automobility is possible, that an accident-free, sustainable automobility can be achieved through new technologies. These technosocial visions need to be evaluated not against their future promises but their embedded ontopolitical assumptions.

In the final chapter we turn to the question of what a post-automobility world might look like and how we might move towards such a future. That will require, we argue, a politics based on what Agamben has called "destituent power," focused on the deconstruction and disassembling of the automobility imaginary.

THE SOCIOTECHNICAL AUTOMOBILITY IMAGINARIES OF THE TWENTY-FIRST CENTURY

Post-automobility is not, we remarked in the preface, a world of autonomous, connected, electric automobiles. Like the automobility sociotechnical imaginaries of the past, we can expect autonomous, connected, electric vehicle sociotechnical imaginary to result in even more automobility. Like the automobility sociotechnical imaginaries of the past, there are many reasons to not believe the promises, not least because automobility, besides being a factory of collective illusion, has been a factory of collective dissimulation. This includes financial support for think tanks and policy institutes that have propagated the view that there is no consensus amongst climate scientists regarding global warming and its causes (McCright and Dunlap 2003). Or the production of diesel automobiles that were designed to identify when they are undergoing emissions tests, changing to a different set of operational parameters that simulated being within legal emissions limits.

The connected, autonomous, electric automobility future may be considered either a single sociotechnical imaginary or three separate, albeit related, sociotechnical imaginaries. In the following sections, we examine the content and claims of these imaginaries, each of which is an exemplary instance of a sociotechnical imaginary of the type described by Jasanoff and Kim.

Electric Dreams: The Electric Vehicle Sociotechnical Imaginary

The electric mobility sociotechnical imaginary is a vision of a future transportation system propelled by electric energy. Co-produced by a variety of different actors (Jasanoff 2004), it is a shared and publicly performed vision of a future embedded in ostensibly sustainable technology. Thinking with Levitas, the electric mobility imaginary addresses one specific aspect of a "good life," that of sustainability.

The first point we would here make is that the technological solution that is being proposed only displaces the negative externalities of automobility to different areas within the (global) political order, from the Global North to the Global South. A number of countries have plans to reduce greenhouse gas (GHG) emissions from automobile transportation by replacing automobiles powered by internal combustion engines with electric vehicles. The logic behind this, viewed from a global perspective, is that if single nations reduce their total automobile GHG emissions, this will result in a reduction in overall planetary GHG emissions. This is false.

Reducing the number of internal combustion-powered cars within a national space will not result in reduced automobile GHG emissions if those vehicles continue to operate elsewhere. The proper unit of analysis, therefore, is not national fleets but the individual automobile. In the hypothetical case of a country that converts to 100 percent electric vehicles, a transition to electric will not contribute to any reduction in automobility GHG emissions if its entire automobile fleet has been exported to other countries. It will have worsened the situation given the GHG emissions associated with new car production, including the production of electric cars. Moreover, many vehicles that are exported from the Global North are no longer considered roadworthy, or no longer comply with local tailpipe emissions standards. There is no "outside" or "away" where externalities may spill over or are to be transferred. Displacement of problems, such as pollution or environmental degradation, does not offer remedies. The individual and collective national satisfaction and righteousness that driving an electric car provides is made possible by transporting entire fleets to the Global South.

Furthermore, if the energy sources are not GHG emission-free, then neither are electric vehicles. In addition, the energy requirements to build an electric vehicle need to be part of the calculation of the GHG emissions across the lifetime of an electric vehicle. There are other environmental and ethical issues relatively unique to electric vehicles, such as forced labor and environmental degradation in locations where raw materials are required, as well as the manufacture of batteries. While some of the raw materials and manufacturing processes are different, such environmental and ethical issues are not absent in the production of automobiles powered by electric motors.

The key commodity behind the current technology, lithium, is a raw material mined in regions that are politically unstable, have limited or no mining industry, are vulnerable to Global North neo-colonizing (Egbue and Long 2012) and use child and slave labor. Life cycle studies also confirm that, currently, battery use accounts for only about 20 percent of the overall life cycle impact, while battery production and disposal, in terms of energy use and waste disposal challenges, have very high environmental impacts (Cusenza et al. 2019).

Non-degradable materials and harmful particles "stick": they stay in the environment or in our bodies and do not degrade or disappear in the course of a human lifespan. "Pseudo-solutions" or "coercive resilience," like changing the propellant or displacing pollution, only prolong the status quo and store up greater environmental and political problems for the future (Chandler 2019). Put another way: environmental or social change cannot be prevented or slowed through the betterment of the situation through engineering "solutions" that derive from developments in technoscience.

Mobility injustice (Sheller 2018; Martens 2016) is reproduced on multiple levels. New infrastructure is required to offer available charging options in urban areas, channeling public monies from the non-automobilized less privileged to the more affluent (electric) automobilized segments of society. Sustainability is viewed through a lens of technological determinism (Mladenović et al. 2020), and thus the challenge is reduced to a technological problem of the propellent as opposed to the "way of life" entangled with the automobility imaginary. The automobile is reduced to an artifact that comes into being when purchased and evaporates when sold. Within this neoliberal ontology, questions regarding the lifeworld options, risks and the ethical values embedded in the utopia of electric mobility are considered irrelevant.

With respect to the climate crisis and sustainability, automobility is a planetary problem that cannot be solved at local levels (Chandler 2018). It is estimated that by 2050, 50 percent of new cars will be electric, but what this estimate does not reveal is that in 2050 there will be more internal combustion engine cars on the roads than there are currently. Looked at solely in terms of GHG emissions, it is clear that 2050 is too late. In short, not even on their own terms are electric vehicles a "solution" to the problem they claim as central to the "good life" they profess.

The solution, clearly, is not to build new cars, but to get the existing cars off the roads. There is, however, no discernible plan to do this. Rather, a new market is being opened up, aided by the State, providing automobile manufacturers the opportunity to continue producing automobiles. Currently, approximately 100 million new automobiles are manufactured each year, which is only twenty million less than the annual increase in the world's population.

The Autonomous Vehicle Sociotechnical Imaginary

Visions surrounding "self-driving" or "autonomous" vehicles are another exemplary instance of an ostensibly "transformational" sociotechnical imaginary (2009; Jasanoff 2015). Like the electric vehicle sociotechnical imaginary, it is a sociotechnical imaginary composed of visions coproduced through the efforts of a multiplicity of epistemic actors—marketing and advertising agencies, the academy, states, intergovernmental organizations, transport and road safety experts, social and mass media, automobile manufacturers and automobiles themselves in the guise of prototypes and concept cars—that are engaged in, either tangentially or as a primary work task, the process of interpreting, defining and predicting the contours of the autonomous automobility future. The autonomous vehicle imaginary is not the first but the most recent of a series of autonomous vehicle sociotechnical imaginaries (Braun 2019; Kidd 1956).

Arguments for an autonomous mobility future revolve mainly around increased road safety and congestion reduction, as well as other potential benefits such as travel-cost reduction and increased parking space (Litman 2019; Fagnant and Kockelman 2015). Central to the increased traffic safety narrative is the frequently cited statistic, discussed in the previous chapter, that 93 percent of automobile "accidents" are due to human error (Treat et al. 1979; Singh 2018). It is argued that if the human driver can be replaced with a computer—or described slightly differently, if the car-driver hybrid entity (Randell 2017; Urry 2006) can be substituted with a machine controlled robot within which humans can be transported—death and injury rates could in principle be reduced by approximately ninety percent (Fagnant and Kockelman 2015, 173).

This claim is based on a mistaken premise. It is mistaken not because the predicted reduction in percentage is questionable on its own terms (Favarò, Eurich, and Nader 2018), or because of the specific ethical questions that have been raised with respect to autonomous vehicles (Himmelreich 2018) or because road death and injury can and does occur for reasons not related to accidents (Balkmar 2018; Sorin 2020; Seo 2019). From an ontopolitical point of view, it is mistaken because the ostensible problem in need of a solution, namely human error as the primary cause of accidents, is a technologically deterministic construct. It is a construct that originates in the codebooks, data collection and analytical procedures of accident-causation methodologies. This statistical construct has become the central political justification for moving towards an autonomous vehicle transport future.

The Dataspaces of Connected Autonomous Vehicles

Within industry and government discourses and visions, autonomous vehicles are seen as one component of a multidimensional connected autonomous vehicle future. A connected, driverless transport vision, based on electricity as propellant—"connected, cooperative and automated mobility" as it is called in policy jargon (European Commission 2021)—will produce a new network space (Castells 2009). Multiplying the dromocratic space of the road, people and data will travel infinitely and freely, together with their assumed "data double" or "data twin." They will no longer move along an autostrada but will travel in network space along what we call a "datastrada," without being confined, but fully controlled (Haggerty and Ericson 2000). In the sociotechnical imaginary of connected autonomous mobility, data becomes the epistemic reality, remaking the world (Wyly 2014) through Big Data architectures based on algorithms and arithmetic deep-learning architectures created by private data regimes. The promise of an autonomous and electric mobility future upholds and extends the ontology of nomocracy.

The multiplicity of lifeworlds become subordinated to what has become known as "Big Data." "Big" not only in the sense of size but also big in the Orwellian sense of "Big." Within Big Data situated knowledges of space, of movement and of semiotic interconnectedness become lost in the quantitative data (Dalton and Thatcher 2015). Small impacts are substituted for, and "autonomous" responsiveness is based on, a quantitative social physics, using Big Data to assess interactions through complexity modelling and algorithmic analyses. Data is removed from the concrete conditions of its production and, as it travels through the datastradas of virtual network-space, is mutated, thinned and transformed (Porter 2020). Its symbolic aspects are lost, black-boxed and transduced. Their algorithmic components render the technology inscrutable (Stilgoe 2018, 30). So-called "raw data"—data that does not exist in the purity its name suggests—is used, naively, as simply a representation of an assumed natural/physical reality. Interconnections are established in network space by arithmetic logic. Symbolic meanings are continuously transformed as data is gathered, stored, combined, moved and deployed (Longino 2020).

The sociotechnical imaginary of autonomous, connected mobility will produce new realities. These regimes and data realities will flatten the complex meanings and interconnections of everyday mobilities, creating a purified politics in what Craig Dalton, Linnet Taylor and Jim Thatcher (2016) call "dataspheres." Dataspheres—data created, stored, deployed, analyzed, transformed by the specific infrastructure of serendipitously interconnected and operated databases in one geographical location (Dalton, Taylor and Thatcher 2016)—are turned into dataspace: an interoperable and standardized, managed and controlled connected infrastructure of data providers and users to produce new spatialities (Cuno et al. 2019). Autonomous mobility will not be individual automobiles maneuvering through autoscapes aided by LIDAR systems and with sensors tracking, mapping and analyzing the environment.

It will be an assemblage of interconnected mobility things transmitting data and accessing all the available data sources: automobiles, surveillance cameras, road and roadside sensors, satellites and other miscellaneous data creating sources, all making journeys within dataspace. Dataspace is yet another mathematically constructed sphere of discipline and control that substitutes the multiple social interactions of everyday life with a functional system of data ordering (Harvey 1990; Deleuze and Lapoujade 2006). In this space, data is made interoperable, standardized and compatible. It creates a reality in which "control and value are indissolubly linked to the machine ensembles that comprise contemporary digital infrastructures" (Larkin 2013, 339). It represents an enlargement and qualitative transformation of the cyborg entity of which we are a component.

Dataspace confines and transfigures the flow of human experience and practice to a black-boxed technosocial configuration of arithmetically managed "Big Data." This will add a new aspect to the confinement of human experience, already conquered and controlled by the production of space on the map and in the dreamscape, by engaging in a technoscientific discourse of abstract, homogenous data universals. A new material semiotic "Big Data network" (Law and Mol 2001; Latour 1999) will emerge. Data are "material-semiotic things" with dimensionality, weight and texture as well as being products of a particular set of cultural practices engraving values and ideologies (Bates, Lin, and Goodale 2016). They are material semiotic inasmuch as they are produced, generated and distributed, embedded in sociocultural practices and deployed by way of an infrastructure that requires specific spatial imaginaries and practices. They are used and transformed by material-political practices: omissions, homogenizations and alterations for better usability, offering a new vantage point for perceiving and appropriating through technoscientific practices of knowledge production. Moving between different sites in dataspace, during its journey, data becomes a mutable mobile through cleaning, adjustment and homogenization procedures, producing new space-time (Law and Mol 2001). Data is reproduced, reconfigured, transduced and mutated cotemporally and simultaneously, put to work in different places, contexts and for diverse purposes. This is the emerging new automobility sociotechnical imaginary, albeit one that, as yet, is rarely performed for general publics but which circulates among engineering elites.

From the vantage point of ontological politics, the deployment of power in dataspace makes it an exemplary sphere of discipline and control (Iveson and Maalsen 2019). Individuals as data-doubles become surveilled and disciplined as they become more visible to authorities as they are readily seen in a more immediate, collective and anonymous gaze (Foucault 1980, 154). The subject of biopower is transformed from the individual—the entity that cannot be divided—to the "dividual," the entity that can be divided into separate parts" (Deleuze 1992). This new subject is comprised of interrelated but independent aspects, distributed in a dataspace that is a technology of control. The dividual, unlike the Foucauldian subject or Agamben's bare life, becomes the coded dividual—divisible and produced through modulatory control effected through arithmetization and the anticipation of flows (Savat 2013).

Injustice is transformed into "simulated justice" (O'Malley 2010, 795) through the fragmentation of individuals into simulated dividuals with commodified privileges—such as "fines" that are automatically administered, calculated and paid for and within a virtual network—becoming more important than liberal rights. The dromocratic process of speed will be controlled by automatic processes: the digitally processed photograph of the registration number of a speed-violating vehicle is transmitted via telematic apparatuses to a police computer that calibrates and issues the fine notice. This fine is then automatically sent to and processed by a bank account, the money transferred and the issue is settled (O'Malley 2010). In this datacratic order, a nascent sphere of discipline and control that resituates nomocracy within Big Data environments, the subject that is bare life becomes non-life. The corporeal discipline of individuals is replaced with the simulated governance of dividuals. It represents a significant qualitative change in the knowledge and practices of the science of dromology.

Smart city discourses create speculative and technological determinist spaces of science fiction instead of facilitating a discussion about the future of urban spaces and how data analytics can be used effectively in complex urban environments (Löfgren and Webster 2020). In constructing the city as a calculable whole, Big Data provides an ironic twist to the positivist epistemic myth of a world perfectly knowable and representable. Smart solutionism—black-boxed, arithmetically produced technical outcomes—turns into a Big Data spectacle that eschews situated, social and historical modes of knowledge production. Smart city discourses engage in a command-and-control illusion that mostly serves corporate interests, which are represented as the interests of the citizenry as a whole. The rhizomatic material semiotic network becomes a flat mathematic semiotic network of inscrutable algorithms. Collective and individual experience is homogenized, bringing places under a single mechanism of calculation, that is a spatial logic forming, but also denying, the diversity of lived-material encounters (Dalton et al. 2020).

This is not, of course, how dataspace is imagined. It is claimed to be a "simple" interoperable, standardized and compatible technology, a virtual infrastructure to create "a seamless digital area with the scale that will enable the development of new products and services based on data" (European Commission 2018). It is an exemplary case of what we have argued throughout this book: material semiotic networks of meaning that are imaginary realities. It is an imaginary composed not only of visions of roads populated by safe, autonomous, computer-driven vehicles but also of vehicles simultaneously travelling within a newly produced neutral and benign third space, the space of Big Data.

In that ostensibly neutral and benign space, the inhabitants of digitally networked environments, which is most of us, are subject to forms of social control enabled by arithmetic and modulatory regulation. In the ontology of simulated justice, it is the dividual—non-life—that is the subject, made visible as a living individual only when s/he shows resistance to simulation and challenges the process, or when a risk threshold is crossed (O'Malley 2010). This risk threshold is discretionary and black-boxed by design as such algorithmic operations also become inscrutable.

These visions—the technoscientific dreams of engineers and corporate executives—contribute to the reproduction of automobility by defining counter-visions of an alternative future as unnecessary and obsolete. The central premise of this new sociotechnical imaginary is that risks, both in terms of general social impacts and as actual power/violence effects, are problems that can be managed through technological solutions (Mladenović et al. 2020).

Dwelling in the new threshold—neither alive nor not dead, a number, coded, produced through modulatory control—the dividual is the muselmann of the datacratic order. This is existence in the ultimate state of exception, existing as both modulated dividual and replicated data-double, managed and processed in dataspace via surveillance cameras, phone records, credit card purchase slips, reassembled as the individual.

To borrow from the language of historical interpretations of totalitarianism, "cumulative radicalization" as an interpretative concept may be applied.

The Holocaust historian Hans Mommsen (1991), explaining how ordinary people were capable of horrendous deeds, claimed that bureaucratic mechanisms played the biggest role in radicalizing German society as opposed to a preordained will of the Führer or a pre-imagined strategy. Post-Weimar Germany, by cumulative radicalization, turned into a totalitarian society based on a totalitarian ontology. Many, Mommsen argues, acted due to blind obeisance, a misguided calculus of efficiency, career motives or simply of a wish to get along (Kershaw 2004). Nazi ontology evolved together with its politics: cumulative radicalization of society in Germany gradually created the Volkkörper as the basis of its corporeal ontology, sacralized its ideology and its embodiment, the Nazi movement, which progressively eliminated other sources of meaning and created Nazism as the ultimate, desirable form of human existence on Earth (Neumann 2009). Cumulative radicalization sits with Arendt's "banality of evil" thesis. It was, she argued, a specific kind of sheer thoughtlessness, not stupidity, that made Adolf Eichmann one of the biggest criminals to have lived on Earth (Arendt 1994).

The vision of connected autonomous mobility also has an element of "cumulative radicalization" and a version of thoughtlessness: space, data, meaning, society are imagined in a purified politics of technological functionalism. The autonomous automobile would be a post-cyborg, computerized car-body entity, looking, seeing, feeling the environment through its sensors as a human would. Indistinguishable from the outside from a car with a human driver, it would pass the Turing test (Turing 1950).

The automobile is entangled into the new space without any ontological awareness of the new spatial setup or the material semiotic architecture that has been created. Data imagined as "raw" becomes, through cumulative technological radicalization, a socio-material construct of mutable mobile flows and yet another political ontology of control. The politics of technological determinism (Mladenović et al. 2020) and solutionism (Dewandre 2018) of autonomous, electric, connected vehicles, to borrow Arendt's (1977) concept, is the *banality of technology,*

As we have argued throughout this book, deployments of power in the automobility imaginary create entangled, multiple, performed nomocratic realities of *closure*, of *control* and of *bare life*. Different versions of the automobility imaginary suggested disruptions, transformations and radical changes. Such versions are iterations of an enduring, albeit constantly transforming, singular, rhizomatic imaginary. Its rhizomatic properties, as well as its mutable mobility, have produced regional and national differences as automobility has expanded across the planet. These should not be thought of as distinct and separate imaginaries, but as variations within the larger rhizomatic network, indicating both material and strategic durability (Law and

Mol 2001). The same applies to these new visions described here. Connected, autonomous and electric automobilities are not only non-transformational, but they are also technological varieties of the same hegemonic imaginary, the same political ontology.

TWENTY-FIRST CENTURY AUTOMOBILITY FUTURES

The connected, autonomous, electric vehicle sociotechnical imaginary assures us that solutions have been found to the problems of automobile death and injury, GHG emissions, traffic congestion and more. Through the promises contained within its publicly performed constructs of an imaginary future world, it constructs a universe in the future perfect tense wherein many of the problems of automobility have been solved. It provides a ready-made rejoinder to automobility's techno-critics. It is a complex of visions promoted and supported by the automobile industry and related interests, amongst which interests their capital accumulation prospects are not incidental (Paterson 2007), aided by states that are no less interested (Manderscheid 2012; 2014).

The success of automobility sociotechnical imaginaries is dependent upon convincing us that there are no alternatives; that automobility pasts and futures have and will be determined by technological innovations; that those pasts and futures were *not* the outcomes of political strategies and decisions. Like the sociotechnical imaginaries of the past, the connected, autonomous, electric vehicle sociotechnical imaginary will contribute to ensuring the reproduction of the totalitarian automobility regime under which we live; it is a regime of continued production of more automobiles and more automobility infrastructure. They represent an imaginary reconstitution of society that would "establish the institutional basis of the good life, of happiness, and the social conditions for grace" (Levitas 2017, 6; 2013, 65). It is a sociotechnical imaginary that ensures the social reproduction and further expansion of automobility. It will result in nothing more than more of the same, namely, more automobility and more ontological totalitarianism.

As a political ontology automobility is not, we argued in chapter 2, co-temporal with the emergence of the car. Cumulative automobility radicalization, with its origins in the totalizing device of the map and the production of space in nineteenth-century capitalism, continued with the railway experience, annihilation of time-space and the creation of the car-driver cyborg inscribing dromocratic experience into Euclidean and material semiotic space. It is a performative, experiential (*functional* in Mommsen's theory) technology game as form of life (Wittgenstein 1953, §19) that is a political ontology.

Chapter Nine

Idiotes

Destituting Automobility and Post-Automobility[*]

In the introductory chapter to *The Crisis of European Sciences and Transcendental Phenomenology*, written between 1934 and 1937, posthumously published in German in 1954, Edmund Husserl (1970, 7–8) wrote that:

> We make our beginning with a change which set in at the turn of the last century in the general evaluation of the sciences. It concerns not the scientific character of the sciences but rather what they, or what science in general, had meant and could mean for human existence. The exclusiveness with which the total worldview of modern man, in the second half of the nineteenth century, let itself be determined by the positive sciences and be blinded by the "prosperity" they produced, meant an indifferent turning-away from the questions which are decisive for a genuine humanity. . . . In our vital need—so we are told—this science has nothing to say to us. It excludes in principle precisely the questions which man, given over in our unhappy times to the most portentous upheavals, finds the most burning: questions of the meaning or meaninglessness of the whole of this human existence. . . . In the final analysis they concern man as a free, self-determining being in his behavior toward the human and extrahuman surrounding world and free in regard to his capacities for rationally shaping himself and his surrounding world.

The "crisis" of the sciences that Husserl refers to is not a crisis of the type described by Thomas Kuhn (1970), namely the breakdown of a scientific paradigm, but instead a rejection of the very validity of the existential question of what the meaning of the sciences could be. "Scientific, objective truth," Husserl remarked, had been reduced to "a matter of establishing what

---

[*] An extended version of this chapter was submitted to the journal *Applied Mobilities*. At the time of writing, it is still under review.

the world, the physical as well as the spiritual world, is in fact." The sciences were concerned only with what Heidegger called the ontic.

Husserl's observation is a lamentation regarding not only what the sciences have become but a lamentation based on a hope that the sciences could be otherwise, that they could in some way be remedied. It is a nostalgia for a past when the individual sciences were understood to be branches of philosophy. The crisis of the sciences is, consequently, at the same time also a crisis for philosophy and, more importantly, a crisis for humanity. Having cut themselves off from what Husserl called the *Lebenswelt*, or lifeworld, the world of everyday existence, the sciences ceased to be seen, and ceased to see themselves, as a human project, the purposes of which are embedded in and derived from the lifeworld. The sciences appear not only to be autonomous from that lifeworld, but they also had, since Galileo, Husserl (1970, 48–9) argued, "[surreptitiously substituted] the mathematically substructed world of idealities for the only real world, the one that is actually given through perception, that is ever experienced and experienceable—our everyday life-world."

What Husserl called the lifeworld, roughly what Heidegger called "Being-in-the-world," we have argued, is an imaginary reality. That imaginary, to quote Husserl, is "the only real world." It is, however, a world of simulacra and simulation wherein what is the real and what is the imaginary have become identical and hence indistinguishable. Science fiction, both as literary genre and as the simulation we inhabit, Jean Baudrillard (1994, 126) observed, "is no longer anywhere, and it is everywhere." *Qua* imaginaries of a future technology, sociotechnical imaginaries are nothing more nor less than science fictions, or rather technoscience fictions. Albeit fictions with concrete plans for which adequate finance has been procured, frequently with assistance from the state, that have been brought into material existence roughly as they were imagined.

If the sciences of Husserl's epoch could not tell us what to do, the technosciences of our own epoch not only tell us what to do but tell us what reality is and what it is not; what is important and what is not; what is beautiful and what is ugly. (The E-Type Jaguar, Enzo Ferrari once opined, was "the most beautiful car ever made.") Like the sciences criticized by Husserl, their public justification is sociotechnical "progress." Self-driving cars have begun to appear on our roads, as automobiles once initially did, and drones are being presented to us as inevitable. There is no meaningful citizen involvement; publics are not asked if that is what they want, nor if they approve of the investment of social resources in these technologies, both our collectively owned social resources as well as those that are privately owned and controlled. To the degree publics are considered, it is to educate them, to dispel their irrational resistance to new technologies, such as autonomous vehicles. This is the realm of the ontopolitical. It is a realm of power, precisely because only those with the power and resources to do so are able to construct and disseminate the visions, material and symbolic, that sustain the automobility imaginary.

The automobility imaginary contains within itself the potential for disillusionment, not just for individuals but also in terms of its publicly performed visions and their associated utopias. Indeed, the automobility imaginary is always subject to disillusionment. It is a disillusionment that threatens to appear with the appearance of a new sociotechnical imaginary. Each newly constructed sociotechnical imaginary contains within itself an admission that something is missing or wrong under the current state of affairs. Currently it is the admission that automobility both kills and contributes to the environmental crisis.

Moving towards a post-automobility future will require the deconstruction and collapse of the automobility imaginary. It requires deconstructing the realism of everyday automobility. The Western metaphysical tradition is not just a metaphysic of interest to philosophers, a tradition that, for those critical of that tradition, leads philosophers into error; it is a metaphysic of everyday life, which governs our most central assumptions about what things are, what the world is and who we are.

Husserl suggested, in *The Crisis of the European Sciences*, that coming to an understanding of phenomenology was akin to the experience of a religious conversion. William Barrett, in his introduction to Daisetz Suzuki's *Zen Buddhism* (1956), wrote that he had been told by a friend of Heidegger, who had once visited Heidegger at his home and found him reading one of Suzuki's books, that Heidegger remarked that if he had correctly understood what Zen Buddhism was, that this was what he had been trying to get at all along, not only in *Being and Time* but in all his writings.

Within the ontology of phenomenology, the world, "reality," is neither independent of us nor something unseen, operating behind or under a veil of appearances, comprised of mechanisms and causal structures. If we have understood Husserl correctly, it is this hermeneutic shift, an alteration in one's understanding of what reality might be, that is what he was trying to get at with the notion of a "religious conversion." Put another way, it is a hermeneutic shift to a phenomenological attitude from an attitude of everyday realism.

A post-phenomenological ontology retains this insight, that reality is none other than the reality of everyday existence but necessitates focusing on the indexical related processes, agents and networks of power by which reality is constructed. If automobility is a quintessential sociotechnical apparatus of modernity, it is to postmodernity that post-automobility would belong. If postmodernity is understood as an intellectual movement that has focused on deconstructing the realist assumptions of modernity, so moving towards a post-automobility future requires the deconstruction of the realist metaphysics that sustain the automobility imaginary, by which we take it to be real and not a dreamscape. That is what we have attempted to do in the preceding pages. What is required is not just the intellectual deconstruction of automobility but its deconstruction in practice, to which we now turn.

A DESTITUTE MOBILITY UTOPIA

Is another kind of ontology and an alternative politics at all imaginable? "The fundamental activity of sovereign power," Agamben (2014, 66) argued,

> is the production of bare life as the originary political element. And it is this bare life (or "sacred" life, if *sacer* designates primarily a life that can be killed without committing murder) that, in the juridical-political machine of the West, acts as a threshold of articulation between *zoē* and *bios*, natural life and politically qualified life. And it will not be possible to think another dimension of life if we have not first managed to deactivate the *dispositif* of the exception of bare life.

How is it possible, then, to "deactivate the *dispositif* of the exception of bare life"? Agamben's answer is to transform the "ontology of the subject" from being a subject that uses an object to a subject that constitutes itself through use (Agamben 2014, 69). The monastic concept of "use" as opposed to "ownership" discussed in *Homo Sacer* (Agamben 2017) is here relevant. "Use," in the Franciscan form of life, is a practice void of ownership of a consumable (food, drink, clothes and so forth that are essential to the life of the monks) which establishes an ontological relationship to the object. Use is "an act of becoming, insofar as a part of it has already passed and another is still to come, does not exist properly in nature, but only in memory or expectation: it is an instantaneous being, which as such can be thought, but not possessed" (Agamben 2017, 991). Franciscans are able to define an existence outside the law, outside the order that establishes the ontological relationship. It is a reality that is psychological and procedural, between subject and object, a form-of-life, a habit and custom (Agamben 2014, 71). Use is "configured as a *tertium* with respect to law and life, potential and act [. . .] the monks' vital practice, their form of life" (Agamben 2017, 998).

We have described automobility as an ontopolitically ordered, deterritorialized, semiotic and rhizomatic space. Being in this ontology is not moving from A to B nor the right to do so. Rather, it is the "right to perform" within the theatron of automobility, to *do automobility*. The "right to perform" is the ontological politics that subjectifies individuals and collectives, and thus establishes a relationship between the living being and the automobility *dispositif* (Agamben 2009). This right to perform is akin to "language itself, which is perhaps the most ancient of apparatuses—one in which thousands and thousands of years ago a primate inadvertently let himself be captured," creating the subject (14). Freeing the subject from what Heidegger called "enframing," the desubjectifying closure and control of technology (Heidegger 1977), is what Agamben calls living "as not": "destitution without refusal" (Agamben 2014, 71). It is to deactivate "juridical and social property" without establishing a new identity, deposing the social conditions in which one finds oneself living, without negating them but simply *using* them. Liberation from enframing for Agamben lies in "inoperativity:" a destituent form of power, a "dance" or "play" (Agamben 2007). It is the "deactivation of existing values and powers" as in the rite of the feast (Agamben 2014) or in the "highest poverty" of monastic life (Agamben 2017, 985–1000).

What is relevant here for our context is that within the idea of law—at the core of the order that provides the "right to perform"—is violence that is already permitted (Schmitt 2003, 73). Being a subject, Agamben (2018, 25) argues, means that one commits a "crimen," an action sanctioned by "the order of responsibility and law." Crimen derives from *karman*, the Sanskrit word that means "action linked with a consequence"—colloquially, "karma." However, when actions are sanctioned by the law, it is a people in its entirety that is subject to legal violence and is made culpable. Punishment is an ontological condition, as the basic concept of the law is that there is "no law without punishment." Sanctionable action creating the culpable individual is the ultimate subjectification by the idea of the law as ontopolitical *dispositif*. In automobility the culpable individual is transformed into a *keropolitical subject* (bare life) through bracketed and normalized violence.

The rite of the feast that Agamben refers to is the Roman carnival, which was later brought to life in the tradition of the *jester* in Shakespearian plays ("This cold night will turn us all to fools and madmen/King Lear") or the *yurodivy* ("fools for Christ") in Eastern Orthodox asceticism. Jesters or fools for Christ employed shocking and unconventional behavior as part of the rite to challenge accepted norms, deliver prophecies or to mask piety. The role is also a connector, the one who makes unusual links, uncovers associations or breaks through walls of assumed and accepted knowledge. As e e cummings (2014 [1953]) explained in a lecture, he is generally opposed to the

> genuine lecturer [who] must obey the rules of mental decency, and clothe his personal idiosyncrasies in collectively acceptable generalities, an authentic ignoramus remains quite indecently free to speak as he feels. This prospect cheers me, because I value freedom; and have never expected freedom to be

anything less than indecent. The very fact that a burlesk addict of long standing (who has many times worshipped at the shrine of progressive corporeal revelation) finds himself on the verge of attempting an aesthetic striptease, strikes me as a quite remarkable manifestation of poetic justice; and reinforces my conviction that since I can't tell you what I know (or rather what I don't know) there's nothing to prevent me from trying to tell you who I am.

"Authentic ignoramus"—to genuinely not to know—is a version of what Agamben suggests as the (new) model of politics: relational, subject-centered *inoperativity* or "destituent power" (Agamben 2014). Destituent inasmuch "as have not": knowledge, rule, authority, social context all "made inoperative." Destituent power creates new, poetic forms of life, "poetic justice," as cummings has it, that is not use-context but the material semiotic embodiment of deactivated social conditions—a "modal ontology." Its focus is "what the human body can do, opening it to new possible use" (Agamben 2014, 70).

This modal ontology is reminiscent of the relational political ontology of Arendt (1958; Walsh 2011; Menge 2019): acting in concert, focusing on "natality" (Ryan 2018). For Arendt it is "natality, and not mortality, [that] may be the central category of [the] political" (Arendt 1958, 9); active life or action-as-beginning is what forges the link between natality and politics. Natality is to begin something, to set something new and unpredictable in motion. Whatever emerges arises between people who coexist in a habituated web of relationships. However, this web is in constant flux and is (re)created instantaneously by action as natality. "What is divine"—writes Agamben— "is not being itself, but [. . .] its own always already modifying and 'naturing'—being born—in the modes" (Agamben 2014, 73). Natality thus is rewritten by Agamben as "acting inoperativity"—making inoperative the biological, economic and social conditions by recreating all and always anew.

Destituent power addresses the irresolvable dialectic of constituent and constituted power, the constitutive power/violence that is the *nomos*. Revolutions establish and constitute new law by violence, but once the law is constituted, power/violence remains in order to preserve the law: "Power that was only just overthrown by violence will rise again in another form, in the incessant, inevitable dialectic between constituent power and constituted power, violence which makes the law and violence that preserves it" (Agamben 2014, 70). Destituent power/violence, in contrast, "the sign and the seal but never the means" (Benjamin 1996, 252), breaks the cycle. It is "action-as-beginning" void of the *dispositif* (imaginary/spectacle/dreamscape/*nomos*) that makes power/violence constitutive and separates bare life from life, being-in from being-with. In doing so, destitute power renders apparatuses that marginalize, exclude and erase inoperative. Resistance would effect the "ungovernmentability" of the form-of-life, enabling new uses and potentialities that withstand, suspend and deactivate the force and techniques of the *dispositif*(s) in play.

Destituent power denotes a way of resisting the profound ontological violence (cf. Andersen 2020) captured in the nomocratic *dispositif*. What Agamben (2017, 1269) calls "sovereign autoconstitution of Being" is a form of power/violence that captures potentiality and action in the perpetual process of abolishing and reinventing ever-new sovereign forms of spatio-political orders. Destituent power mobilizes a peculiar modality of power (as potentiality and action) which not only remains independent of the mythic violence of constituted and constituent law (Benjamin 1996) but, by doing so, also creatively aims to ensure the continuity of everyday natality, or mundane life, that is not governed by the power/violence that is the *nomos*. Such destituent power is evoked, in a different everyday life context, by the resistance to modern day colonizing violence, being coerced into a spatial existence that can only result in being either victim or enemy (Joronen 2017).

What does this mean for a shared future addressing the looming question of "what it means to be human" in nomocracy? What might a future look like from which we could reflect upon what we *could* or *should* do? How can such destituent modalities of power or "pockets of resistance" (Jensen and Richardson 2004) be imagined in post-automobility? How would a world of destituent power look like, and what do we need to do if we wanted to get there? How can the *dispositif* of nomocracy be deactivated?

To destitute, used as a verb, is to forsake the imaginary of automobility (with the awareness that we are still captured by the picture), and open up what Agamben calls the "sphere of pure means": "a means that appears as such, only insofar as it emancipates itself from every relation to an end [. . .] it is attested only as exposition and destitution of the relationship between violence and juridical order, between means and end" (Agamben 2017, 1270–71). Instead of constructing a new imaginary, destituent power aims for slowdowns, wherein everyday life "continue[s] its steady course for a finite period of time" (Joronen 2017, 94). These slowdowns resist, upend *dromos* and *nomos*—speed, power/violence—while remaining vigilant to new nomocratic techniques so that they are unable to efficiently execute their totalitarian intrusions. Destituency creates dysfunctionality in the ways nomocracy governs. Its aim is to ensure the continuity of everyday, mundane forms-of-life through promoting new means and ways of resisting. Destituent natality would disrupt biopolitical governmentality without creating new *nomoi*.

As *nomos* is of space, our material semiotic counter-narrative revolves around interfering with the entangled complex of Euclidean, network and virtual spatialities, which are entangled not only in a situational logic but also in a form of life that we have described in this book using different metaphors.

However, there are multiple realities, performed and entangled setups of different objects and subjects, not only one singular, coherent and tenuous reality that we can have perspectives *on*. Realities, in the plural, are enacted in relations: automobility realities are performed in automobility-related practices—what we have called mundane, everyday automobility reality. This empirical ontology—enacted, relational realities—is multistable. As Michel Callon has shown in his study of scallops and fishermen of Saint-Brieuc Bay who took turns in exchanging active and passive periods, the enactment of two sets of relations created two symmetrical versions of fishermen and scallops, two realities, two ontologies (Callon 1984). What destitute power suggests is an enacted relational entanglement that does *not* create another reality or subject-object ontology. To destitute is to permanently disrupt the entanglement.

DESTITUTE COMMONING AND THE IDIŌTĒS

The Greek *nemein*, from which nomos is derived, means "[to] accord [to] each his own—not in relationship to the soil, but in relationship to the people who settle it" (Arendt 1958, 68). At the center of the Arendtian *nomos* is plurality ("men, not Man, live on the earth and inhabit the world" [Arendt 1958, 7]), the primary condition of the political. While nomocracy operates by violence and appropriation of space, an Arendtian, human-centered post-automobility requires shared space as the precondition for "action-as-beginning." This place would be shared by those who inhabit the man-made world together. The automobility *nomos* is one in which a dangerous human-machine cyborg entity has appropriated space, and it is with that entity that we are obliged to share space.

Politics, the mode of being in the place we share, for Arendt "requires a *nomos* because without it the space of action would have no structure, and no world" (Arendt 2005, 267). *Nomos* is a topographical metaphor for the space of appearance, the precondition for, but not an apparatus of, plurality and political freedom. Post-automobility would spring from people, from intersubjective action, not the blood-filled asphalt of the *nomos* of automobility. Disrupting the automobility *nomos* requires disrupting the triad of power/violence/justice of which the *nomos* is comprised. Bracketed violence needs to be unveiled for what it is: sovereign power that dehumanizes by reducing political being to bare life. Post-automobility is not, to refer to the current debates surrounding driverless futures, a world of automated vehicles but one where humans re-acquire the political to act freely in concert (Arendt 1958). While Foucauldian automobility scholarship has moved in this direction under the concept of autonomobility—active, collectivized and socialized mobility modalities (Cass and Manderscheid 2018)—this needs to be located within the spatial politics of post-automobility.

Nemein, we noted earlier, also means "to dwell." The version of post-automobility we are proposing emphasizes a phenomenological reordering of the space in which we dwell. The space, in Heideggerian terms, that is Being-in-the-world, with the proviso that concrete Being-in-the-world is always Being-in-the-world as constructed through networks of power. The post-automobility "place we share," a politico-topographical metaphor, is the name of the "dimension in which the linguistic and corporeal, material and immaterial, biological and social operations are made inoperative and contemplated as such" (Agamben 2014, 74).

Such a sphere in a city could be an actual "shared space" (Chan and Zhang 2018; Hamilton-Baillie 2008b; Hamilton-Baillie 2008a), ungoverned by current systems of traffic control and spatial appropriation strategies, open to potentiality and void of coercive control. The concept of "shared space," that of all street users moving and interacting in their use of space on the basis of informal social protocols and negotiation, is not new in urban design. Such arrangements existed before the introduction of segregation associated with urban roads in Mediterranean hill towns or market squares, which were organized around the informal sharing of space by vehicles and other users. From an urban design perspective, experimentation with and the conscious application of the concept of shared space was made by Joost Vàhl and his colleagues in the Netherlands in the late 1960s and early 1970s. Vàhl and others eliminated standard road signing, marking, curbs and barriers. They created a new, playful vocabulary of street design full of local references, surprise and intrigue (Hamilton-Baillie 2008b). In 1976 the Dutch government recognized and formalized the approach, defining the concept of the *woonerf* ("yard for living") as a means to design low-speed residential roads.

However, once the shared-space concept entered the regulatory dictionary as yet another *dispositif* of urban design governmentality, that is as constituent regulatory power, the demise of the *woonerf* began. As soon as there were standards established, with guidance on the number and spacing of "traffic calming devices," and a formal sign to identify such spaces, enthusiasm for the concept began to fade. Although not so articulated, at the core of the original concept was a shift to a destituent modality of everyday enacted reality. However, as it emerged as an accepted design concept, just another category in the standard road hierarchy, its appeal started to fade. When shared space entered as *dispositif*—"with a major function at a given historical moment responding to an urgent need [. . . with . . .] a dominant strategic function" (Foucault 1980, 194–28)—it became a failed regulatory intervention; just another component of the *dispositif* of the mobility regime in the city. Post-automobility could be conceptualized as the revival of the concept of "shared space," not as design concept or a regulatory effect, but as a mode of post-automobility Being. This would mean a shift from a technosocial ordering of space to spatial reordering focusing on the human condition: the phenomenological (re)construction of human speed, rhythm and spatial distribution in the city as the space of (mobile) action (Dewandre 2018).

The empirical examples of destituent play shown by Joronen (2017, 96) in Israeli colonial coercion point to a modality in which the way of resistance "is not with violence, not with resignation, and not with giving up. We [. . .] refuse to be enemies [. . .] we are dealing with our frustration in a positive way committed to non-violent resistance." For the locals trying to survive against all odds, "[f]our things are important. Refusing to be a victim. Refusing to hate. Act that way what we believe in, [and] not take nonviolent resistance as strategy, but a way-of-life." Translating this to urban coercion (Urry 2006), similar simple everyday practices of not falling prey to a victim/enemy dichotomy or letting violence become the way of life in the insurrection against biopolitical coercion come to mind. Biking in the middle of the road slowing down traffic; setting up temporary urban gardens on parking spots during the weekend; driving at low speeds—not breaking the rules but also not conforming with the coercive practices that determine the realities of the road; signaling the space around the bicycle to those who cross over the imaginary line in their cars. These individual actions of destitute resistance to automobility are forms of commoning (Nikolaeva et al. 2019). Human and political geography has been moving towards an appreciation of the concept of the commons (Hardin 1968) that focuses on socio-spatial practices and social relationships that break the neoliberal imaginary and political practices of privatized (urban) space.

We may reformulate the commons as the Arendtian spatio-political place we share:

> the common wealth of the material world—the air, the water, the fruits of the soil, and all nature's bounty—which in classic European political texts is often claimed to be the inheritance of humanity as a whole, to be shared together [. . .] also and more significantly those results of social production that are necessary for social interaction and further production, such as knowledges, languages, codes, information, affects, and so forth (Hardt and Negri 2009, viii).

Commoning, following Hardt and Negri (2009), is a modality of participation that is a subject-centered, biopolitical "struggle over the control or autonomy of the production of subjectivity" (Hardt and Negri 2009, x). This move displaces the debate surrounding the commons and commoning from the spatio-political to that of political ontology: to biopolitics as a struggle for power over administering and producing life.

The struggle takes the form of a biopolitical "event:" action-as-beginning that has the potential to disrupt the historical order. This rupture in the fabric of the dispositif is an act of freedom that produces a new subjectivity with the potential, as Walter Benjamin put it in the context of the destruction of World War I, that forces us "to start from scratch; to make a new start; to make a little go a long way; to begin with a little and build up further" (Benjamin 2005, 732). Commoning is a political strategy to create and maintain the biopolitical event: the production of life as an act of destitute resistance, innovation and freedom. It is a partisan relationship between subjectivity and dispositif; partisan not in the telluric or traditional political sense of friend-foe political theology (Schmitt 2004) but as a political mode of resistance in the struggle of the construction of biopolitical bodies (Hardt and Negri 2009, 61). Destitute partisanship is a version of what Deleuze calls "rebellious spontaneity," which creates "events that can't be explained by the situations that give rise to them, or into which they lead. They appear for a moment, and it's that moment that matters, it's the chance we must seize. [. . .] If you *believe in the world* you precipitate events, however inconspicuous, that elude control, you engender new space-times, however small their surface or volume " (Deleuze 1995, 176, our emphasis). To paraphrase Deleuze in an Arendtian vein, commoning is destitute partisan political Being, starting from scratch anew as a form of natality. It is an example of what Vaneigem called a revolution of everyday life: "passionate break-outs from the factories of collective illusion." Automobility is one of those factories, and its product is the collective illusion that is the automobility imaginary.

The locus of modern political being is the city, which provides possibilities for metropolitan rebellion. The new subjectivity would be the insurgent citizen (Holston 2019). To Tim Cresswell's (2013) characterization of the mobile modern citizen who stands at the intersection of geographical imaginations of a sedentary nation, a dense city and an interconnected world, we would add that she also dwells in the imaginary of nomocratic automobility. Cityscapes are made legible and interpreted as the automobility citizen enacts them. Avoiding jaywalking and following the law (Cresswell 2013, 106) are ensured within the imaginary through being coerced into accepting normalized violence.

As Holston (2019, 129) has argued, urban citizenship complements national citizenship as its substance is belonging to and being resident in the metropolis "where right-claims addressing the production of the city and related civic performances make up the agenda, mobilization, and passions of association" that make citizens members of a political community. In its less romantic formulation, urban citizenship is also coercion into being party to conflicts that evoke definite forms and meanings of violence that are specific to the city (Holston and Appadurai 1999). The metropolis as the locus of the biopolitical production of modern political being is not (only) the built environment of urban buildings, the thoroughfares, public or semi-public spaces and nodes of urban metabolism or urban channels of communication but also the living dynamic of cultural practices, intellectual circuits, affective networks and social institutions that spill over the well-defined borders of the city and become entangled with local, national as well as global flows (Hardt and Negri 2009, 154). Automobility citizenship is a form of residence in and belonging to the geography of these flows, making claims upon the metropolis and using the metropolis to make violent claims normalized in the entangled imaginary. The appropriation of space, order made visible, is the political mode of declaring where citizens of automobility belong by making violent claims, constantly and continuously also violating space which others claim. Such violence is legible and visible not only in the "fortified residential enclaves," "corporate luxury zones," "quarantined war zones," "forbidden sectors" or illegally constructed shanties (Holston and Appadurai 1999, 202). The violence is everywhere, as it is not only constitutive of the space of the city or its politics but of the biopolitical production of automobility citizenship.

Destitution is disowning automobility citizenship, something that is not earned or claimed but into which the individual is coerced by the dispositif that is the ontopolitical imaginary of automobility. To destitute this imaginary is a modality of insurgent citizenship (Holston 1999), a deactivation of the *nomos* "not law as rights, but law as disadvantage and humiliation [. . .] expressed in the Brazilian maxim 'for friends everything; for enemies, the law'" (Holston 2009, 252). This insurgent politics is based on commoning not only stemming from people acting together but "also of a sense that they have contributor rights to the commons thus created" (Holston 2019, 136). Instead of violent claims and claims to violence that originate from and are constitutive of the space of automobility that is the *nomos*, it would be a process, commoning, through which contributor rights are articulated and exercised. This enactment becomes commoning of mobile solidarities: sharing, nurturing and non-violently interpreting the common in-between. What is relevant here is that such insurgency would be directed not only against the modern city and its order but also the ontopolitical imaginary of automobility.

To start anew is a destitute form of Being in the deactivated dispositif, engendering new, small, in-between space-time. Commoning mobility is the creating of new, small space-times in concert. It is partisan and destitute politics not connected to the soil but to a post-automobility insurrection that offers *doing* mobility free of the automobility dispositif (Manderscheid 2014). Translating this to a "mobility commons" concept means reflecting on and organising mobilities that embrace communal decision-making processes, openness to new forms of appreciating "the right to mobility as well as the right to immobility (the right not to be displaced), the awareness of the social production of mobility and the power relations inherent in it, as well as a commitment to creating equity and working in the interest of the public good, contested as it may be" (Nikolaeva et al. 2019). Commoning mobility not only recreates mobility as commons but also produces destitution as commons. Destitution is the ultimate commons: to "have not" is to have nothing to enclose, to appropriate, to privatize or to own. It is a poetic form of life, rebellious spontaneity of the event as situation (Debord 1959). The situation is the map of the moment: social relations, politics of space not inscribed in a geometrical order or frozen in a material semiotic network but open to situational natality (Debord 2002). Commoning destitution cuts through, as Hardt and Negri (2009, viii) suggest, the dichotomies of private and the public, socialism or capitalism. It focuses on new space-time: knowledge, rule, authority, social context all made inoperative; open not enframed in the *dispositif* and not enclosed in the order made visible by the *nomos*. Destitute, embodied spacetime as commons, inoperative acting as commoning.

Reflecting on the survivors of camps, stateless, in danger because lacking (national) citizenship, Arendt (1973, 300) observed that their "*abstract nakedness of being* was their greatest danger." She argues that being "nothing but human"—destitute in the face of political rights or nationhood—necessarily means that one is confined to the private sphere and is forced to live outside, deprived of expression within, and action upon a common world. In the Greek tradition of the polis, treasured by Arendt as the sphere of freedom, exclusively located in the political realm as opposed to the realm of the private (Arendt 1958, 31), there existed a form-of-life that was both an individual withdrawn from political life, confined or reserved to the private sphere, while at the same time having a special form of expression and action upon the common world. This is the figure of the idiōtēs.

The word derives from the Greek adjective *idios*, meaning "private" or "personal." Thus, *idiōtēs* is often translated as "private individual," opposed to a magistrate or a member of the community who was more actively involved in political life. Contrary to standard understandings of the idiōtēs as a private, non-political person, Rubinstein (1998) argues that idiōtēs was a generic name for the individual citizen, the smallest unit of the citizen-body as opposed to the collective whole, *ko koinon* or *polis*. Although participants of the political-institutional framework of Athenian democracy, they were nor to be confused with the more powerful political actors, such as magistrates or rhetors, who held an elevated status as opposed to ordinary citizens. To be an idiōtēs did not necessarily imply a total retreat or exclusion from politics but referred to a group of amateur citizens who participated in some political activities but not in others, whose participation did not surpass some ill-defined threshold (Landauer 2014). Demosthenes differentiated between magistrates who speak frequently and those who do not, identifying the latter group as idiōtai. The amateur magistrate was "a poor man," an "ordinary citizen" as opposed to a rich and powerful member of the Athenian political elite. Aeschines, who was a leading political figure in Athens portrayed himself as idiōtēs (Preus 2012). This and other references to idiōtēs may be read as a democratic version of the Platonic idea that those who exercise political power should not be lovers of political rule. Idiōtai were not excluded from political life but participated less and were not suspected of exploiting their position. Therefore, "idiōtai [were] not held to the same strict standards of accountability as the more politically active members of the polis" (Landauer 2014, 146). The "popular unaccountability" of idiōtēs meant that they were not held accountable, as were magistrates, when making political decisions as jurors. When defendants, they were treated more leniently and lower standards of culpability were applied as they were seen as politically "amateur, and [not having] the power to harm the city" (148).

Thus, idiōtēs, like *homo sacer*, dwell at a political threshold. They occupy the private realm ("private citizen") but are also active politically and participate in the life of the polis. However, their actions were not sanctioned by "the order of responsibility and law," thus idiōtēs were both part of the political community but void of the originary crimen of being held culpable for their political actions and speech. They were not orators who were trained, professional and, typically, wealthy; as jurors they could not be punished for their decisions; as citizens they were not held culpable for political acts encapsulated in their speech. They were not subject to legal violence and in the face of the law it was permitted to "forbear judgement" (ibid., 146). Popular unaccountability, powerless to do harm to the political community but powerful enough to make decisions on behalf of its citizens, is the destitute political being of the idiōtēs, a political-ontological condition. The insurgent citizenship of the idiōtēs is grounded in the rebellious ontological politics of their amateurish participation in the polis: powerful to common, powerless to harm.

It is surprising that Agamben dealt with the figure of "the idiot" only in reference to an early essay of Walter Benjamin on Dostoevsky's *The Idiot*, in which Benjamin argues that the life of Prince Mishkin must remain unforgettable, even if no one remembers it (Agamben 2010, 39). The idiot is a representative, for Agamben, of the political modality of exigency, someone whose life has completely been forgotten but remains unforgettable. This political modality is a strategic "as not," an exigency of the messianic vocation that dislocates and nullifies the subject. It is different from that of the idiōtēs who is a political subject not subjectified by the dispositif, having "deactivated the apparatus" by the sheer force of being an amateur and not aspiring to have power. Being an amateur is to live "as have not" in relation to power. It is to use power but not to possess it; to act at the threshold between *zoē* and *bios,* private life and political life; to deactivate the dispositif through being a subject that constitutes itself through action and speech; whose existence outside of accountability to the law. The idiōtēs, an occasional speaker, a politically non-professional citizen, does not *own* politics as a rhetor or magistrate would, He is a subject who constitutes himself through the politics of use. In the polis that he is a member of, he has the potential to exercise power in the moment of speaking but retreating to the position of political destitution the moment he becomes silent.

As discussed above, the Greek stem *idios* refers to private interests in opposition to the public, and while both *idios* and *idiōtēs* have a wide range of meanings, the word also implied the notion of private property for the Greeks. The figure of the idiōtēs is, of course, the etymological origin of the modern concept of the "idiot": "an obsolete term for a person with profound mental retardation, also an abusive term for a fool" as the Oxford Reference Dictionary informs its readers. While traditional renderings of the emergence of divisions between the "rational" and the "mad" or the social exclusion of the "mentally retarded" are connected to the social critique of power/knowledge that is the characteristic of the medical profession or of psychiatry (Foucault 2009), there is another element at play closer to the discussion here and why the figure of the idiōtēs is relevant for our context: private property and the freedom to act in public. As Buhrer (2014, 83) notes, criteria for describing specific competencies in relation to property first emerged in "competency inquisitions held in England during the later Middle Ages, centuries before a concept of intellectual disability existed in medical or psychiatric thought." In the fourteenth and sixteenth centuries, English royal courts oversaw hundreds of inquisitions involving individuals called upon as idiots or fools. In these inquisitions officials, acting on behalf of the Crown, asked alleged idiots, their friends and their families questions to determine whether they were able to manage their own affairs, specifically their property. If it was deemed that they were not, they lost all the rights associated with legal adulthood—"the ability to possess or sell property, make contracts, marry and testify in court." The Crown then seized their property and sold their wardships to people that were often the same people who brought the allegations to Court in the first place. Thus, legally speaking, to be an idiot in the Middle Ages in England was less related to being mentally fit as to being legally judged able to manage the property, to calculate profits and be able to use calendar-time as a tool to operate (Buhrer 2014, 96).

Our inquiry began with the ruts of the *diolkos* in ancient Greece which, through the sociotechnical imaginings of a professional politician, changed perceptions of far and near by connecting Corinth with Athens as an early dromological event. It created a durable technosocial network that altered power structures enabling a Roman proconsul to reestablish rule by inscribing a dromoscopic illusion *into* space as well as *of* space. We followed the transformation of time and of space through war-, land- and cityscapes, and then the ontopolitical imaginaries that is the keropolitical order that is signified by the ill-name of "automobility." These imaginaries were developed, disseminated and constituted by, as Jasanoff and Kim (2015, 2) note, an assemblage of "social roles, institutions, and practices spawned by modernity: scientists, engineers, and designers; patents and trademarks; autoworkers and big corporations; regulators; dealers and distributors; advertising companies; and users, from commuters to racers." They are all, in the terms of Athenian politics, professional rhetors and *hoi politeuomenoi* (politicians), working with imaginaries, minding the business of the polis that is Western (post-Enlightenment Global North) late-modernity; producing space-time perceptions and the ontopolitics of social durability attained through advances in Western science and technology. Here we can only suggest that the figure of the idiōtēs—lay as opposed to private, powerful to act in concert with the destitute modality of commoning but powerless to be a threat to the commons, performing politics that create worlds as well as realities in the multiverse of material semiotic networks, but not creating imaginaries that become autopoietic world-makers—has the potential to deactivate the automobility dispositif.

We argued in our analysis of nomocracy that to dwell in automobility—the "biopolitical metropolis" (Hardt and Negri 2009, 250–60), the human condition in late modernity—means to live in a reality that is a dreamscape, with new rules, norms and deployments of power that are made visible in the alienated spectacle. Automobility, the new *nomos* of the Earth, is bracketed violence that has become the state of normality, creating the biopolitical metropolis as the camp in which bare life dwells as permanent survivor. Put another way, the "right to the city" (Lefebvre 2005, 150)—the commons as a culturally creative, open and free social world, a "framework within which we all can dwell" (Harvey 2011)—has been degraded, banalized and abused. Destitute commoning suggests an alternative modality: the re-creating of the metropolis as the site of a new "biopolitical production," of people living together, sharing resources, communicating, exchanging goods and ideas.

Constructing a post-automobility utopia in the present is to do things such as put a vase of roses in a spot where cars usually park; constructing spontaneous *lieux de mémoire* (sites of memory) (Nora 1998) such as white bicycles commemorating accident victims in the city, thus making power/violence visible; moving in a vehicle at slow, human speed and blocking traffic on a main street; putting up a bench, creating a small garden, placing a plant in a pothole, using a "walking tool" (Knopflacher 2006, 394) to show what would happen if people had as much space as automobiles. Walking all the streets of a metropolis without an explicit goal as Matt Green does in New York City; reoccupying urban space for eating and being together as the bicycle chef Morten Kryger Wulff does in Copenhagen (https://www.cykelkokken.dk/), who, with his patrons for the meal, set themselves down in a park, on the boardwalk or in a side street, cooking, serving and eating food together, not renting but using space and taking back the city for its people. It requires destituting the automobility nomos, reclaiming the road as a public space, as it was before the convergence of nomos and dromos and the imaginary in the first half of the twentieth century (McShane 1994; Norton 2008).

All of this and more: what spontaneous, partisan, amateur idiōtēs of the city think up and do. For those who wished to read about a new imaginary, a better nomos or a more beautiful dreamscape, we cannot offer one. It might be likened to Wittgenstein's imaginary of language—"an ancient city: a maze of little streets and squares, of old and new houses, and of houses with additions from various periods; and this surrounded by a multitude of new boroughs with straight regular streets and uniform houses" (Wittgenstein 1953, §18). Starting constantly anew, destitute post-automobility commoning would be acting inoperatively, not breaking or creating the law but deactivating the dispositif of nomocratic power/violence; profaning bare life and moving political life back into the city. Post-automobility is in the present, now. It is one reality of multiple potentialities; a spontaneous entanglement of rebellious amateur idiotai who create mobility as commons one step at a time.

Epilogue

In the introduction we remarked that not only is there no politically neutral location from which automobility could be represented as it "really is," from which a representation could be constructed that would correspond to that presumed reality, but there is also no independently existing "automobility as it really is." Our answer to the question "What is automobility?"—which is this book in its entirety—is neither more nor less disinterested than the answers provided by those whose activities sustain and reproduce the automobility imaginary.

"The purpose of a book," Paul Ricoeur (1970, 3) wrote in *Freud and Philosophy*, "is never entirely justified. In any event, no one is required to display his motives or to entangle himself in a confession. To attempt it would be self-delusion." Ricoeur's hesitation was, however, immediately taken back. "Yet, more than anyone," he continued, "the philosopher cannot refuse to give his reasons." Here at the end, we would like to share with the reader some personal reasons.

The foreword by Tedros Adhanom Ghebreyesus, Director-General of the World Health Organization, to the 2018 WHO *Global Status Report on Road Safety* opens with the following image: "There is a phone call or a knock on the door that we all dread, in which we are told that a loved one has been killed or seriously injured in a road traffic crash." Our reasons include the dread of which Adhanom Ghebreyesus spoke, that the phone call or the knock on the door might be *that* phone call or *that* knock on the door. This dread is the generalized epistemic violence of automobility. It is not an individual fear but the collective fear described by Virilio (2012) in *The Administration of Fear*.

One of us was involved in an accident that seriously injured a passenger in the car he was driving. The other received the call of which Adhanom

Ghebreyesus spoke. These two events and experiences—grief for one of us and guilt for the other—have been in the background of what we have written.

After the fact of grief, when its immediate presence, which is the presence of absence, has passed, it is possible to wonder if one properly, or even minimally adequately, brought to some kind of conclusion what Freud in *Mourning and Melancholia* called "grief work." To put the matter in the past tense—"after the fact of grief"—is to assume one has concluded the work. The same can be said of guilt. But what if both turn out to be ongoing processes, an ever-present repressed? If for one of us writing this book turned out to be more reconciliation work, for the other it turned out to be more grief work. Work on the unfinished and never finishable business that is grief work and guilt work, intellectualized and sublimated guilt and grief work, but that is what the task that is this book, for better or worse, demanded, although we did not know that at the beginning.

Automobile victims do not simply "die"; they are violently killed. We have cited it in several places, but here it is appropriate to again mention Joseph Furnas's (1935) essay, "—And Sudden Death," first published in 1935 in *The Reader's Digest*. Automobility ensures it happens frequently.

The dead are dead and can no longer be witnesses to death; only the living can. Objects of pity, and few emotions are less welcome than pity, witnesses to road deaths are treated as epistemologically flawed. Those who have been spared being witnesses are the normal ones, those with a sensible and proper attitude towards cars and driving. We think the reverse. Automobility is not an individual repression; it is a collective repression of the grief and guilt associated with the almost ninety million people who have been killed not by an automobile but by that ill-named thing that is automobility, for whom less than a handful of relatively unknown public memorials have been erected.

For Freud, dreams were a space where the repressed could articulate itself. In automobility this is reversed: it is the dreamscape that thwarts articulation of the repressed. Grief and guilt are central to the experience of automobility. Grief and its pre-mortem—necrophobia and mortal fear—are biopolitical operators of control through which fear is administered. They are the dread of which Adhanom Ghebreyesus spoke, and it is the dread we all dread. Feeling wholly responsible, as well as possibilities for exoneration, are apparatuses of power. Automobility makes us fearful, apprehensive and culpable as a collectivity. Power and violence—nomos and policing—become normalized as the universal human condition of late modernity.

The power and violence of automobility are unique to our epoch, the epoch of nomocracy. Grief and responsibility are core, repressed experiences. Road grief and responsibility are privatized and individualized. That privatization allows the CEOs of automobile corporations, policymakers, advertising agencies, road safety experts and the many others who participate in the financial and moral economy of automobility to sleep soundly at night. Not they, it is "the environment," "the vehicle" and, above all, "the driver" that are responsible.

Even this expanded list of agents serves to individualize blame. We all live within the imaginary. Whether those who occupy the centers of power of automobility know that the utopian visions they disseminate are lies we do not know. If they do not know, they should know. Who and what then are responsible? In the end, is not everyone responsible? But if everyone is responsible, as Arendt observed in *Eichmann in Jerusalem*, no one is responsible. This is the thoughtless banality of automobility.

There is no other cause to these events in our own lives or to those millions of other similar events in other lives across the globe, one every twenty-three seconds (World Health Organization 2018), happening as you read this sentence, or the causes of the ecological destruction of our planet. It is automobility: the dreamscape, spectacle, imaginary and nomos—the ontological politics and paradigm of late modernity—that is the cause. Bruno Latour once observed that it is not airplanes that fly but instead airlines that fly. So also it is with automobility. It is neither automobiles nor drivers that kill, nor, for that matter, as Lewis Mumford put it, is it automobiles that are turning our planet into a wasteland, but an imaginary, a nomos, a dromos and a dreamscape which together fall under the ill-named sign that is "automobility."

To the degree we are able to imagine the specificities of individual crimes against humanity, they outrage and offend us because we are fellow human beings. It is precisely this that marks these crimes not solely as crimes committed against individuals but as crimes against all of us. Automobility death and injury always happen to "someone else." They have been rendered banal by their numbing regularity, ceasing to outrage and offend us, reported in newspapers only when they involve someone famous or are unusual in some other way. Physical causality and *ipso facto* moral responsibility have been constructed as laying with "the driver," a psychological displacement that allows others who are also responsible to sleep in peace. The death and injury and environmental destruction caused by automobility are no less crimes against humanity than other recognized crimes against humanity.

Humans are not the only inhabitants of this planet. Post-humanism asks that we acknowledge that automobility is both an ecocide crime and an ongoing multiple genocide against our fellow terrestrials, not so different from us, nor we from them. As Jacques Derrida (2009, 56) has pointed out,

> One must not be content to mark the fact that what is attributed as "proper to man" also belongs to other living beings if you look more closely, but also, conversely, that what is attributed as proper to man does not belong to him

in all purity and all rigor; and that one must therefore restructure the whole problematic.

As Aldo Leopold (1949, 204) more than seventy years ago in *A Sand County Almanac* put it, it requires an ethic that "changes the role of *Homo sapiens* from conqueror of the land-community to plain member and citizen of it. It implies respect for his fellow-members, and also respect for the community as such."

And here, at the end, we ask ourselves if Ricoeur was right, if we are simply being delusional. And we, of course, wonder if exposing our souls in an academic text is appropriate or not. Émile Durkheim died of grief for his son who was killed in the First World War, yet he refused to talk of it, while Paul Ricoeur chose to speak of his father who died in that same war. The exposing of our souls has not been to share something uniquely personal but to describe something that is flattened by road accident statistics and which is known to many millions of people. It is a form of knowing that might be described as existential epistemology. And if the "baring" of one's soul is to expose the bare life—*nuda vita*—which, as Agamben has argued, is within us all, felt as the dread of the phone call or the knock on the door, then we have revealed nothing personal which, out of decency and respect for public decorum that demands one not appear naked in public, we should have kept to ourselves, but only what is common to all of us. We are all *homo sacer*.

We conclude where we began. Like others before us, we would be very happy if the publication of this book contributes not only to resistance to automobility but to its destitution, not only to this ill-named thing called "automobility," but also to the destitution of the ontopolitics of our time—late-modernity—of which automobility is symptom and constitutive thereof.

References

Achterhuis, Hans. 2001. *American Philosophy of Technology: The Empirical Turn*. Bloomington: Indiana University Press.
Adorno, Theodor W. 2010. *Minima Moralia: Reflections on a Damaged Life*. London: Verso.
Agamben, Giorgio. 1998. *Homo Sacer*. Stanford, CA: Stanford University Press.
Agamben, Giorgio. 2007. *Profanations*. New York: Zone Books.
Agamben, Giorgio. 2009. *What is an Apparatus and Other essays*. Edited by Warner Hamacher, *Crossing Aesthetics*. Stanford, CA: Stanford University Press.
Agamben, Giorgio. 2014. "What is a Destituent Power?" *Environment and Planning D: Society and Space* 32 (1): 65–74. doi: 10.1068/d3201tra.
Agamben, Giorgio. 2017. *The Omnibus Homo Sacer*. Stanford, CA: Stanford University Press.
Agamben, Giorgio. 2018a. *Karman. A Brief Treatise on Action, Guilt, and Gesture*. Stanford, CA: Stanford University Press.
Agamben, Giorgio. 2018b. *What is Real?* Edited by Werner Hamacher, *Crossing Aesthetics*. Stanford, CA: Stanford University Press.
Agamben, Giorgio, and Patricia Dailey. 2010. *The Time that Remains: A Commentary on the Letter to the Romans*. Stanford, CA: Stanford University Press.
Alam, Yunis. 2020. *Race, Taste, Class and Cars: Culture, Meaning and Identity*. Bristol, UK: Policy Press.
Althusser, Louis. 2014. *On the Reproduction of Capitalism: Ideology and Ideological State Apparatuses*. London: Verso.
Ambrose, Stephen E. 2000. *Nothing Like It In the World: The Men Who Built the Transcontinental Railroad, 1863–1869*. New York: Simon and Schuster.
Andersen, Tawny. 2020. "Ontological Violence: Catherine Malabou on Plasticity, Performativity, and Writing the Feminine." *Culture, Theory and Critique* 61 (1): 4–21. doi: 10.1080/14735784.2020.1761414.
Anderson, Benedict. 1991. *Imagined Communities: Reflections on the Origin and Spread of Nationalism*. London: Verso.

Appadurai, Arjun. 1990. "Disjuncture and Difference in the Global Cultural Economy." *Theory, Culture & Society* 7 (2–3): 295–310. doi: 10.1177/026327690007002017.

Appadurai, Arjun. 1998. *Modernity at Large: Cultural Dimensions of Globalization.* Minneapolis: University of Minnesota Press.

Appadurai, Arjun. 2015. "Afterword: The Dreamwork of Capitalism." *Comparative Studies of South Asia, Africa and the Middle East* 35 (3): 481–85. doi: 10.1215/1089201x-3426325.

Aptiv Services US LLC, AUDI AG, Bayrische Motoren Werke AG, Ltd Beijing Baidu Netcom Science Technology Co., Continental Teves AG & Co oHG, Daimler AG, FCA US LLC, HERE Global B.V., Infineon Technologies AG, Intel, and Volkswagen AG. 2019. "Safety First for Automated Driving." In. https://www.daimler.com/documents/innovation/other/safety-first-for-automated-driving.pdf (accessed 21 Oct 2020).

Archer, Neil. 2017. "Genre On the Road: The Road Movie as Automobilities Research." *Mobilities* 12: 509–19.

Ardente, F., J-P. Aurambout, G. Baldini, R. Braun, P. Christidis, A. Christodoulou, A. Duboz, et al. 2019. The Future of Road Transport—Implications of Automated, Connected, Low-Carbon and Shared Mobility. Edited by M. Alonso Raposo and B. Ciuffo. Luxembourg: Publications Office of the European Union. doi:10.2760/9247.

Arendt, Hannah. 1958. *The Human Condition*. Chicago: Chicago University Press.

Arendt, Hannah. 1970. *On Violence*. New York: Harcourt.

Arendt, Hannah. 1973. *The Origins of Totalitarianism*. New York: Harcourt Brace Jovanovich.

Arendt, Hannah. 1994. *Eichmann in Jerusalem: A Report on the Banality of Evil.* New Edition. London: Penguin Classics. Original edition, 1965.

Arendt, Hannah. 2005. "Introduction Into Politics." In *The Promise of Politics*, edited by J. Kohn. New York: Schocken.

Aristotle and W. D. RossD. 1981. *Aristotle's Metaphysics*. Oxford: Clarendon Press.

Austin, J. L. 1965. *How to Do Things with Words*. New York: Oxford University Press.

Badiou, Alain. 2007. *The Century*. Cambridge, UK: Polity Press.

Baehr, Peter. 2002. "Identifying the Unprecedented: Hannah Arendt, Totalitarianism, and the Critique of Sociology." *American Sociological Review* 67 (6): 804–31. doi: 10.2307/3088971.

Balkmar, Dag 2018. "Violent Mobilities: Men, Masculinities and Road Conflicts in Sweden." *Mobilities* 13 (5): 717–32. doi: 10.1080/17450101.2018.1500096.

Balkmar, Dag. 2019. "Towards an Intersectional Approach to Men, Masculinities and (Un)sustainable Mobility: The Case of Cycling and Modal Conflicts." In *Integrating Gender into Transport Planning*, edited by C. Scholten and T. Joelsson. London: Palgrave Macmillan.

Barnes, Trevor J., and Claudio Minca. 2013. "Nazi Spatial Theory: The Dark Geographies of Carl Schmitt and Walter Christaller." *Annals of the Association of American Geographers* 103 (3): 669–87. doi: DOI: 10.1080/00045608.2011.653732.

Barthes, Roland. 1972. "The New Citroën." In *Mythologies*. New York: Hill and Wang.
Bates, Jo, Yu-Wei Lin, and Paula Goodale. 2016. "Data Journeys: Capturing the Socio-Material Constitution of Data Objects and Flows." *Big Data & Society* 3 (2): 2053951716654502. doi: 10.1177/2053951716654502.
Baudrillard, Jean. 1994. *Simulacra and Simulation*. Ann Arbor: University of Michigan Press.
Baudrillard, Jean. 2005. *The System of Objects*. Translated by J. Benedict. London: Verso.
Beaumont, Matthew, and Michael Freeman. 2007. *The Railway and Modernity: Time, Space, and the Machine Ensemble*. Oxford: Lang.
Beckmann, Jörg. 2004. "Mobility and Safety." *Theory, Culture & Society* 21 (4/5): 81–100. doi: 10.1177/0263276404046062.
Bednar, Robert. 2020. *Road Scars: Place, Automobility, and Road Trauma*. Lanham: Rowman & Littlefield.
Bendersky, Joseph. 1979. "The Expendable Kronjurist: Carl Schmitt and National Socialism, 1933–36." *Journal of Contemporary History* 14 (2): 309–28. doi: 10.1177/002200947901400207.
Benjamin, Walter. 1991. *Gesammelte Schriften, Suhrkamp-Taschenbuch Wissenschaft*. Frankfurt am Main: Suhrkamp.
Benjamin, Walter. 1996. "Critique of Violence." In *Walter Benjamin: Selected Writings*, edited by M. Bullock and M. W. Jennings, 236–52. Cambridge, MA: Harvard University Press.
Benjamin, Walter. 1999. *The Arcades Project*. Translated by Howard Eiland and Kevin McLaughlin. Cambridge, MA: Harvard University Press.
Benjamin, Walter. 2005. "Experience and Poverty." In *Selected Writings*. Cambridge, MA: Harvard University Press.
Berger, Peter L, and Thomas Luckmann. 1990. *The Social Construction of Reality: A Treatise in the Sociology of Knowledge*: Anchor Books.
Bergson, Henri. 2005. *Creative Evolution*. New York: Cosimo Books. Original edition, 1911.
Bergson, Henri. 2013. *Time and Free Will: An Essay on the Immediate Data of Consciousness*. London: Routledge. Original edition, 1910.
Bernard, Andreas. 2014. *Lifted: A Cultural History of the Elevator*. New York: NYU Press.
Bertoncello, Michele, and Dominik Wee. 2015. "Ten Ways Autonomous Driving Could Redefine the Automotive World." London: McKinsey.
Bhaskar, Roy. 1978. *A Realist Theory of Science*. Atlantic Highlands, NJ: Humanities Press.
Bhaskar, Roy. 2015. *The Possibility of Naturalism: A Philosophical Critique of the Contemporary Human Sciences*. London: Routledge.
Birch, Kean, and Fabian Muniesa. 2020. *Assetization: Turning Things into Assets in Technoscientific Capitalism*. Cambridge, MA: The MIT Press.
Birtchnell, Thomas, Satya Savitzky, and John Urry. Eds. 2015. *Cargomobilities: Moving Materials in a Golden Age*. New York: Routledge.

Blaser, Mario. 2013. "Ontological Conflicts and the Stories of Peoples in Spite of Europe: Toward a Conversation on Political Ontology." *Current Anthropology* 54 (5): 547–68. doi: 10.1086/672270.

Boccioni, Umberto, Carlo Carrà, Luigi Russolo, Giacomo Balla, and Gino Severini. 1910. "Manifesto of the Futurist Painters." https://www.unknown.nu/futurism/painters.html.

Bogard, William. 2009. "Mobilities." *Surveillance & Society* 6: 188–89.

Böhm, Steffen, Campbell Jones, Chris Land, and Matthew Paterson. 2006. "Conceptualizing Automobility." In *Against Automobility*, edited by Steffen Böhm, Campbell Jones, Chris Land and Matthew Paterson, 3–16. Oxford: Blackwell.

Böhm, Steffen, Campbell Jones, Chris Land, and Matthew Paterson. 2006. "Introduction: Impossibilities of Automobility." In *Against automobility*, edited by Steffen Böhm, Campbell Jones, Chris Land and Matthew Paterson, 3–16. Malden, MA: Blackwell.

Bonham, Jennifer. 2006. "Transport: Disciplining the Body that Travels." In *Against Automobility*, edited by Stephen Böhm, Campbell Jones, Chris Land and Mat Paterson, 57–74. Oxford: Blackwell.

Bonneuil, Christophe, and Jean-Baptiste Fressoz. 2016. *The Shock of the Anthropocene: The Earth, History and Us*. London: Verso.

Bourdieu, Pierre. 2014. *Distinction: A Social Critique of the Judgement of Taste*. London: Routledge.

Braun, Robert. 2019. "Autonomous Vehicles: From Science Fiction to Sustainable Future." In *Mobilities, Literature, Culture*, edited by Marian Aguiar, Charlotte Mathieson and Lynne Pearce, 259–80. London: Palgrave Macmillan.

Braun, Robert, and Richard Randell. 2020. "Futuramas of the Present: The 'Driver Problem' in the Autonomous Vehicle Sociotechnical Imaginary." *Humanities and Social Sciences Communications* 7 (1):163. doi: 10.1057/s41599-020-00655-z.

Braun, Robert, and Richard Randell. 2021. "Getting Behind the Object We Love the Most: Cars: Accelerating the Modern World Victoria and Albert Museum." *Transfers* 11 (1):138–42. doi: 10.3167/trans.2021.110108.

Braun, Robert, and Richard Randell. 2022. "The Vermin of The Street: The Politics of Violence and the Nomos of Automobility." *Mobilities* 17(1): 53–68. https://doi.org/10.1080/17450101.2021.1981118

Breton, André. 1993. *Earthlight, Sun & Moon*. Los Angeles: Sun & Moon Press.

Brown, Wendy. 2017. *Undoing the Demos: Neoliberalism's Stealth revolution*. New York: Zone Books.

Bufacchi, Vittorio. 2007. *Violence and Social Justice*. London: Palgrave Macmillan UK.

Bufacchi, Vittorio. 2013. "Introduction: Philosophy and Violence." *Revue internationale de philosophie* 265 (3): 233–35.

Buhrer, Eliza. 2014. "Law and Mental Competency in Late Medieval England." *Reading Medieval Studies* 40: 83–100.

Bullard, Robert D. 1990. *Dumping in Dixie: Race, Class, and Environmental Quality*. Boulder, CO: Westview Press.

Burgess-Jackson, Keith. 2003. "Violence in Contemporary Analytic Philosophy." In *International Handbook of Violence Research*, edited by Wilhelm Heitmeyer and John Hagan, 989–1004. Dordrecht: Springer Netherlands.
Burnham, John Chynoweth. 1961. "The Gasoline Tax and the Automobile Revolution." *Mississippi Valley Historical Review* 48 (3): 435–59.
Cadena, Marisol de la, and Mario Blaser, editors. 2018. *A World of Many Worlds*. Durham, NC: Duke University Press.
Callon, Michel. 1984. "Some Elements of a Sociology of Translation: Domestication of the Scallops and the Fishermen of St Brieuc Bay." *The Sociological Review* 32: 196–233. doi: 10.1111/j.1467-954X.1984.tb00113.x.
Campbell, David. 2005. "The Biopolitics of Security: Oil, Empire, and the Sports Utility Vehicle." *American Quarterly* 57: 943–72.
Capra, Fritjof. 1996. *The Web of Life: A New Synthesis of Mind and Matter*. New York: Harper Collins.
Capra, Fritjof. 2002. *The Hidden Connections: A Science for Sustainable Living*. New York: Anchor.
Carayannis, Elias, and David. F. J. Campbell. 2009. "'Mode 3' and 'Quadruple Helix': Toward a 21st Century Fractal Innovation Ecosystem." *International Journal of Technology Management* 46 (3–4): 201–34.
Cass, Noel, and Katharina Manderscheid. 2018. "The Autonomobility System: Mobility Justice and Freedom Under Sustainability." In *Mobilities, Mobility Justice and Social Justice*, edited by N. Cook and D. Butz, 101–15. London, New York: Routledge.
Castellano, Katey. 2018. "Anthropomorphism in the Anthropocene: Reassembling Wildlife Management Data in Bear 71." *Environmental Humanities* 10 (1): 171–86. doi: 10.1215/22011919-4385516.
Castells, Manuel. 2009. *The Rise of the Network Society*. Oxford: Wiley-Blackwell.
Castoriadis, Cornelius. 1997. *The Imaginary Institution of Society*. Cambridge, MA: MIT Press.
Chambers, Peter. 2018. *Border Security: Shores of Politics and Horizons of Justice*. 1st ed. Oxon: Routledge.
Chambers, Peter, and Tom Andrews. 2019. "Never Mind the Bollards: The Politics of Policing Car Attacks through the Securitisation of Crowded Urban Places." *Environment and Planning D: Society and Space* 37 (6): 1025–44. doi: 10.1177/0263775818824343.
Chan, Jeffrey Kok Hui, and Ye Zhang. 2018. "Sharing Space: Urban Sharing, Sharing a Living Space, and Shared Social Spaces." *Space and Culture*. doi: 10.1177/1206331218806160.
Chandler, David. 2008. "The Revival of Carl Schmitt in International Relations: The Last Refuge of Critical Theorists?" *Millennium* 37 (1): 27–48. doi: 10.1177/0305829808093729.
Chandler, David. 2018. *Ontopolitics in the Anthropocene: An Introduction to Mapping, Sensing and Hacking*. London; New York: Routledge.

Chandler, David. 2019. "Forum 2: The Migrant Climate: Resilience, Adaptation and the Ontopolitics of Mobility in the Anthropocene." *Mobilities* 14 (3): 381–87. doi: 10.1080/17450101.2019.1609194.

Chenisbest, Bernard, Norbert Jähn, and Jean-Yves Le Coz. 1998. *European Accident Causation Methodology (EACS)*. France. Paper number 98-S2-O-08.

Clarsen, Georgine. 2014. "Feminism and Gender." In *The Routledge Handbook of Mobilities*, edited by Peter Adey, Bissell David, Hannam Kevin, Peter Merriman and Mimi Sheller. London: Routledge.

Clynes, Manfred E., and Nathan S. Kline. 1960. "Cyborgs and Space." *Astronautics* 5 (9):26–27, 74–76.

Coady, C. A. J. 1986. "The Idea of Violence." *Journal of Applied Philosophy* 3 (1): 3–19.

Coeckelbergh, Mark. 2018. "Technology Games: Using Wittgenstein for Understanding and Evaluating Technology." *Science and Engineering Ethics* 24: 1503–19.

Condit, Carl W. 1977. *The Railroad and the City: A Technological and Urbanistic History of Cincinnati*. Cincinnati: Ohio State University Press.

Conley, Jim. 2012. "A Sociology of Traffic: Driving, Cycling, Walking." In *Technologies of Mobility in the Americas*, edited by Phillip Vannini, Lucy Budd, Ole B Jensen, Christian Frisker and Paola Jirón. New York: Peter Lang.

Connell, Raewyn, and Rebecca Pearse. 2015. *Gender: In World Perspective*. Cambridge, UK: Polity Press.

Connolly, William E. 2004. *The Ethos of Pluralization*. Minneapolis: Minnesota University Press.

Cormier, Brendan, and Elizabeth Bisley. 2019. *Cars: Accelerating the Modern World*. London: Victoria and Albert Museum.

Cottrill, Caitlin D., and Piyushimita Thakuriah. 2010. "Evaluating Pedestrian Crashes in Areas with High Low-Income or Minority Populations." *Accident Analysis & Prevention* 42 (6): 1718–28. doi: 10.1016/j.aap.2010.04.012.

Cowen, Deborah. 2014. *The Deadly Life of Logistics: Mapping the Violence of Global Trade*. Minneapolis: University of Minnesota Press.

Cresswell, Tim. 2001. "The Production of Mobilities." *New Formations* 43 (Spring): 3–25.

Cresswell, Tim. 2010. "Towards a Politics of Mobility." *Environment and Planning D: Society and Space* 28: 17–31.

Cresswell, Tim. 2013. "Citizenship in Worlds of Mobility." In *Critical Mobilities*, edited by O. Soderstrom, D. Ruedin, G. D'Amato and F. Panese, 105–24. London: Routledge.

Culver, Greg. 2018. "Death and the Car: On (Auto)Mobility, Violence, and Injustice." *ACME: An International Journal for Critical Geographies* 17 (1): 144–70.

cummings, e e 2014 (1953). "e e cummings Tries to Answer the Question 'Who Am I?' in This Delightful Lecture." *The New Republic*, October 14, 2014 (November 2).

Cuno, Silke, Lina Bruns, Nikolay Tcholtchev, Philipp Lämmel, and Ina Schieferdecker. 2019. "Data Governance and Sovereignty in Urban Data Spaces Based

on Standardized ICT Reference Architectures." *Data* 4 (16). doi: 10.3390/data4010016.
Curts, Kati. 2015. "Temples and Turnpikes in 'The World of Tomorrow': Religious Assemblage and Automobility at the 1939 New York World's Fair." *Journal of the American Academy of Religion* 83: 722–49. doi: 10.1093/jaarel/lfv041.
Cusenza, Marie Anna, Silvia Bobba, Fulvio Ardente, Maurizio Cellura, and Franco Di Persio. 2019. "Energy and Environmental Assessment of a Traction Lithium-Ion Battery Pack For Plug-In Hybrid Electric Vehicles." *Journal of Cleaner Production* 2015: 634–49. doi: 10.1016/j.jclepro.2019.01.056.
Dalakoglou, Dimitris 2017. *The Road: An Ethnography of (Im)mobility, Space, and Cross-border Infrastructures in the Balkans*Manchester: Manchester University Press.
Dalton, Craig M., and Jim Thatcher. 2015. "Inflated Granularity: Spatial "Big Data" and Geodemographics." *Big Data & Society* 2: 1–15.
Dalton, Craig M., Linnet Taylor, and Jim Thatcher. 2016. "Critical Data Studies: A Dialog on Data and Space." *Big Data & Society* 3 (1). doi: 10.1177/2053951716648346.
Dalton, Craig, Clancy Wilmott, Emma Fraser, and Jim Thatcher. 2020. "'Smart' Discourses, the Limits of Representation, and New Regimes of Spatial Data." *Annals of the American Association of Geographers* 110 (2): 485–96. doi: 10.1080/24694452.2019.1665493.
Dant, Tim. 2004. "The Driver-car." *Theory, Culture and Society* 21: 61–79. doi: 10.1177/0263276404046061.
Davenport, John, and Julia L. Davenport. 2006. *The Ecology of Transportation: Managing Mobility for the Environment*. Netherlands: Springer.
Dawson, Andrew, Jennifer Day, and David Ashmore. 2020. "Multiautoculturalism: Reconceptualising Conflict on the Roads." *The Asia Pacific Journal of Anthropology* 21 (3): 205–28. doi: 10.1080/14442213.2020.1754894.
De Certeau, Michel. 1980. "On the Oppositional Practices of Everyday Life." *Social Text* 3 (Autumn): 3–43.
Dean, Mitchell. 2010. "Power at the Heart of the Present: Exception, Risk and Sovereignty." *European Journal of Cultural Studies* 13 (4): 459–75. doi: 10.1177/1367549410377147.
Debord, Guy. 1959. "Situationist Theses on Traffic." In *Situationist International: Anthology*, edited by Ken Knabb, 69–70. Berkeley, CA: Bureau of Public Secrets.
Debord, Guy. 2002. "The Situationists and the New Form of Action in Politics or Art." In *Guy Debord and The Situationist International: Texts and Documents*, edited by Tim McDonough, 159–66. Cambridge, MA: MIT Press.
Debord, Guy. 2014. *The Society of the Spectacle*. Translated by Ken Knabb. Berkley, CA: Bureau of Public Secrets. Original edition, 1967.
DeLanda, Manuel. 2004. *Intensive Science and Virtual Philosophy*. London: Continuum.
Deleuze, Gilles. 1992. "Postscript on the Societies of Control." *October* 59: 3–7.
Deleuze, Gilles. 1995. *Negotiations*. Translated by Martin Joughin. New York: Columbia University Press.

Deleuze, Gilles, and Félix Guattari. 1987. *A Thousand Plateaus*. Minneapolis: University of Minnesota Press.
Deleuze, Gilles, and David Lapoujade. 2006. *Two Regimes of Madness: Texts and Interviews, 1975–1995, Semiotext(e)*. London: MIT Press.
Derrida, Jacques. 1988. *Limited Inc*. Evanston, IL: Northwestern University Press.
Derrida, Jacques. 1998. *The Monolingualism of the Other, or the Prosthesis of Origin*. Translated by Patrick Mensah. Stanford, CA: Stanford University Press.
Derrida, Jacques. 2008. *The Animal that Therefore I Am*. New York: Fordham University Press.
Derrida, Jacques. 2009. *The Beast and the Sovereign, Seminars of Jacques Derrida*. Chicago: The University of Chicago Press.
Derrida, Jacques. 2015. *Of Grammatology*. Baltimore, MD: Johns Hopkins University Press.
Dewandre, Nicole. 2018. "Political Agents as Relational Selves: Rethinking EU Politics and Policy-Making with Hannah Arendt." *Philosophy Today* 62 (2): 493–519. doi: 10.5840/philtoday2018612222.
Dewey, John. 1929. *Experience and Nature*. London: George Allen & Unwin.
Dickens, Charles. 1848. *Dombey and Son*. London: Bradbury and Evans.
Dubbini, Rachele 2010. "Agones on the Greek Agora between Ritual and Spectacle: Some Examples from the Peloponnese." Ritual dynamics and the science of ritual, Wiesbaden, 2010.
Edensor, Tim. 1997. "National Identity and the Politics of Memory: Remembering Bruce and Wallace in Symbolic Space." *Environment and Planning D: Society and Space* 15 (2): 175–94. doi: 10.1068/d150175.
Edensor, Tim. 2004. "Automobility and National Identity:Representation, Geography and Driving Practice." *Theory, Culture & Society* 21 (4–5): 101–20. doi: 10.1177/0263276404046063.
Egbue, Ona, and Suzanna Long. 2012. "Critical Issues in the Supply Chain of Lithium for Electric Vehicle Batteries." *Engineering Management Journal* 24 (3): 52–62. doi: 10.1080/10429247.2012.11431947.
Ehn, Billy, and Orvar Löfgren. 2010. *The Secret World of Doing Nothing*. Berkeley: University of California Press.
Elvebakk, Beate. 2007. "Vision Zero: Remaking Road Safety." *Mobilities* 2: 425–41.
Elvik, Rune. 2005. "Speed and Road Safety: Synthesis of Evidence from Evaluation Studies." *Transportation Research Record* 1908 (1): 59–69. doi: 10.1177/0361198105190800108.
Epstein, Reid J., and Patricia Mazzei. 2021. "How the GOP Is Creating Harsher Penalties for Protesters." *New York Times*, April 21.
Eskin, Michael. 1999. "A Survivors Ethics: Levinas' Challenge to Philosophy." *Dialectical Anthropology* 24 (3/4): 407–50.
Esposito, Roberto. 2008. "Totalitarianism or Biopolitics? Concerning a Philosophical Interpretation of the Twentieth Century." *Critical Inquiry* 34 (4):633–44. doi: 10.1086/592537.
European Commission. 2017. "EU Action to Curb Air Pollution by Cars: Questions and Answers." Brussels: European Commission.

European Commission. 2018. "Towards a Common European Data Space." Brussels: European Commission.
European Commission. 2021. "Cooperative, Connected and Automated Mobility (CCAM)." [Government document online] European Commission, accessed 08 March 2021. https://ec.europa.eu/transport/themes/its/c-its_en.
Everuss, Louis. 2020. "The New Mobilities Paradigm and Social Theory." In *Routledge Handbook of Social and Cultural Theory*. Edited By Anthony Elliott. New York: Routledge.
Fagnant, Daniel J., and Kara Kockelman. 2015. "Preparing a Nation for Autonomous Vehicles: Opportunities, Barriers and Policy Recommendations." *Transportation Research Part A: Policy and Practice* 77: 167–81. doi: 10.1016/j.tra.2015.04.003.
Favarò, Francesca, Sky Eurich, and Nazanin Nader. 2018. "Autonomous Vehicles' Disengagements: Trends, Triggers, and Regulatory Limitations." *Accident Analysis & Prevention* 110: 136–48.
Featherstone, Mike. 2004. "Automobilities: An Introduction." *Theory, Culture & Society* 21: 1–24.
Ferrando, Francesca. 2020. *Philosophical Posthumanism*. New York: Bloomsbury Academic.
Finlay, Christopher J. 2017. "The Concept of Violence in International Theory: A Double-Intent Account." *International Theory* 9 (1): 67–100. doi: doi:10.1017/S1752971916000245.
Fish, Stanley. 1994. *There's No Such Thing as Free Speech, and It's a Good Thing, Too*. New York: Oxford University Press.
Flink, James J. 1972. "Three Stages of American Automobile Consciousness." *American Quarterly* 24 (4): 451–73. doi: 10.2307/2711684.
Flonneau, Mathieu 2012. "Automobilismes. Visite des clichés de l'immobilité." *e-Phaïstos* I (2): 71–75.
Fortun, Kim, and Mike Fortun. 2005. "Scientific Imaginaries and Ethical Plateaus in Contemporary U.S. Toxicology." *American Anthropologist* 107: 43–54.
Foucault, Michel. 1969. *The Archaeology of Knowledge*. New York: 1st American.
Foucault, Michel. 1980. *Power/Knowledge: Selected Interviews and Other Writings, 1972-1977*. New York: Pantheon Books.
Foucault, Michel. 1986. "Space, Knowledge and Power." In *The Foucault Reader*, 239–56. Harmondsworth, UK: Penguin.
Foucault, Michel. 1995. *Discipline & Punish: The Birth of the Prison*. New York: Random House.
Foucault, Michel. 2007. *Security, Territory, Population: Lectures at the College de France, 1977-78*. Basingstoke: Palgrave Macmillan.
Foucault, Michel. 2009. *History of Madness*. New York: Routledge.
Fraedrich, Eva, Sven Beiker, and Barbara Lenz. 2015. "Transition Pathways to Fully Automated Driving and Its Implications for the Sociotechnical System of Automobility." *European Journal of Futures Research* 3 (1): 1–11. doi: 10.1007/s40309-015-0067-8.

Fraedrich, Eva, and Barbara Lenz. 2016. "Societal and Individual Acceptance of Autonomous Driving." In *Autonomous Driving. Technical, Legal and Social Aspects*, edited by M Maurer, J Gerdes, B Lenz and H Winner, 621–640. Berlin: Springer.

Freud, Sigmund. 1959. *The Question of Lay Analysis*. Translated by James Strachey. New York: W. W. Norton & Company.

Freud, Sigmund. 1985. *The Complete Letters of Sigmund Freud to Wilhelm Fliess, 1887–1904*. Translated by J. M. Masson. Cambridge, MA: Harvard University Press.

Freud, Sigmund. 1999. *The Interpretation of Dreams*. Oxford: Oxford University Press.

Freud, Sigmund. 2010. *The Interpretation of Dreams*. Translated by James Strachey. New York: Basic Books.

Fricker, Miranda. 2011. *Epistemic Injustice: Power and the Ethics of Knowing*. Oxford: Oxford University Press.

Furnas, Joseph. 1935. "—And Sudden Death." *Reader's Digest*, 21–26.

Gabbatiss, Josh. 2018. "Alarming Photos Reveal Devastating Scale of Rainforest Destruction in Papua New Guinea." *Independent*, March 21. https://www.independent.co.uk/environment/papua-new-guinea-rainforest-destruction-photos-deforestation-global-witness-illegal-logging-a8265451.html.

Galli, Carlo. 2015. *Janus's Gaze: Essays on Carl Schmitt*. Durham NC: Duke University Press.

Gartman, David. 2004. "Three Ages of the Automobile: The Cultural Logics of the Car." *Theory, Culture & Society* 21: 169–95.

Gentile, Emilio. 1990. "Fascism as Political Religion." *Journal of Contemporary History* 25 (2/3): 229–51.

Gentile, Emilio. 2004. "Fascism, Totalitarianism and Political Religion: Definitions and Critical Reflections on Criticism of an Interpretation." *Totalitarian Movements and Political Religions* 5 (3): 326–75. doi: 10.1080/14690760420003121177.

Goffman, Erving. 1963. *Behavior in Public Places*. New York: Free Press.

Gorz, André. 1980. "The Social Ideology of the Motorcar." In *Ecology as Politics*. Montréal: Black Rose Books.

Graham, James. 2007. "Exploding Johannesburg: Driving in a Worldly City." *Transtext(e)s Transcultures* 跨文本跨文化 3: 67–83.

Green, Matt. 2020. "I am Just walkin'." Accessed 6 August, 2020. https://imjustwalkin.com/nyc-details/.

Gregory, Derek. 2006. "The Black Flag: Guantánamo Bay and the Space of Exception." *Geografiska Annaler. Series B, Human Geography* 88 (4): 405–27.

Grilo, Clara, Elena Koroleva, Richard Andrášik, Michal Bíl, and Manuela González-Suárez. 2020. "Roadkill Risk and Population Vulnerability in European Birds and Mammals." *Frontiers in Ecology and the Environment* 18 (6): 323–28. doi: 10.1002/fee.2216.

Gundler, Bettina. 2013. "Promoting German Automobile Technology and the Automobile Industry: The Motor Hall at the Deutsches Museum, 1933–1945." *Journal of Transport History* 34: 117–39. doi: 10.7227/TJTH.34.2.3.

Gusfield, Joseph R. 1989. "Constructing the Ownership of Social Problems: Fun and Profit in the Welfare State." *Social Problems* 36 (5): 431–41.

Haddon, W. 1968. "The Changing Approach to the Epidemiology, Prevention, and Amelioration of Trauma: The Transition to Approaches Etiologically rather than Descriptively Based." *American Journal of Public Health* 58 (8): 1431–38.

Haggerty, Kevin D., and Richard V. Ericson. 2000. "The Surveillant Assemblage." *The British Journal of Sociology* 51: 605–22. doi: 10.1080/00071310020015280.

Halberstam, Judith. 1998. *Female Masculinity*. Durham, NC: Duke University Press.

Hall, Tom, and Robin James Smith. 2013. "Stop and Go: A Field Study of Pedestrian Practice, Immobility and Urban Outreach Work." *Mobilities* 8: 272–92.

Hamilton-Baillie, Ben. 2008a. "Shared Space: Reconciling People, Places and Traffic." *Built Environment* 34: 161–81.

Hamilton-Baillie, Ben. 2008b. "Towards Shared Space." *URBAN DESIGN International* 13 (2): 130–38. doi: 10.1057/udi.2008.13.

Hannam, Kevin, Mimi Sheller, and John Urry. 2006. "Editorial: Mobilities, Immobilities and Moorings." *Mobilities* 1: 1–22. doi: 10.1080/17450100500489189.

Haraway, Donna. 2015. "Anthropocene, Capitalocene, Plantationocene, Chthulucene: Making Kin." *Environmental Humanities* 6 (1): 159–65. doi: 10.1215/22011919-3615934.

Haraway, Donna. 2016a. "The Cyborg Manifesto." In *Manifestly Haraway*, 5–90. Minneapolis: University of Minesota Press.

Haraway, Donna. 2016b. *Staying with the Trouble: Making Kin in the Chthulucene*. Durham, NC: Duke University Press.

Hardin, Garrett. 1968. "The Tragedy of the Commons." *Science* 162 (3859): 1243–48. doi: 10.1126/science.162.3859.1243.

Hardt, Michael, and Antonio Negri. 2009. *Commonwealth*. Cambridge, MA: Harvard University Press.

Harvey, David. 1990a. "Between Space and Time: Reflections on the Geographical Imagination." *Annals of the Association of American Geographers* 80 (3):418–34.

Harvey, David. 1990b. *The Condition of Postmodernity*. Cambridge, MA: Basil Blackwell.

Harvey, David. 2001. *Spaces of Capital*. New York: Routledge.

Harvey, David. 2003. "The Fetish of Technology: Causes and Consequences." *Macalester International* 13.

Harvey, David. 2007. "Neoliberalism as Creative Destruction." *The ANNALS of the American Academy of Political and Social Science* 610: 21–44.

Harvey, David. 2011. "The Future of the Commons." *Radical History Review* (109): 101–7.

Heidegger, Martin. 1977. "The Question Concerning Technology." In *The Question Concerning Technology and Other Essays*, 3–35. New York: Harper and Row Publishers.

Heidegger, Martin 1962. *Being and Time*. London: Blackwell.

Heidegger, Martin. 2002. *Off the Beaten Track*. Cambridge, UK: Cambridge University Press.

Heinrich, Herbert W. 1931. *Industrial Accident Prevention: A Scientific Approach.* New York: McGraw-Hill.

Himmelreich, Johannes. 2018. "Never Mind the Trolley: The Ethics of Autonomous Vehicles in Mundane Situations." *Ethical Theory and Moral Practice* 21: 669–84. doi: 10.1007/s10677-018-9896-4.

Hodgetts, Timothy, and Jamie Lorimer. 2020. "Animals' Mobilities." *Progress in Human Geography* 44 (1): 4–26. doi: 10.1177/0309132518817829.

Hollnagel, Erik. 1998. *Cognitive Reliability and Error Analysis Method: CREAM.* New York: Elsevier.

Holston, James. 1999. "Spaces of Insurgent Citizenship." In *Cities and Citizenship*, edited by J Holston, 155–73. Durham, NC: Duke University Press.

Holston, James. 2009. "Insurgent Citizenship in an Era of Global Urban Peripheries." *City & Society* 21 (2): 245–67. doi: 10.1111/j.1548-744X.2009.01024.x.

Holston, James, and A. Appadurai. 1999. "Introduction: Cities and Citizenship." In *Cities and Citizenship*, edited by James Holston, 1–18. Durham, NC; London: Duke University Press.

Holston, James. 2019. "Metropolitan Rebellions and the Politics of Commoning the City." *Anthropological Theory* 19 (1): 120–42. doi: 10.1177/1463499618812324.

Holzapfel, Helmut. 2000. "The Outside World as a Learning Environment: Perspectives from Child-oriented Town Planning." *World Transport Policy and Practice* 6: 5–7.

Hook, Derek, and Vlad Petre Glaveanu. 2013. "Image Analysis: An Interactive Approach to Compositional Elements." *Qualitative Research in Psychology* 10: 355–68.

Hornborg, Alf. 2006. "Footprints in the cotton fields: The Industrial Revolution as time–space appropriation and environmental load displacement." *Ecological Economics* 59 (1): 74–81. doi: 10.1016/j.ecolecon.2005.10.009.

Husserl, Edmund. 1970. *The Crisis of European Sciences and Transcendental Phenomenology.* Evanston, IL: Northwestern University Press.

Ihde, Don. 1993. "Postphenomenology: Essays in the Postmodern Context." *Northwestern University Studies in Phenomenology and Existential Philosophy.*

Ihde, Don. 2009. *Postphenomenology and Technoscience: The Peking University Lectures.* Albany: State University of New York Press.

Illich, Ivan. 1974. *Energy and Equity.* New York: Harper & Row.

IPCC. 2014. *Climate Change 2014: Synthesis Report.* Contribution of Working Groups I, II and III to the Fifth Assessment Report of the Intergovernmental Panel on Climate Change. Geneva.

IRTU. 2007. *A Scientific Study "ETAC" European Truck Accident Causation.*

Iveson, Kurt, and Sophia Maalsen. 2019. "Social Control in the Networked City: Datafied Dividuals, Disciplined Individuals and Powers of Assembly." *Environment and Planning D: Society and Space* 37 (2): 331–49. doi: 10.1177/0263775818812084.

Jacobs, Jane. 1961. *The Death and Life of Great American Cities.* New York: Random House.

Jacques, Johanna. 2015. "From Nomos to Hegung: Sovereignty and the Laws of War in Schmitt's International Order." *Modern Law Review* 78 (3): 411–30. doi: 10.1111/1468-2230.12122.

Jacquette, Dale. 2013. "Violence as Intentionally Inflicting Forceful Harm." *Revue internationale de philosophie* 265 (3): 293–322.

Jain, Sarah. 2005. "Violent Submission: Gendered Automobility." *Cultural Critique* 61: 186–214.

Jam Handy Organization. 1940. *To New Horizons*. Detroit: General Motors Corporation, Department of Public Relations.

Jasanoff, Sheila. 2004. *States of Knowledge: The Co-Production of Science and the Social Order*. London: Routledge.

Jasanoff, Sheila. 2015. "Future Imperfect: Science, Technology, and the Imaginations of Modernity." In *Dreamscapes of Modernity: Sociotechnical Imaginaries and the Fabrication of Power*, edited by Sheila Jasanoff and Sang-Hyun Kim, 1–33. Chicago: University of Chicago Press.

Jasanoff, Sheila, and Sang-Hyun Kim. 2009. "Containing the Atom: Sociotechnical Imaginaries and Nuclear Power in the United States and South Korea." *Minerva* 47: 119–46. doi: 10.1007/s11024-009-9124-4.

Jasanoff, Sheila, and Sang-Hyun Kim. 2015. *Dreamscapes of Modernity: Sociotechnical Imaginaries and the Fabrication of Power*. Chicago: University of Chicago Press.

Jensen, Ole B., and Tim Richardson. 2004. *Making European Space*. London: Routledge.

Joly, Auguste. 1912. "Sur le Futurisme." *La Belgique artistique et littéraire* 82: 68–74.

Joronen, Mikko. 2017. "'Refusing to Be a Victim, Refusing to Be an Enemy': Form-of-life as Resistance in the Palestinian Struggle Against Settler Colonialism." *Political Geography* 56: 91–100.

Kahneman, Daniel. 2011. *Thinking, Fast and Slow*. London: Penguin.

Kant, Immanuel. 2000. *Critique of the Power of Judgment*. Cambridge, UK: Cambridge University Press.

Katz, Jack. 1999. "Pissed Off in L.A." In *How Emotions Work*. Chicago: University of Chicago Press.

Kaufmann, Vincent. 2002. "Re-Thinking Mobility: Contemporary Sociology." *Transport and Society* 6 (4): 8–17.

Keats, John. 1958. *The Insolent Chariots*. Philadelphia, PA: Lippincott Williams & Wilkins.

Keith, Tamara. 2016. "Commander-In-Tweet: Trump's Social Media Use And Presidential Media Avoidance." accessed April 27, 2021. https://www.npr.org/2016/11/18/502306687/commander-in-tweet-trumps-social-media-use-and-presidential-media-avoidance?t=1619541869557.

Kershaw, Ian. 2004. "Understanding Nazi Germany." *Journal of Contemporary History* 39 (2): 239–54.

Kidd, Michael. 1956. *Key to the Future*. Dudley Pictures Corporation.

Kitchin, Rob, and Martin Dodge. 2011. *Code/Space: Software and Everyday Life*. Cambridge, MA: MIT Press.

Klinkenborg, Verlyn. 2007. "Millions of Missing Birds, Vanishing in Plain Sight." *The New York Times*, 20.

Knabb, Ken, ed. 2006. *The Situationist International Anthology*. Berkeley, CA: Bureau of Public Secrets.

Kopenawa, Davi, and Bruce Albert. 2013. *The Falling Sky: Words of a Yanomami Shaman*. Cambridge, MA: Harvard University Press.

Koskenniemi, Martti. 2004. "International Law as Political Theology: How to Read Nomos der Erde?" *Constellations* 11 (4): 492–511. doi: 10.1111/j.1351-0487.2004.00391.x.

Koskenniemi, Martti. 2005. *From Apology to Utopia: The Structure of International Legal Argument: Reissue with a New Epilogue*. Cambridge, UK: Cambridge University Press.

Koskenniemi, Martti. 2012. "Letter in Response to Michael Salter's Recent Paper on Carl Schmitt's Grossraum." *Chinese Journal of International Law* 12 (1): 201–2. doi: 10.1093/chinesejil/jms053.

KPMG. 2012. "Self-driving Cars: The Next Revolution."

Kramer, Anna. 2018. "The Unaffordable City: Housing and Transit in North American Cities." *Cities* 83: 1–10. doi: 10.1016/j.cities.2018.05.013.

Kuhn, Thomas Samuel. 1970. *The Structure of Scientific Revolutions*. Chicago: University of Chicago Press.

Lacan, Jacques. 1977. *Ecrits: A Selection by Jacques Lacan*. New York: Norton.

Lamont, Mark. 2012. "Accidents Have No Cure! Road Death as Industrial Catastrophe in Eastern Africa." *African Studies* 71: 174–94.

Lancaster, William. 1995. *The Department Store: A Social History*. London; New York: Leicester University Press.

Landauer, Matthew. 2014. "The Idiōtēs and the Tyrant:Two Faces of Unaccountability in Democratic Athens." *Political Theory* 42 (2): 139–66. doi: 10.1177/0090591713499763.

Larkin, Brian. 2013. "The Politics and Poetics of Infrastructure." *Annual Review of Anthropology* 42 (1): 327–43. doi: 10.1146/annurev-anthro-092412-155522.

Latimer, Joanna, and Rolland Munro. 2006. "Driving the Social." In *Against Automobility*, edited by Steffen Böhm, Campbell Jones, Chris Land and Matthew Paterson, 32–52. Oxford: Blackwell Publishing.

Latour, Bruno. 1990. "Technology is Society Made Durable." *The Sociological Review* 38 (1): 103–31. doi: 10.1111/j.1467-954X.1990.tb03350.x.

Latour, Bruno. 1999. "On Recalling ANT." *The Sociological Review* 47: 15–25. doi: 10.1111/j.1467-954X.1999.tb03480.x.

Latour, Bruno. 2000. *Pandora's Hope: Essays on the Reality of Science Studies*. Cambridge, MA: Harvard University Press.

Latour, Bruno. 2005. *Reassembling the Social: An Introduction to Actor-Network-Theory*. New York: Oxford University Press.

Latour, Bruno, and Steve Woolgar. 2013. *Laboratory Life: The Construction of Scientific Facts*. Princeton, NJ: Princeton University Press.

Latour, Bruno. 2018. *Down to Earth: Politics in the New Climatic Regime*. English edition. Cambridge, UK: Polity Press.
Law, John. 1986. "On the Methods of Long Distance Control: Vessels, Navigation, and the Portuguese Route to India." In *Power, Action and Belief: A New Sociology of Knowledge?*, edited by John Law, 234–63. London: Routledge, Henley.
Law, John. 1990. "Power, Discretion and Strategy." *The Sociological Review* 38 (1):165–91. doi: 10.1111/j.1467-954X.1990.tb03352.x.
Law, John. 2009. "Actor Network Theory and Material Semiotics." In *The New Blackwell Companion to Social Theory*, edited by Bryan S. Turner, 141–58. Oxford: Wiley-Blackwell.
Law, John, and Annemarie Mol. 2001. "Situating Technoscience: An Inquiry into Spatialities." *Environment and Planning D: Society and Space* 19 (5):609–21. doi: 10.1068/d243t.
Law, John, and Annemarie Mol. 2002. *Complexities: Social Studies of Knowledge Practices*. Durham, NC: Duke University.
Lee, Nick, and Steve Brown. 1994. "Otherness and the Actor Network: The Undiscovered Continent." *American Behavioral Scientist* 37 (6): 772–90. doi: 10.1177/0002764294037006005.
Lefebvre, Henri. 1991 (1947). *The Critique of Everyday Life*. Translated by John Moore. Vol. 1. London: Verso.
Lefebvre, Henri. 2005. *The Urban Revolution*. Minneapolis: Minnesota University Press.
Lefebvre, Henri. 2013. *Rhythmanalysis: Space, Time and Everyday Life*. Translated by Gerald Moore and Stuart Elden. London: Bloomsbury.
Lefebvre, Henri. 1992. *The Production of Space*: Wiley-Blackwell.
Legg, Stephen, and Alexander Vasudevan. 2011. "Introduction." In *Spatiality, Sovereignty and Carl Schmitt: Geographies of the Nomos*, 1–18. London; New York: Routledge.
Leopold, Aldo. 1949. *A Sand County Almanac, and Sketches Here and There*. New York: Oxford University Press.
Levi, Primo. 1991. *If This is a Man*. London: Abacus.
Levinas, Emanuel. 1990. *Difficile liberté : essais sur le judaïsme*. Paris: Albin Michel.
Levitas, Ruth. 2011. *The Concept of Utopia*. Student ed.New York: Witney: Peter Lang.
Levitas, Ruth. 2013. *Utopia as Method: The Imaginary Reconstitution of Society*. London: Palgrave Macmillan.
Levitas, Ruth. 2017. *Where There Is No Vision, the People Perish: A Utopian Ethic for a Transformed Future*. London, UK: Center for the Understanding of Sustainable Prosperity.
Lewis, M. J. T. 2001. "Railways in the Greek and Roman World." In *Early Railways. A Selection of Papers from the First International Early Railways Conference*, edited by A. Guy and J. Rees, 8–19. London: Newcomen Society.
Lindegaard, Laura Bang. 2016. "The Discursive Accomplishment of Rationalities in the Automobility Regime." In *The Mobilities Paradigm: Discourses and*

Ideologies, edited by Marcel Endres, Katharina Manderscheid and Christophe Mincke. London: Routledge.
Lindenlauf, Astrid. 2014. "Agora in the Greek World." In *Encyclopedia of Global Archaeology*, edited by Claire Smith, 69–78. New York: Springer New York.
Lipson, Hod, and Melba Kurman. 2016. *Driverless: Intelligent Cars and the Road Ahead*. Cambridge, MA: MIT Press.
Litman, Todd. 2019. "Autonomous Vehicle Implementation Predictions: Implications for Transport Planning." Victoria Transport Policy Institute.
Ljung, Michael. 2002. "DREAM – Driving Reliability and Error Analysis Method." Masters, Linköping University.
Loberg, Molly. 2018. *The Struggle for the Streets of Berlin*. Cambridge, UK: Cambridge University Press.
Löfgren, Karl C., and William R. Webster. 2020. "The Value of Big Data in Government: The Case of 'Smart Cities.'" *Big Data & Society* 7 (1): 2053951720912775. doi: 10.1177/2053951720912775.
Löfgren, Orvar. 2008. "Motion and Emotion: Learning to be a Railway Traveller." *Mobilities* 3 (3): 331–51. doi: 10.1080/17450100802376696.
Longino, Helen E. 2020. "Afterword: Data in Transit." In *Data Journeys in the Sciences*, edited by Sabina Leonelli and Niccolò Tempini, 391–99. Cham: Springer International Publishing.
Luhmann, Niklas. 1995. *Writing Science*. Standford, CA: Standford University Press.
Lukács, Georg. 1972. *History and Class Consciousness: Studies in Marxist Dialectics*. Cambridge, MA: MIT Press.
Lupton, Deborah. 1999. "Monsters in Metal Cocoons: 'Road Rage' and Cyborg Bodies." *Body & Society* 5: 57–72. doi: 10.1177/1357034X99005001005.
Lynas, Mark. 2020. *Our Final Warning: Six Degrees of Climate Emergency*. London: 4th Estate.
Maier, Charles S. 2016. *Once Within Borders: Territories of Power, Wealth, and Belonging since 1500*. Cambridge, MA: The Belknap Press of Harvard University Press.
Maier, Hans. 2007. "Political Religion: A Concept and its Limitations." *Totalitarian Movements and Political Religions* 8 (1): 5–16. doi: 10.1080/14690760601121614.
The Manchester Guardian. 1896. "Bridget Driscoll, on a day trip to Crystal Palace, was bewildered by the car's approach, got in its way and was knocked down." Accessed 20 Oct 2020. https://www.theguardian.com/world/2014/aug/26/uk-first-fatal-car-accident-archive-1896.
Manderscheid, Katharina. 2012. "Automobilität als raumkonstituierendes Dispositiv der Modeme." In *Die Ordnung der Räume*, edited by H Füller and B Michel, 145–78. Münster: Westphälisches Dampfboot.
Manderscheid, Katharina. 2016. "Who Does the Move?" In *The Mobilities Paradigm: Discourses and Ideologies*, edited by Marcel Endres, Katharina Manderscheid and Christophe Mincke. London: Routledge.
Manderscheid, Katharina 2014. "The Movement Problem, the Car and Future Mobility Regimes: Automobility as Dispositif and Mode of Regulation." *Mobilities* 9 (4): 604–26. doi: 10.1080/17450101.2014.961257.

Marcus, George E. 1995. *Technoscientific Imaginaries: Conversations, Profiles, and Memoirs*. Chicago: University of Chicago Press.
Marinetti, Filippo Tommaso. 1909. "The Futurist Manifesto." https://www.society-forasianart.org/sites/default/files/manifesto_futurista.pdf.
Martens, Karel. 2016. *Transport Justice: Designing Fair Transportation Systems*. New York: Routledge.
Marx, Karl. 1973. *Grundrisse*. Translated by Martin Nicolaus. London: Penguin.
Marx, Karl. 1976. "Capital. Vol 1." *Pelican Marx Library*.
Marx, Karl. 1977. *Economic and Philosophic Manuscripts of 1844*. 5th rev ed. Moscow: Progress Publishers.
Marx, Karl, and Friedrich Engels. 1976a. "The Communist Manifesto." In *Collected Works*, 477–519. London: Lawrence and Wishart.
Marx, Karl, and Friedrich Engels. 1976b. *The German Ideology*. 3rd. Rev. ed. [S.l.]: Progress Pubs.
Massey, Doreen. 1994. *Space, Place and Gender*. Minneapolis: University of Minnesota Press.
Massey, Doreen. 2005. *For Space*. London: Sage.
Massey, Doreen. 2009. "Concepts of Space and Power in Theory and in Political Practice." *Documents d'Anàlisi Geogràfica* 55: 15–26.
Mate, Geraldine, and Celmara Pocock. 2018. "A Disconnected Journey." *International Journal of Heritage Studies* 24 (4): 374–89.
Mathieson, Charloette. 2015. "'Flying From the Grasp': Embodying the Railway Journey." In *Mobility in the Victorian Novel*, 57–86. London: Palgrave Macmillan.
May, Jon, and Nigel Thrift. 2001. "Introduction." In *Timespace: Geographies of temporality*, edited by Jon May and Nigel Thrift, 1–46. New York: Routledge.
McCarthy, Tom. 2007. *Auto Mania: Cars, Consumers, and the Environment*. New Haven, CT; London: Yale University Press.
McCright, Aaron M., and Riley E. Dunlap. 2003. "Defeating Kyoto: The Conservative Movement's Impact on U.S. Climate Change Policy." *Social Problems* 50 (3): 348. doi: 10.1525/sp.2003.50.3.348.
McDonough, Thomas F. 1994. "Situationist Space." *October* 67: 58–77.
McIlvenny, Paul. 2019. "How Did the Mobility Scooter Cross the Road? Coordinating with Co-Movers and Other Movers in Traffic." *Language & Communication* 65: 105–30.
McKibben, Bill. 2020. "130 Degrees." *New York Review of Books*. August 20.
McKinsey & Company. 2013. *The Road to 2020 and Beyond: What's driving the global automotive industry?*
McNeill, William. 1982. "The Industrialization of War." *Review of International Studies* 8 (3): 203–13.
McShane, Clay. 1994. *Down the Asphalt Path: The Automobile and the American City*. New York: Columbia University Press.
The Melbourne Age. 2008. "Angry Driver Takes out 50-Strong Cycle Pack." May 8.
Menge, Torsten. 2019. "Violence and the Materiality of Power." *Critical Review of International Social and Political Philosophy*: 1–26. doi: 10.1080/13698230.2019.1700344.

Mercedes-Benz. 2020. "Autonomous." Accessed 20 Oct. https://www.mercedes-benz.com/en/exhibitions/iaa/autonomous/.

Merleau-Ponty, Maurice. 2012. *Phenomenology of Perception*. London: Routledge.

Merriman, Peter. 2009. "Automobility and the Geographies of the Car." *Geography Compass* 3 (2): 586–99. doi: 10.1111/j.1749-8198.2009.00219.x.

Merriman, Peter, and Lynne Pearce. 2017. "Mobility and the Humanities." *Mobilities* 12 (4): 493–508.

Miller, Clark A. 2015. "Globalizing Security: Science and the Transformation of Contemporary Political Imagination." In *Dreamscapes of Modernity: Sociotechnical Imaginaries and the Fabrication of Power*, edited by Sheila Jasanoff and Sang-Hyun Kim, 277–99. Chicago: University of Chicago Press.

Mills, C. Wright. 1959. *The Sociological Imagination*. New York: Oxford University Press.

Minca, Claudio, and Rory Rowan. 2015. *On Schmitt and Space, Interventions*. New York: Routledge.

Mitchell, Timothy. 2013. *Carbon Democracy: Political Power in the Age of Oil*. London: Verso.

Mitchell, Timothy 2020. "The Body Politic that Captured the Future." In *A Book of the Body Politic: Connecting Biology, Politics and Social Theory*, edited by Bruno Latour, Simon Schaffer and Pasquale Gagliardi, 49–59. Fondazione Giorgio Cini.

Mladenović, Miloš N., Dominic Stead, Dimitris Milakis, Kate Pangbourne and Moshe Givoni. 2020. "Governance Cultures and Sociotechnical Imaginaries of Self-Driving Vehicle Technology: Comparative Analysis of Finland, UK and Germany." *Advances in Transport Policy and Planning* 5: 235–62. doi: 10.1016/bs.atpp.2020.01.001.

Mol, Annemarie. 1999. "Ontological Politics: A Word and Some Questions." *The Sociological Review* 47: 74–89. doi: 10.1111/j.1467-954X.1999.tb03483.x.

Mol, Annemarie, and John Law. 1994. "Regions, Networks and Fluids: Anaemia and Social Topology." *Social Studies of Science* 24 (4): 641–71. doi: 10.1177/030631279402400402.

Mommsen, Hans. 1991. *From Weimar to Auschwitz*. Translated by Philip O'Conner. Princeton, NJ: Princeton University Press.

Moore, Charles. 2015. *Margaret Thatcher: The Authorized Biography, Volume Two: Everything She Wants*. London ed: Penguin.

Moraglio, Massimo 2017. *Driving Modernity: Technology, Experts, Politics, and Fascist Motorways, 1922–1943*. Translated by Erin O'Loughlin. Oxford: Berghahn.

Morris, Blake, and Rose Morag. 2019. "Pedestrian Provocations: Manifesting an Accessible Future." *Global Performance Studies* 2 (2).

Möser, Kurt. 2003. "The Dark Side of 'Automobilism', 1900–30." *Journal of Transport History* 24: 238–58.

Mumford, Lewis. 1957. "Babel in Europe." *New Yorker*.

Mumford, Lewis. 1961. *The City In History: Its Origins, Its Transformations, and Its Prospects, Harvest/HBJ book*. New York: Harcourt Brace Jovanovich.

Mumford, Lewis. 1963. *The Highway and the City*. New York: Harcourt, Brace.

Muniz Jr., Albert. M., and Thomas C. O'Guinn. 2001. "Brand Community." *Journal of Consumer Research* 27 (4): 412–32.

Murphy, Ann V. 2012. *Violence and the Philosophical Imaginary*. New York: State University of New York Press.

Nader, Ralph. 1965. *Unsafe at Any Speed: The Designed-in Dangers of the American Automobile*. New York: Grossman.

National Trust. No Date. "Mary Ward." https://www.nationaltrust.org.uk/castle-ward/features/mary-ward.

Neiman, Susan. 2019. *Learning from the Germans: Confronting Race and the Memory of Evil*. New York: Farrar, Straus and Giroux.

Neumann, Boaz. 2009. "The Phenomenology of the German People's Body (Volkskörper) and the Extermination of the Jewish Body." *New German Critique* (106): 149–81.

NHTSA, National Highway Traffic Safety Administration. 2015. *National Motor Vehicle Crash Causation Report*. Washington, DC: US Department of Transportation.

Nicholson, Judith A. 2016. "Don't Shoot! Black Mobilities in American Gunscapes." *Mobilities* 11 (4): 553–63. doi: 10.1080/17450101.2016.1211823.

Nikolaeva, Anna, Peter Adey, Tim Cresswell, Jane Yeonjae Lee, Andre Nóvoa, and Cristina Temenos. 2019. "Commoning Mobility: Towards a New Politics of Mobility Transitions." *Transactions of the Institute of British Geographers* 44 (2): 346–60. doi: 10.1111/tran.12287.

Noland, Robert B. 2013. "From Theory to Practice in Road Safety Policy: Understanding Risk versus Mobility." *Research in Transportation Economics* 43 (1): 71–84.

Nora, Pierre. 1998. *Realms of Memory: Rethinking the French Past*. Chicago: University of Chicago Press.

North American International Auto Show. 2019. "AutoMobili-D." Accessed 20 Oct. https://naias.com/planetm-exhibition.

Norton, Peter D. 2007. "Street Rivals: Jaywalking and the Invention of the Motor Age Street." *Technology and Culture* 48 (2): 331–59.

Norton, Peter D. 2008. *Fighting Traffic: The Dawn of the Motor Age in the American city*. Cambridge, MA: MIT Press.

Novitzky, Peter, Michael J. Bernstein, Vincent Blok, Robert Braun, Tung Tung Chan, Wout Lamers, Anne Loeber, Ingeborg Meijer, Ralf Lindner, and Erich Griessler. 2020. "Improve Alignment of Research Policy and Societal Values." *Science* 369 (6499): 39–41. doi: 10.1126/science.abb3415.

O'Malley, Pat. 2010. "Simulated Justice: Risk, Money and Telemetric Policing." *The British Journal of Criminology* 50 (5): 795–807. doi: 10.1093/bjc/azq036.

Odysseos, Louiza, and Fabio Petito. 2007. *The International Political Thought of Carl Schmitt: Terror, Liberal War and the Crisis of Global Order*, Routledge Innovations in Political Theory. London; New York: Routledge.

Ojakangas, Mika. 2005. "Impossible Dialogue on Bio-power: Agamben and Foucault." *Foucault Studies* 2 (May).

Oster, Sharon B. 2014. "Impossible Holocaust Metaphors: The Muselmann." *Prooftexts* 34 (3): 302–48.

Ostler, Jeffrey. 2019. *Surviving Genocide: Native Nations and the United States from the American Revolution to Bleeding Kansas.* New Haven, CT: Yale University Press.

Ostrom, Elinor. 1990. *Governing the Commons: The Evolution of Institutions for Collective Action.* Cambridge, UK: Cambridge University Press.

Packard, Vance. 1961. *The Waste Makers.* New York: D. McKay Co.

Parsons, Talcott, Robert Bales, and Edward Shils. 1953. *Working Papers in the Theory of Action.* New York: The Free Press.

Parsons, Talcott, and Edward A Shils. 1962. *Toward a General Theory of Action.* New York: Harper Torchbooks.

Paterson, Matthew. 2007. *Automobile Politics: Ecology and Cultural Political Economy.* Cambridge, UK: Cambridge University Press.

Pattinson, Jo-Ann, Haibo Chen, and Subhajit Basu. 2020. "Legal Issues in Automated Vehicles: Critically Considering the Potential Role of Consent and Interactive Digital Interfaces." *Humanities and Social Sciences Communications* 7 (1): 153. doi: 10.1057/s41599-020-00644-2.

Paulsson, R. 2005. "Deliverable 5.2: In-depth Accident Causation Data Study Methodology Development Report." In *SafetyNet.*

Pearce, Lynne. 2012. "Automobility in Manchester Fiction." *Mobilities* 7: 93–113. doi: 10.1080/17450101.2012.631813.

Pellow, David Naguib, and Robert J. Brulle. 2007. "Poisoning the Planet: The Struggle for Environmental Justice." *Contexts* 6 (1): 37–41. doi: 10.1525/ctx.2007.6.1.37.

Pesses, Michael W. 2017. "Road Less Traveled: Race and American Automobility." *Mobilities* 12: 677–91.

Petridou, E., and M. Moustaki. 2000. "Human Factors in the Causation of Road Traffic Crashes." *Eurporean Journal of Epidemiology* 16 (9): 819–26. doi: 10.1023/A:1007649804201.

Pettegrew, David K. 2016. *The Isthmus of Corinth.* Ann Arbor: University of Michigan Press.

Plant, Sadie. 1992. *The Most Radical Gesture.* London: Routledge.

Pordzik, Ralph. 2009. *Futurescapes: space in utopian and science fiction discourses.* Amsterdam: Rodopi.

Porter, Bryan E. (ed.). 2012. *Handbook of Traffic Psychology.* Amsterdam: Elsevier.

Porter, Theodore M. 2020. "Most Often, What Is Transmitted Is Transformed." In *Data Journeys in the Sciences*, edited by Sabina Leonelli and Niccolò Tempini, 229–36. Cham: Springer International Publishing.

Preus, Christian Abraham. 2012. "The Art of Aeschines: Anti-Rhetorical Argumentation in the Speeches of Aeschines." PhD, Classics, University of Iowa.

Prigogine, Ilya. 1997. *The End of Certainty: Time, Chaos, and the New Laws of Nature.* New York: The Free Press.

Puricelli, Piero. 1922. *Rete stradale per autoveicoli Milano–Lago di Como Milano–Varese–Milano–Lago Maggiore, Relazione.* Milano: Umberto Grioni.

Rainey, Lawrence, Christine Poggi, and Laura Wittman. 2009. *Futurism: An Anthology.* New Haven, CT; London: Yale University Press.

Rajan, Sudhir Chella. 1996. *The Enigma of Automobility: Democratic Politics and Pollution Control*. Pittsburgh, PA: University of Pittsburgh Press.

Randell, Richard. 2017. "The Microsociology of Automobility: The Production of the Automobile Self." *Mobilities* 12 (5): 663–76. doi: 10.1080/17450101.2016.1176776.

Randell, Richard. 2020a. "The Cathedrals of Automobility: How to Read a Motor Show." In *Material Mobilities*, edited by Ole B. Jensen, Claus Lassen and Ida Sofie Gøtzsche Lange. London: Routledge.

Randell, Richard. 2020b. "No Paradigm to Mobilize: The New Mobilities Paradigm is Not a Paradigm." *Applied Mobilities* 5 (2): 206–23. doi: 10.1080/23800127.2018.1493063.

Reason, James. 2000. "Human Error: Models and Management." *BMJ* 320 (7237):768–70. doi: 10.1136/bmj.320.7237.768.

Reid, Amanda. 2015. "Place, Meaning, and the Visual Argument of the Roadside Cross." *Savannah Law Review* 2 (265).

Richardson, Tina. 2015. *Walking Inside Out: Contemporary British Psychogeography*. London: Rowman & Littlefield International.

Ricoeur, Paul. 1970. *Freud and Philosophy: An Essay on Interpretation*. New Haven, CT: Yale University Press.

Rieger, Bernhard. 2013. *The People's Car: A Global History of the Volkswagen Beetle*. Cambridge, MA; London: Harvard University Press.

Rochet, Guénot et Mesnager. 1900. "Rapport sur l'automobilisme." In *Bulletin de la Société d'encouragement pour l'industrie nationale*. Paris.

Rogoff, Seth. 2018. "Freud's Conquest of the Dreamscape: Legibility and Power in Freud's 'Specimen Dream'." In *Legibility in the Age of Signs and Machines*, edited by P. Hesselberth, J. Houwen, E. In Peeren, and R. Vos, (2018). 51–65. Leiden: Brill.

Rolfes, Steven J., and Douglas R. Weise. 2014. *Cincinnati Art Deco*. Mount Pleasant, NC: Arcadia Publishing.

Rorty, Richard. 1982a. *Consequences of Pragmatism*. Minneaplois: University of Minnesota Press.

Rorty, Richard. 1982b. "Philosophy as a Kind of Writing: An Essay on Derrida." In *Consequences of Pragmatism*. Minneapolis: University of Minnesota Press.

Rorty, Richard. 1989. *Contingency, Irony, and Solidarity*. Cambridge, UK: Cambridge University Press.

Rose, Morag. 2006. "The LRM." LRM, accessed 22.02.2021. http://thelrm.org/index.

Rowan, Rory. 2011. "A New Nomos of Post-Nomos?" In *Spatiality, Sovereignty and Carl Schmitt: Geographies of the Nomos*, edited by Stephen Legg, xiv, 306. London: Routledge.

Rubinstein, Lene. 1998. "The Athenian Political Perception of the Idiotes." *Kosmos: Essays in Order, Conflict, and Community in Classical Athens*: 125–43.

Ryan, Kevin. 2018. "Refiguring Childhood: Hannah Arendt, Natality and Prefigurative Biopolitics." *Childhood* 25 (3): 297–310. doi: 10.1177/0907568218777302.

Salmon, Paul M., Michael G. Lenné, Neville A. Stanton, Daniel P. Jenkins, and Guy H. Walker. 2010. "Managing Error on the Open Road: The Contribution of Human Error Models and Methods." *Safety Science* 48 (10): 1225–35.

Salzani, Carlo. 2015. "From Benjamin's *bloßes Leben* to Agamben's Nuda Vita: A Genealogy." In *Towards the Critique of Violence: Walter Benjamin and Giorgio Agamben*, edited by Brendan Moran and Carlo Salzani, 1 online resource (xii, 251 pages). London: Bloomsbury Academic.

Sanders, Guy D. R. 1996. "Portage of Ships Across the Isthmus." *Tropis* 4: 423–28.

Sant'Elia, Antonio 1914. "Manifesto of Futurist Architecture." https://evolutionaryurbanism.com/2017/02/28/manifesto-of-futurist-architecture/.

Savat, David. 2013. "The Human-Machine Assemblage." In *Uncoding the Digital: Technology, Subjectivity and Action in the Control Society*, 63–82. London: Palgrave Macmillan UK.

Schepers, Paul, Marjan Hagenzieker, Rob Methorst, Bert van Wee, and Fred Wegman. 2014. "A Conceptual Framework for Road Safety and Mobility Applied to Cycling Safety." *Accident Analysis & Prevention* 62: 331–40.

Schivelbusch, Wolfgang. 2014. *The Railway Journey: The Industrialization of Time and Space in the Nineteenth*. Berkeley: University of California Press.

Schmitt, Carl. 1923. "Soziologie des Souveränitätsbegriffes und politische Theologie." In *Hauptprobleme der Soziologie: Erinnerungsgabe für Max Weber*, edited by Melchior Palyi, 3–35. München: Duncker & Humblot.

Schmitt, Carl. 2001. *Land und Meer: eine weltgeschichtliche Betrachtung*. Stuttgart: Klett-Cotta. Original edition, 1942.

Schmitt, Carl. 2003. *The Nomos of the Earth in the International Law of the Jus Publicum Europaeum*. Edited by G. L. Ulmen. New York: Telos Press. Original edition, 1950.

Schmitt, Carl. 2004. *The Theory of the Partisan: A Commentary/Remark on the Concept of the Political*. Translated by A. C. Goodson. Ann Arbor: Michigan State University Press.

Schmitt, Carl. 2005. *Political Theology: Four Chapters on the Concept of Sovereignty*. University of Chicago Press ed. Chicago: University of Chicago Press.

Schmitt, Carl. 2015. *Land and Sea: A World-historical Meditation*. Candor, NY: Telos Press Publishing.

Searle, John R. 2018. "Constitutive Rules." *Argumenta* 4 (1): 51–4. doi: 0.14275/2465-2334/20187.sea.

Seo, Sarah A. 2019. *Policing the Open Road: How Cars Transformed American Freedom*. Cambridge, MA: Harvard University Press.

Sheller, Mimi. 2014. "The New Mobilities Paradigm for a Live Sociology." *Current Sociology* 62: 789–811.

Sheller, Mimi. 2018. *Mobility Justice: The Politics of Movement in an Age of Extremes*. London: Verso.

Sheller, Mimi, and John Urry. 2000. "The City and the Car." *International Journal of Urban and Regional Research* 24 (4): 737–57. doi: 10.1111/1468-2427.00276.

Sheller, Mimi, and John Urry. 2006. "The New Mobilities Paradigm." *Environment and Planning A: Economy and Space* 38 (2): 207–26. doi: 10.1068/a37268.

Sheller, Mimi, and John Urry. 2016. "Mobilizing the New Mobilities Paradigm." *Applied Mobilities* 1 (1): 10–25. doi: 10.1080/23800127.2016.1151216.

Short, John Rennie, and Luis Pinet-Peralta. 2010. "No Accident: Traffic and Pedestrians in the Modern City." *Mobilities* 5: 41–59. doi: 10.1080/17450100903434998.
Singh, Santokh. 2015. *Critical Reasons for Crashes Investigated in the National Motor Vehicle Crash Causation Survey*. Washington DC: National Highway Traffic Safety Administration.
Singh, Santokh. 2018. *Critical Reasons for Crashes Investigated in the National Motor Vehicle Crash Causation Survey*. Washington, DC: National Highway Traffic Safety Administration.
Sitze, Adam. 2015. "Introduction." In *Janus's Gaze: Essays on Carl Schmitt*, edited by Carlo Galli. Durham NC: Duke University Press.
Soja, Edward W. 1989. *Postmodern Geographies. The Reassertion of Space in Critical Social Theory*. London: Verso.
Soja, Edward W. 1996. *Thirdspace: journeys to Los Angeles and other real-and-imagined places*. Cambridge, MA: Blackwell.
Solomon, Brian. 2015. *Railway Depots, Stations & Terminals*. Hull, Canada: Voyageur Press.
Sorin, Gretchen Sullivan. 2020. *Driving while Black: African American Travel and the Road to Civil Rights*. New York: Liveright Publishing Corporation.
Spiteri, Raymond. 2015. "From Unitary Urbanism to the Society of the Spectacle: The Situationist Aesthetic Revolution." In *Aesthetic Revolutions and Twentieth-Century Avant-Garde Movements*, edited by Aleš Erjavec. Durham, NC: Duke University Press.
Spivak, Gayatri Chakravorty. 1988. "Can the Subaltern Speak?" In *Colonial Discourse and Post-Colonial Theory*, edited by Patrick Williams and Laura Chrisman, 66–111. New York: Columbia University Press.
Stanton, Neville A., and Paul M. Salmon. 2009. "Human Error Taxonomies Applied to Driving: A Generic Driver Error Taxonomy and its Implications for Intelligent Transport Systems." *Safety Science* 47 (2): 227–37.
Stilgoe, Jack. 2018. "Machine Learning, Social Learning and the Governance of Self-Driving Cars." *Social Studies of Science* 48 (1): 25–56.
Strauss, Claudia. 2006. "The Imaginary." *Anthropological Theory* 6: 322–44.
Streeck, Wolfgang. 2016. *How Will Capitalism End?: Essays on a Failing System*. London: Verso.
Sumantran, Venkat, Charles Fine, and David Gonsalvez. 2017. *Faster, Smarter, Greener: The Future of the Car and Urban Mobility*. Cambridge, MA: MIT Press.
Taylor, Charles. 2004. *Modern Social Imaginaries, Modern Social Imaginaries*. Durham, NC: Duke University Press.
Taylor, Lisa, and Boff Whalley. 2018. "Real Change Comes from Below!': Walking and Singing about Places that Matter; the Formation of Commoners Choir." *Leisure Studies* 38: 58–73. doi: 10.1080/02614367.2018.1521465.
Taylor, Nigel. 2003. "The Aesthetic Experience of Traffic in the Modern City." *Urban Studies* 40 (8): 1609–25.
Thomas, Pete, Andrew Morris, Rachel Talbot, and Helen Fagerlind. 2013. "Identifying the Causes of Road Crashes in Europe." *Annals of Advances in Automotive Medicine* 57 (September 22–25):13–22.

Thornton, Robert. 2002. "The Peculiar Temporality of Violence: a Source of Perplexity about Social Power." *KronoScope* 2 (1): 41–69. doi: 10.1163/15685240260186790.

Thrift, Nigel. 1994. "Globalisation, Regulation, Urbanisation: The Case of the Netherlands." *Urban Studies* 31 (3): 365–80. doi: 10.1080/00420989420080381.

Thrift, Nigel. 1996. *Spatial Formations*. London: Sage.

Thrift, Nigel. 2004. "Driving in the City." *Theory, Culture & Society* 21: 41–59. doi: 10.1177/0263276404046060.

Thrift, Nigel. 2007. "Overcome by Space: Reworking Foucault." In *Space, Knowledge and Power: Foucault and Geography*, 53–58. Farnham, UK: Ashgate.

Thrift, Nigel, and Steve Pile. 1995. "Mapping the Subject." In *Mapping the Subject: Geographies of Cultural Transformation*, edited by Nigel Thrift and Steve Pile, 13–56. London: Routledge.

Times of India. 2019. "93% accidents in HP caused due to human error." *Times of India*, Jun 13, 2019, 07:06 IST. Accessed 1 Sept, 2020. https://timesofindia.indiatimes.com/city/shimla/93-accidents-in-hp-caused-due-to-human-error/articleshow/69763927.cms.

Topham, Gwyn 2020. "Self-driving cars could be allowed on UK motorways next year." *The Guardian*, August 18. https://www.theguardian.com/technology/2020/aug/18/self-driving-cars-allowed-motorways-industry-risk.

Treat, John R., N. John Castellan, R. L. Stansifer, R. E. Mayer, Rex D. Hume, David Shinar, Stephen T. McDonald and Nicholas S. Tumbas. 1977a. *Tri-level study of the causes of traffic accidents: final report. Volume I: causal factor tabulations and assessments*. Bloomington: Indiana University Press.

Treat, John R., N. John Castellan, R. L. Stansifer, R. E. Mayer, Rex D. Hume, David Shinar, Stephen T. McDonald, and Nicholas S. Tumbas. 1977b. *Tri-level study of the causes of traffic accidents: final report. Volume II: special analyses*. Bloomington: Indiana University Press.

Treat, John R., N. John Castellan, R. L. Stansifer, R. E. Mayer, Rex D. Hume, David Shinar, Stephen T. McDonald, Nicholas S. Tumbas, United States. National Highway Traffic Safety Administration., and University of Michigan. Library. Deep Blue. 1979. *Tri-level study of the causes of traffic accidents: final report. Executive summary*. Bloomington: Indiana University Press.

Trier, James 2019. *Guy Debord, the Situationist International, and the Revolutionary Spirit*. Leiden: Brill.

Tully, James. 1988. *Meaning and Context: Quentin Skinner and His Critics*. New Haven, CT: University of Yale Press.

Tumarkin, Maria 2005. *Traumascapes: The Power and Fate of Places Transformed by Tragedy*. Melbourne: Melbourne University Publishing.

United States Central Intelligence Agency. "World Fact Book." https://www.cia.gov/library/publications/the-world-factbook/rankorder/2085rank.html.

United States Department of Transportation, National Highway Traffic Safety Administration. 2008. "National Motor Vehicle Crash Causation Survey (NMVCCS) Field coding manual." In Washington, DC: US Deptarement of Trasportation, National Highway Traffic Safety Administration. http://www-nrd.nhtsa.dot.gov/Pubs/811051.PDF.

United States National Highway Traffic Safety Administration. 2008. "National Motor Vehicle Crash Causation Survey Report to Congress." In Washington, DC: US Deptarement of Trasportation, National Highway Traffic Safety Administration. http://www-nrd.nhtsa.dot.gov/Pubs/811059.PDF.
Urry, John. 1994. "Time, Leisure and Social Identity." *Time & Society* 3 (2):131–49. doi: 10.1177/0961463x94003002001.
Urry, John. 2000. *Sociology Beyond Societies*. London: Routledge.
Urry, John. 2004. "The 'System' of Automobility." *Theory, Culture & Society* 21 (4–5): 25–39. doi: 10.1177/0263276404046059.
Urry, John. 2005a. "The Complexities of the Global." *Theory, Culture & Society* 22:235–54.
Urry, John. 2005b. "The Complexity Turn." *Theory, Culture & Society* 22:1–14.
Urry, John. 2006. "Inhabiting the Car." *Sociological Review* 54 (1): 17–31. doi: 10.1111/j.1467-954x.2006.00635.x.
Urry, John. 2007. *Mobilities*. New York: Wiley.
Vaneigem, Raoul 1983. *The Revolution of Everyday Life*. London: Left Bank Books and Rebel Press. Original edition, 1967.
Vattimo, Gianni. 1984. "La situazione della filosofia." In *Enciclopedia Europea*. Milan: Garzanti.
Verbeek, P. 2005. *What Things Do: Philosophical Reflections on Technology, Agency, and Design*. University Park, PA: Penn State University Press.
Victoria and Albert Museum. 2019. "About Cars Accelerating the Modern World." accessed 03 November. https://www.vam.ac.uk/articles/about-the-cars-accelerating-the-modern-world-exhibition.
Virilio, Paul. 2006. *Speed and Politics*. Cambridge, MA: MIT Press.
Virilio, Paul. 2007a. *Open Sky*. Translated by Julie Rose. London: Verso.
Virilio, Paul. 2007b. *The Original Accident*. Translated by Julie Rose. Cambridge, UK: Polity Press.
Virilio, Paul. 2012. *The Administration of Fear, Semiotext(e)*. Cambridge, MA: MIT Press.
Voegelin, Eric. 2000 (1938). "Modernity without Restraint." In *The Collected Works of Eric Voegelin*, edited by M. Henningsen. Columbia: University of Missouri Press.
Vohra, Karn, Alina Vodonos, Joel Schwartz, Eloise A. Marais, Melissa P. Sulprizio, and Loretta J. Mickley. 2021. "Global Mortality from Outdoor Fine Particle Pollution Generated by Fossil Fuel Combustion: Results from GEOS-Chem." *Environmental Research* 195: 110754. doi: 10.1016/j.envres.2021.110754.
Wacquant, Loïc. 2016. "A Concise Genealogy and Anatomy of Habitus." *The Sociological Review* 64 (1): 64–72. doi: 10.1111/1467-954X.12356.
Wadhwa, Vivek, and Alex Salkever. 2017. *The Driver in the Driverless Car: How Our Technology Choices Will Create the Future*. Oakland, CA: Berrett-Koehler.
Walker-Smith, Brian. 2013. "Human Error as the Cause of Vehicle Crashes." 1 September. http://cyberlaw.stanford.edu/blog/2013/12/human-error-cause-vehicle-crashes.

Walks, Alan. 2015. "Driving Cities: Automobility, Neoliberalism, andUrban Transformation." In *The Urban Political Economy and Ecology of Automobility*, edited by Alan Walks, 3–20. New York: Routledge.
Wallerstein, Immanuel Maurice. 2004. *World-Systems Analysis: An Introduction*. Durham, NC: Duke University Press.
Walsh, Philip. 2011. "The Human Condition as Social Ontology: Hannah Arendt on Society, Action and Knowledge." *History of the Human Sciences* 24 (2): 120–37. doi: 10.1177/0952695110396289.
Walter, E. 1964. "Power and Violence." *American Political Science Review* 58 (2): 350–60. doi: 10.2307/1952867.
Warner, H. W., M. Ljung Aust, J. Sandin, E. Johansson, and G. Björklund. 2008. "DREAM 3.0, Driving Reliability and Error Analysis Method."
Watkins-Hughes, Peter 2009. *Cow* (movie trailer).
Weber, Max. 1925. *Wirtchaftsgeschichte: Abriss der universalen Sozial- und Wirtchaftgeschichte*. Munich und Leipzig.
Werfel, Franz. 1946. "Können wir ohne Gottesglauben leben?" In *Zwischen oben und unten*, 65–148. Stockholm.
Whitehead, Alfred North, and Oliver Wendell Holmes Collection (Library of Congress). 1925. *Science and the Modern World. Lowell Lectures, 1925*. New York: The Macmillan Company.
Williams, Richard. 2020. *Race With Love and Death: The Story of Richard Seaman*. London: Simon & Schuster.
Wilson, Thomas P., and Don H. Zimmerman. 1979. "Ethnomethodology, Sociology and Theory." *Humboldt Journal of Social Relations* 7: 52–88.
Wittgenstein, Ludwig. 1953. *Philosophical Investigations*. Translated by G. E. M. Anscombe. Oxford: Basil Blackwell..
Wittgenstein, Ludwig. 2009. *Philosophical Investigations*. Rev. 4th / by P.M.S. Hacker and Joachim Schulte. ed. Chichester: Wiley-Blackwell. Original edition, 1953.
Wittgenstein, Ludwig, and Cyril Barrett. 1967. *Lectures and Conversations on Aesthetics, Psychology, and Religious Belief*. Berkeley: University of California Press.
Wolfe, Patrick. 2006. "Settler Colonialism and the Elimination of the Native." *Journal of Genocide Research* 8 (4): 387–409. doi: 10.1080/14623520601056240.
World Health Organization. 2004. "World report on road traffic injury prevention." Geneva: World Health Organization.
World Health Organization. 2015. "Global status report on road safety." Geneva: World Health Organization.
World Health Organization. 2018. "Global status report on road safety." Geneva: World Health Organization.
Wright, Erik Olin. 2010. *Envisioning Real Utopias*. New York: Verso.
Wyly, Elvin 2014. "The New Quantitative Revolution." *Dialogues in Human Geography* 4 (1): 26–38.
Wynne, Brian. 2005. "Reflexing Complexity: Post-genomic Knowledge and Reductionist Returns in Public Science." *Theory, Culture & Society* 22: 67–94.

Zimmerman, Patricia. 1995. "Boys and Their Indestructible Toys." In *Beyond the Car: Essays on the Auto Culture*, edited by Sue Zielinski and Gordon Laird, 32–39. Toronto: Steel Rail Publishing.

Index

Adhanom Ghebreyesus, Tedros, 161, 162
Adorno, Theodor, 56, 95
Agamben, Giorgio, xxv, 65, 69, 88, 93, 94, 96, 102, 104, 109, 110, 111, 122, 132, 138, 146, 147–149, 157, 164
agones, 61, 62
agora, 61, 62, 68
Althusser, Louis, 16
Anderson, Benedict, 16, 47, 72
annihilation: of space, 50; of space and time, 39, 41, 53, 55, 59, 65, 68, 72, 74; of space by time, 45, 57; of time, 42, 53; of time-space, 57, 58
Anthropocene, xxi, xxvi
Appadurai, Arjun, 72, 73, 78, 79, 154
appropriation of land and space, 88, 91, 99
Arendt, Hannah/Arendtian, xv, xxiv, 56, 58, 59, 62, 98, 99, 124, 148, 150, 152, 153, 155, 163
Aristotle, 119
automobile pollutants, 101
automobile violence, 86, 87, 97
automobility: apparatus, 8, 27; (as) police state, 115, 116; as political religion, 113; avant la lettre, 9, 13, 16; conception/concept of, xxii, 4, 12, 13,15; construction of, xxi, 15, 27; death(s) (and injury), 85, 102, 103, 111, 163; dreamscape, xxv, 71, 78, 83, 86; imaginary/ies, xxii, xxiv, xxvi, 9, 14, 15, 17, 20–30, 33, 55, 59, 69, 75, 82, 83, 110, 115, 122, 128, 131, 132, 134, 140, 145, 146, 153; moral economy of, 95, 96, 163; nomocracy of, 122; regime, 6, 9, 141; studies, xiii, xv, xix–xxii, 3–6, 9, 13, 14, 21, 25, 28, 34, 83, 108, 125, 195, 196; system of, xix, 5–9, 14, 16, 24, 75, 100; violence, 89, 94, 96–99, 103
autonomous: mobility, 7, 135–137, 140; vehicle imaginary, 135
autoscapes, 26, 73, 74, 137
autostrada, 55, 56, 58, 78, 129, 136

Badiou, Alain, 54
Baehr, Peter, 124
bare life, 59, 88, 89, 94, 95, 101, 102, 110, 113, 117, 121, 122, 129, 138, 140, 146–148, 150, 158, 159, 164
Barrett, William, 145
Baudrillard, Jean, 28, 44, 144
Being-in-the-world, xxi, 27, 30, 101, 109, 132, 144, 151
Benjamin, Walter, xv, 44, 58, 98, 153, 156, 157
Bergson, Henri, 42, 54

Bia (Violence), 34, 68
Big Data, 136–139; network, 137; spectacle, 139
biopolitical: constellation, 41; control, 110; control society, 60; governmentality, 149; logics, 59; metropolis, 158; operators, 162; order, 69, 124; power, 59; reality, 129; shift in the political ontology, 122; sovereign(ty), 110
biopolitics, 62, 110, 111, 128, 153
Blaser, Mario, 126
Boccioni, Umberto, 53–55, 114
Böhm, Steffen, xiv, 3–8, 14, 25, 28, 86
Breton, André, 28
Brulle, Robert, 101
Buhrer, Eliza, 157
Burnham, John, C., 13

Callon, Michel, 150
Campbell, Jones, xiv, 3
capitalism, xxiv, 41, 46, 48, 51, 64, 65, 72, 141, 155
Capra, Fritjof, 5
car-driver, 7, 79, 88, 95, 99, 110–113, 115, 122, 135, 141; hybrid, 79, 88, 95, 135
Carrá, Carlo, 53
Castells, Manuel, 123
Chandler, David, xxi, xxvi
Chaplin, Charlie, 48, 63
choros, 61
Christie, Agatha, 44
climate change, 24, 28, 101; crisis, 134; emergency, xiii
Corinth, 36–40, 158; diolkos of, 36, 37, 39, 40, 45, 158; isthmus of, 36–40
Cratos, 33–35, 54
Cresswell, Tim, 153
critical automobility studies, 195
Critical Automobility Studies Lab, 196
Culver, Gregg, 86, 87, 104
cummings, e e, 147, 148
cyborg, 7, 42, 43, 48, 51, 52, 53, 54, 58, 59, 65, 88, 95, 110, 111, 113–115, 117, 121, 122, 137, 141, 150; car-driver, 7, 110, 111, 113, 115, 141; consumer, 58; customer, 48; entity, 43, 51, 95, 111, 137; human-car assemblage, 88; human-machine, xxv, 54, 121, 150; locomotive-body hybrid, 42, 43, 58; locomotive-passenger entity, 43,51; human-machine, 52, 53, 59, 114; techno-human, 65, 87; technology/human, 52; worker, 48

Dadaist, 63, 64
dataspace, 137–139
De Ambris, Alceste, 55
Debord, Guy, xxiv, 51, 62–67
De Certeau, Michel, 62
Deleuze, Gilles, 59–64, 72, 74, 100, 110, 153
Derrida, Jacques/Derridean, xxii, 21, 109, 163
destituent (power/violence), 132, 147–149, 151, 152
destitute, 149, 150, 154, 155, 158, 159; commoning, 150, 158; mobility, 146; modality, 158; partisan(ship), 153; power, 148, 150; resistance, 152, 153
dispositif, 8, 9, 57, 69, 75, 83, 110, 146–155, 157, 158, 159
Dostoevsky, 156
dreams of automobility, 27, 77
dreamscape(s), xxiv, xxv, xxvi, 16–18, 71, 72, 75, 77–84, 86, 107, 109, 114, 128, 129, 137, 146, 148, 158, 159, 162, 163; of modernity, xxiv, 16–18, 72, 78, 84
driver error, 87, 118, 119
dromocracy, xxiv, 33–35, 41, 45, 47, 51, 54, 57, 62, 68, 74–87, 100, 109, 114, 115, 121, 128
dromocratic: automobility, 57; control, 59, 65; era, 52; in-between, 74; lifeworld, 36; military technologies, xxiv; order, 35, 57, 59, 95, 107; revolution, 33, 52, 114, 129; social

order, 55, 65; space, 136; space-time, 41; spectacle, 58, 62, 65, 67–69; speed, 40, 88; technoscientific apparatus, 51; violence, 88, 98
dromologist(s), 33
dromology, 33, 40, 56, 73, 138
dromos, xxiv, xxvi, 33–35, 41, 44, 45, 54, 58, 59, 61, 62, 68, 86, 88, 107, 109, 122, 129, 130, 149, 159, 163
dromoscape, 75
dromoscopic illusion, 39, 40, 158
dromosphere, politics of, 35
Duchamp, Marcel, 63
Durkheim, Émile, 164

ecocide, 163
Edensor, Tim, 73
electric mobility, 133, 134, 136
electric vehicle sociotechnical imaginary, 19, 132, 133, 135, 141
Engels, Friedrich, 46
environmental degradation, 28, 133, 134
environmental destruction, 163
Eris, 71
Esposito, Roberto, 108
Euclidean, 50, 66, 69, 81, 82, 124, 130, 141, 149, 150
Everuss, Louis, 125, 126, 127

fascism/fascist, xxv, 55, 56, 111, 112, 113, 115, 129
Ferrari, Enzo, 144
Flink, James, 10, 13
Fordism, 30, 123
Foucault('s), Michel/Foucauldian, xxi, 7–9, 13, 27, 30, 57, 60, 69, 73, 75, 78, 86, 109, 110, 138, 150
Freud, Sigmund/Freudian, 44, 64, 77–80, 82, 162
Furnas, Joseph, 162
Futurism, 51, 52, 54, 114
Futurist: annihilation of time and space, 53; automobile/driver hybrid, 54; city, 53; movement, 35; revolution, 58; utopia, 78; vision, 129

Futurists, 41, 53–55, 57, 114, 115

Galilei, Galileo, 127, 144
Galli, Carlo, 91
Gentile, Emilio, 113, 115
Goebbels, Joseph, 68
Graham by Patricia Piccini, 114
Green, Matt, xviii, 66, 67, 159
greenhouse gas(es) (GHG) emissions, xiii, 101, 102, 133
Grosz, George, xiv

Haraway, Donna, 18, 42
Hardt, Michael, 152, 155
Haussmannisation, 49
Heidegger, Martin/Heideggerian, xxi, 15, 16, 22, 24, 26, 27, 126, 132, 144, 145, 147, 151
Hephaestus, 34
Hera, 71
Hesiod, 71
Hollnagel, Erik, 120
Hollyband, Claudius, 105
Holston, James, 153, 154
Homer, 61, 71
homo sacer/homines sacri, xxv, 69, 88, 94, 95, 101, 102, 104, 110, 146, 156, 164
hoplitodromos, 34
human error, 96, 97, 118, 119, 120, 135, 136
Husserl, Edmund, 27, 132, 143–145
Hypnos, 71, 72, 77

idios, 155, 157
idiōtēs/idiōtai, 131, 150, 155–159
ikria, 61, 62
Iliad, 71
Illich, Ivan, 12, 13, 56
ill-named, xvi, 69, 107
ill-named thing/sign, xxii, xxiii, 3, 13, 14, 30, 31, 57, 107, 108, 129, 130, 162, 163, 164
imaginary/ies, xxii, xxiv–xxvi, 9, 14–30, 33, 34, 36, 38–40, 43, 46–50, 55,

57, 59, 62,64, 66, 68, 69, 72–83, 107–110, 114, 115, 122, 126, 128–141, 144–149, 152–154, 158, 159, 161, 163; scientific, 16
Isou, Isadore, 63

Jacobs, Jane, 11, 13
Jasanoff, Sheila, xxiv, 16–21, 23, 25, 29, 30, 64, 72, 77, 133, 158
Joly, Auguste, 54
Joronen, Mikko, 152

Kahneman, Daniel, 131, 132
Kant, Immanuel, 48, 89
Keats, John, 11, 67
Ker/Keres, 71, 107, 111
keropolitical, 112, 113, 122, 128, 147, 158; operator, 112; order, 113, 158; regime, 128; subject, 147; threshold, 122
keropolitics, 111, 128
Kim, Sang-Hyun, xxiv, 16–21, 23, 30, 64, 72, 77, 133, 158
Kratos (Power/Might), 34, 68
Kuhn, Thomas/Kuhnian, xx, xxiii, xxiv, 34, 67, 75, 108, 127, 143

Lacan, Jacques, 16
Lamont, Mark, 97
Land, Chris, xiv, 3–8, 14
Lapoujade, David, 60, 64
Latimer, Joanna, 6, 96
Latour, Bruno, 40, 163
Latourian trick, 81
Law, John, xxi, 7, 37, 81
Lefebvre, Henri, 77, 78, 80
Legg, Stephen, 90
Leopold, Aldo, 164
Letterists, 63
letting-go, 65, 66
Levi, Primo, 121
Levitas, Ruth, xv, 131, 133
lifeworld, 33, 36, 41, 57, 75, 80, 129, 132, 134, 136, 144
Ljung, Michael, 120

Luhmann, Niklas, 5, 76

Macquarrie, John, xxi
Maier, Charles, 93
Manderscheid, Katharina, 8
Marcus Antonius, 36, 38–40
Marinetti, Filippo Tommaso, 51–56, 58, 59, 114, 115
Marx, Karl, xv, 45, 46, 48, 108
McShane, Clay, 10, 85, 91, 92, 95
Merleau-Ponty, Maurice, 27
metapherein, 34
metron, 131
mobile ontology, 125–127
mobilities paradigm, 67, 76, 125–127
Mol, Annemarie, xxi, 7, 81
Mommsen, Hans, 140, 141
moral economy, 75, 95, 96, 108, 122
Morten Kryev Wulff, 159
Movement for an Imaginist Bauhaus, 63
Mumford, Lewis, xiv, xxiv, 10–13, 99, 163
Munro, Rolland, 6, 96
Mussolini, Benito, 55

Nader, Ralph, 11–13
natality, 148, 149, 153, 155
Negri, Antonio, 152, 155
Nemesis, 71
nomocracy, 107, 109, 110, 112, 113, 121, 122, 128, 136, 138, 149, 150, 158, 162; of automobility, 122
nomocratic power/violence, 159
nomos, xxv, xxvi, 26, 47, 85, 88–90, 92–99, 101–104, 107, 109, 110, 111, 114, 128, 129, 148–150, 154, 155, 158, 159, 162, 163; of automobility/automobility nomos,26, 47, 88, 90, 93–99, 101–103, 110, 111, 128, 129, 150 Nomos of the Earth, xxv, 88, 89, 91, 93, 114, 129, 158
non-automobility future, xxvi
non-keropolitical ontology, 131
Norton, Peter, 10, 92
Nyx, 71

Octavian, 40
Odyssey, 61
ontic, xxi, xxii, 132, 144; question, xxi
ontical inquiry, xxi
ontological, xxi, xxii, 20, 21, 27, 75, 77, 78, 146, 147, 149, 156, 163; dualism, 20, 79; inquiry, xxi; networks, 126; order, 75; politics, 147, 156, 163; totalitarianism, 129, 141, 159; violence, 149
ontology: of automobility, xxi, 22, 28, 108, 122, 195; of nomocracy, 136; of realism, xxii, 107
ontopolitical, xxii, xxvi, 28, 83, 108, 128, 129, 132, 136, 145, 147, 154, 158; analysis, 128; dispositif, 147; imaginary(ies), xxii, 28, 108, 154, 158; order, 159
ontopolitics, 83, 128, 158; of automobility, xxi, xxvi, 1, 57, 128, 158; of dromocracy, xxiv, 57; of mobility, xxi
orkhēstra, 61, 62
othering, 112

Packard, Vance, 11–13
Palsgrave, John, 105
paradigm of late modernity, 163
Parsons, Talcott, 6, 76
Paterson, Matthew, xiv, 3–9, 14
Pellow, David, 101
Piccini, Patricia, 114
Pinet-Peralta, Luis, 86, 87
police state, xxv, 115, 116, 121
political ontology, 22, 40, 54, 55, 59, 60, 107–109, 112, 122, 126, 127, 129, 140, 141, 148, 153, 195; of automobility, 108, 195; of control, 140; of Futurism, 129; of violence, 109
political religion(s), 107, 112, 113, 115, 121
politics of the dromosphere, 35
politics of technosocial ontologies, 195
Polybius, 38

Portuguese vessel, 81
post-automobility, xiii, xiv, xv, xviii, xix, xxiv, xxv, xxvi, 65, 83, 105, 108, 131, 132, 143, 145, 146, 149–152, 155, 159
post-cyborg, 140
postmodernity, 145, 146
post-phenomenological, 28, 132, 145; ontology, 145
power/violence, xxi, 35, 68, 99, 122, 128, 129, 139, 148, 149, 159; /justice, 150; /speed, 35, 49; automobilized, 129; automobility, 99, 122
Prigogine, Ilya, 5
Prometheus, 34
Puricelli, Piero, 55, 78

Reason, James, 120
rhizomatic: automobility imaginary, 20, 30; biopolitical order, 69, 124; delocalized flows of time, 59; expansion, 26, 88, 100; imaginary, 22, 140; material, 139; network, 22, 59, 81, 130, 140; space, 146; spatial reordering, 99; technosocial space, 69, 124; topography, 55
Ricoeur, Paul, 78, 161, 164
Rivera, Diego, 48, 54
road safety research, 96, 103, 118
Robinson, Edward, xxi
Rorty, Richard, 9, 30
Rousseau, Jean Jacques, 48
Rowan, Rory, 90
Rubinstein, Lene, 155

Saint Bernard, xv
sameing, 126
Sant'Elia, Antonio, 53
Schivelbusch, Wolfgang, 41, 43
Schmitt, Carl, xxv, 88–93, 95, 96, 98, 101, 102, 110, 111, 114
scientific imaginaries, 16
Searle, John, 98
Seo, Sarah, 111, 115

Sheller, Mimi, 5, 6, 14, 26, 67, 68, 108, 127
Short, John Rennie, 86, 87
Situationists, xxiv, 62–65, 67, 73, 128
socialism, 155
sociotechnical: apparatus, 84, 110, 145; imaginary(ies), xxiv, xxv, 16–21, 24, 25, 29, 30, 38, 57, 64, 72, 78, 131–133, 135, 136–139, 141, 144, 145
Soja, Edward, 73
spectacle, xxiv, 34, 51, 58–69, 72–74, 107, 109, 115, 128, 129, 139, 148, 158, 163
Sphynx, 34, 41
Spivak, Gayatri, 126
Streeck, Wolfgang, 46, 48, 82, 83
Styx, 34
Surrealist, 63, 64
sustainability, 81, 133, 134
sustainable automobility (future), xxv, 132
Suzuki, Daisetz, 145
system of automobility, xix, 5–9, 14, 16, 24, 75, 100

technoscience(s), 46, 48, 49, 57, 58, 134, 144
technoscientific: advancements, 51; age, 35; being, 54, 110; capitalism, 46, 51; dreams, 139; imaginaries, 16; management of space, 49; order, 54; political ontology, 60; realty, 47; society, 46; space, 50, 86; transformation, 110; world, xxvi
technosocial: configuration,137; hybrid, 112; lifeworlds, 129; machinery, 56; necessity, 96; network, 39, 158; object, 57; ontologies, 195; ordering, 152; politics, 36; reality, 74; relativism, 123; space, 69, 124; vision, 132
temenos, 61
Thanatos, 71, 111
Thatcher, Margaret, 22
theatron, 58, 61, 62, 68, 146
The Manifesto of Futurism, 51, 52, 54
Theogony, 71
The Spectacle, xxiv
The 'System' of Automobility, xix, 5, 7
time-space, 35, 36, 39, 45–51, 54–63
transitory space, 35, 44, 68
Trump, Donald, 68

Urry, John, xix, xx, xxiii, 5–8, 14, 16, 24, 26, 67, 68, 75, 88, 95, 100, 107, 108, 111, 121, 123, 124, 127
US National Highway Traffic Safety Administration (NHTSA), 118

Vàhl, Joost, 151
Vaneigem, Raoul, 63–65, 78, 153
Vasudevan, Alexander, 90
violence of speed, 33, 35, 68, 109
Virilio, Paul, xxiv, 33, 35, 39, 42, 51, 68, 73, 82, 86, 109, 112, 121, 129, 161
Voegelin, Eric, 113

Weber, Max, 41, 68, 75, 111
Weir, Peter, 83
Werfel, Franz, 113
Wilde, Oscar, 1, 14
Wittgenstein, Ludwig/Wittgensteinian, vii, xiv, 9, 21, 76, 79, 81, 108, 159
Wolfe, Patrick, 90
woonerf, 151
worlding, 126, 127
Wright, Erik Olin, xv
Wynne, Brian, 7

Zeus, 34, 71

About the Authors

Robert Braun is associate professor and senior researcher at the Institute for Advanced Studies in Vienna, Austria. He is deputy head of the research group Science, Technology and Social Transformation. He teaches at the Technical University in Vienna, Austria, and at Masaryk University in Brno, the Czech Republic. He completed his PhD in philosophy. He has authored several books and book chapters and has published in *Science, Mobilities, Journal of Responsible Innovation, Transfers, Humanities & Social Sciences Communications,* and other academic journals. His main research focus is the politics of technosocial ontologies. He is also engaged in policy debates related to responsible innovation, research and engineering ethics, and the confluence of technology and society in general.

Richard Randell is Fellow at the Institute for Advanced Studies in Vienna, Austria, and teaches sociology at the Geneva campus of Webster University. He completed his PhD in sociology at the University of Wisconsin–Madison. His principal research interest is critical automobility studies. In addition to a book chapter on international motor shows, he has published in *Mobilities, Applied Mobilities, Humanities & Social Sciences Communications*, and *Transfers*. His current research projects include a historical reconstruction of the Futurama exhibit at the 1939–40 New York World's Fair, as well as why automobility needs to be taken more seriously by sociologists.

***

In addition to this book and several jointly written essays that are amongst those listed above, the authors are currently collaborating on several essays on the political ontology of automobility. Additionally, they are co-curators of the recently established Critical Automobility Studies Lab at the Institute for Advanced Studies in Vienna. The lab aims to act as a forum where scholars and activists can collaborate, exchange ideas, and reflect on how we might break ourselves away from this mode of existence called "automobility," which, as is argued in this book, is much more than simply cars or a mode of transportation.